Presented to

יונתן

Jonathan "Yoni" Kahn

On the occasion of his graduation from

Levey Day School

Portland, Maine

17 סיון 5772

June 7, 2012

LEVEY
Day School

# Text
# Messages

# Text
# Messages

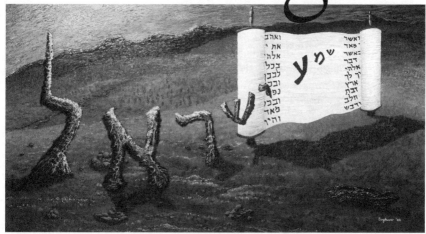

# A Torah
# Commentary
# for Teens

Edited by **Rabbi Jeffrey K. Salkin**

*For People of All Faiths, All Backgrounds*

JEWISH LIGHTS Publishing

Woodstock, Vermont:

*Text Messages:*
*A Torah Commentary for Teens*

2012 Hardcover, First Printing
© 2012 by Jeffrey K. Salkin

**Library of Congress Cataloging-in-Publication Data**
Text messages : a Torah commentary for teens / edited by Jeffrey K. Salkin.
    p. cm.
 Includes bibliographical references.
 ISBN 978-1-58023-507-5
 1. Bible. O.T. Pentateuch—Commentaries. 2. Jewish teenagers—Conduct of life. I. Salkin, Jeffrey K., 1954–
 BS1225.53.T49 2012
 222'.107—dc23

                2012013946

Manufactured in the United States of America
Jacket Design: Tim Holtz
Jacket Art: Shema © Michael Bogdanow

Published by Jewish Lights Publishing
A Division of LongHill Partners, Inc.
Sunset Farm Offices, Route 4, P.O. Box 237
Woodstock, VT 05091
Tel: (802) 457-4000    Fax: (802) 457-4004
www.jewishlights.com

# Contents

Introduction     xv

## *Bereshit* / Genesis

---

**Bereshit** (1:1–6:8)

What If I Don't Like My Brother?
Rabbi Sherre Z. Hirsch     3

Look in the Mirror; Now Look Again
Danny Maseng     6

**Noach** (6:9–11:32)

Even Righteous People Make Mistakes
Rabbi Aaron Bisno     8

Being the "Un-Noah"
Rabbi Nina Beth Cardin     10

**Lech Lecha** (12:1–17:27)

Get Going!
Rabbi Carl M. Perkins     12

A GPS for Compassion
Rabbi Rami Shapiro     14

**Vayera** (18:1–22:24)

Answering the World's Oldest Question
Rabbi Brad Hirschfield     16

Be Present
Rabbi Judith Schindler     18

# Contents

*Chayei Sarah* (23:1–25:18)

A Story of Prayer and Love
Rabbi Elie Kaunfer                                    20

Getting the Order Wrong—or Right
Rabbi Steven Z. Leder                                 22

*Toldot* (25:19–28:9)

The Most Serious Thing That Ever Happened to Me,
by Esau Isaacson
Rabbi Mordecai Finley, PhD                            24

Esau's Tears
Rabbi Dana Saroken                                    27

*Vayetzei* (28:10–32:3)

Jacob's Stairway
Rabbi Sandy Eisenberg Sasso                           29

Jacob's Life Is Our Own
Rabbi David J. Wolpe                                  31

*Vayishlach* (32:4–36:43)

How to Become *Yisrael*
Rabbi Vernon Kurtz                                    33

Each of Us Has a Name
Rabbi Amy Joy Small                                   35

*Vayeshev* (37:1–40:23)

Not Your Plans—God's
Rabbi Lawrence Kushner                                38

That Man Is You
Rabbi Jack Moline                                     40

*Miketz* (41:1–44:17)

Truth or Consequences
Rabbi Cherie Koller-Fox                               43

The Tests of Adulthood
Rabbi Kerry M. Olitzky                                46

***Vayigash*** (44:18–47:27)

   Joseph Comes Out of the Closet
     Rabbi Eve Rudin     49

   Joseph or Moses: Who Do You Want to Be?
     Barry Shrage     52

***Vayechi*** (47:28–50:26)

   Both Kindness to Others and Loyalty to Ourselves
     Rabbi John Moscowitz     55

   *Sababa*!
     Rabbi Avi Weiss     57

# *Shemot*/Exodus

***Shemot*** (1:1–6:1)

   No Such Thing as an Innocent Bystander
     Rabbi William G. Hamilton     63

   So, When Do You Really Grow Up?
     Rabbi Jeffrey K. Salkin     65

***Va'era*** (6:2–9:35)

   Conviction, Yes; Stubbornness, No
     Rabbi Howard L. Jaffe     67

   Hard Hearts—For Real
     Dr. Ron Wolfson     70

***Bo*** (10:1–13:16)

   Being a Global Team Player
     Lisa Exler and Ruth W. Messinger     73

   Does God Fight Fair?
     Rabbi Avi S. Olitzky     76

***Beshalach*** (13:17–17:16)

   Finding Our Voice
     Cantor Benjie Ellen Schiller     78

   That Nachshon Moment
     Rabbi Sid Schwarz     80

Contents

*Yitro* (18:1–20:23)

Rules Are Jewish Love
Rabbi Angela Warnick Buchdahl     82

What Kind of Leader Do You Want to Be?
Rabbi Jonah Pesner     84

*Mishpatim* (21:1–24:18)

"… And Another Thing!"
Rabbi Lester Bronstein     86

God Sweats the Small Stuff
Rabbi Debra Newman Kamin     88

*Terumah* (25:1–27:19)

What Kind of Sanctuary Are You Building?
Rabbi Amy Schwartzman     90

Inside Out
Dr. Ira H. Schweitzer, RJE     92

*Tetzaveh* (27:20–30:10)

Dress Code
Rabbi Sue Levi Elwell, PhD     94

Someone Is Always Watching
Rabbi Michael Pincus     96

*Ki Tisa* (30:11–34:35)

Our Duty to One Another
Rabbi Julie Schonfeld     98

No Free Lunch
Rabbi Daniel G. Zemel     100

*Vayakhel* (35:1–38:20)

Finding Your Life's Purpose
Rabbi Spike Anderson     102

Who Else Is Coming?
Rabbi Pamela Jay Gottfried     105

*Pekudei* (38:21–40:38)

Are You Accountable?
Rabbi Jill Jacobs                                                    107

No Boat
Rabbi Paul Yedwab                                            109

# *Vayikra*/Leviticus

*Vayikra* (1:1–5:26)

Who's Calling, Please?
Rabbi Elyse Frishman                                        113

Sacrifice Play
Rabbi Stuart Weinblatt                                      115

*Tzav* (6:1–8:36)

A Perpetual Fire
Rabbi Jeremy Kalmanofsky                              118

Time for a God Upgrade
Rabbi Jamie Korngold                                        120

*Shemini* (9:1–11:47)

The Gold Standard for Kashrut
Rabbi Morris J. Allen                                          122

A Time for Silence
Rabbi Zoë Klein                                                  125

*Tazria* (12:1–13:59)

Deep and Looking Up:
How a Weird Story of Skin Disease Can Tell Us about Life over
Death and Seeking Inner Peace
Rabbi Peretz Wolf-Prusan and Rabbi Asher Lopatin        127

*Metzora* (14:1–15:33)

When Words Become Contagious
Rabbi Norman M. Cohen                                  130

Sacred Graffiti
Rabbi Shira Stern                                              133

# Contents

*Acharei Mot* (16:1–18:30)

    The Physical Is Also Spiritual
      Rabbi Dr. Bradley Shavit Artson           136

    Never Stand Idly By
      Rabbi Steven Greenberg           138

*Kedoshim* (19:1–20:27)

    Tattoo, Taboo, and the Jew:
    Can I Be Buried in a Jewish Cemetery?
      Rabbi Peter Berg           142

    Sacred Sexuality
      Rabbi Danya Ruttenberg           146

*Emor* (21:1–24:23)

    Animals: What's Cruel, and What's Not So Cruel?
      Stan J. Beiner           148

    God Said **What**?
      Shulamit Reinharz, PhD, and Ellen Golub, PhD           151

*Behar* (25:1–26:2)

    God's Reset Button
      Rabbi Mike Comins           155

    Shabbat and the Power of the "Regular" and "Routine"
      Rabbi Michael L. Feshbach           158

*Bechukotai* (26:3–27:34)

    "Girls Rule! Boys Drool."
      Rabbi Marshal Klaven           160

    A Big "If"
      Rabbi Shira Stutman           162

# *Bemidbar*/Numbers

*Bemidbar* (1:1–4:20)

    Standing Guard
      Rabbi Jonathan E. Blake           167

"They've Given You a Number, and Taken Away Your Name"
Rabbi Joshua Hammerman                                        169

*Naso* (4:21–7:89)

Accessing Your Superpowers
Rabbi Sarah Mack                                              172

Jealousy Is Like Poison
Ethan Klaris and Rabbi Burt Visotzky                         174

*Behaalotecha* (8:1–12:16)

Facing the Wilderness
Rabbi Elliot J. Cosgrove, PhD                                177

What Makes a Leader Powerful?
Deborah Meyer                                                180

*Shelach-Lecha* (13:1–15:41)

They Could Be Giants—So Could You!
Dr. Erica Brown                                              182

Don't Be a Grasshopper!
Rabbi Sheldon Zimmerman                                      185

*Korach* (16:1–18:32)

Rebels for What?
Rabbi Jessica Brockman                                       188

Teaching Lasts Longer Than Politics
Rabbi Michael Paley                                          190

*Chukat* (19:1–22:1)

Speak Up and Speak Out!
Emilia Diamant                                               193

No Leading While Angry!
Rabbi Edward Feld                                            195

*Balak* (22:2–25:9)

Because That's What Jews Do
Robert Bildner                                               198

How Good Are Your Tents!
Cantor Ellen Dreskin                                         201

Contents

*Pinchas* (25:10–30:1)

    It's Not Fair!
        Rabbi B. Elka Abrahamson      203

    A Fanatic Named Pinchas
        Jerry Kaye      206

*Mattot* (30:2–32:42)

    Silence Is Consent
        Rabbi Laura Geller      208

    *Dugma* Is Dogma
        Ira J. Wise, RJE      211

*Maasei* (33:1–36:13)

    Second Chances
        Rabbi William Cutter, PhD, and Georgeanne Cutter      213

    Are We There Yet?
        Rabbi Baruch Frydman-Kohl      216

# *Devarim*/Deuteronomy

*Devarim* (1:1–3:22)

    Trust the Rebellion
        Rabbi Ken Chasen      221

    Angry at God
        Rabbi Harold S. Kushner      224

*Va'etchanan* (3:23–7:11)

    Skydiving and Torah
        Rabbi Marc Gellman, PhD      226

    Curb Your Appetites
        Rabbi Elaine Zecher      229

*Ekev* (7:12–11:25)

    Everything We Do Matters
        Dr. Arnold M. Eisen      232

    The Two-Chambered Heart
        Rabbi Micah D. Greenstein      234

*Re'eh* (11:26–16:17)

The Vision Thing
Wayne L. Firestone                                       237

To See Even (and Especially) Those Who Cannot
Rabbi Loren Sykes                                        239

*Shoftim* (16:18–21:9)

Judging Ourselves, Judging Others
Rabbi Felipe Goodman                                     242

War Isn't All It's Cracked Up to Be
Rabbi Laurence E. Milder                                 244

*Ki Tetzei* (21:10–25:19)

You Must, Because You Can
Rabbi Edward Feinstein                                   247

The Ties That Bind
Rabbi Joseph B. Meszler                                  250

*Ki Tavo* (26:1–29:8)

An Unholy Mash-Up
Rabbi Joseph Black                                       253

Remember Who You Are (and Then, Party)
Rabbi David Steinhardt                                   255

*Nitzavim* (29:9–30:20)

The Ultimate Network
Rabbi Dr. Analia Bortz, MD                               257

Standing for Civility
Rabbi Peter J. Rubinstein                                259

*Vayelech* (31:1–30)

Tunes
Joel Lurie Grishaver                                     261

Facing the End
Rabbi James Ponet                                        263

Contents

*Haazinu* (32:1–52)

Driven to Non-distraction
Rabbi Denise L. Eger                                          266

Listening—with Our Eyes
Rabbi David B. Rosen                                          268

*Ve-zot Ha-brachah* (33:1–34:12)

Building a Better World: A Vision, a Plan, and the Workers
Rabbi Andrew Davids                                          270

... And Ready to Start Again
Rabbi Elie Kaplan Spitz                                       272

Notes                                                        275

# Introduction

Come and see how the voice of God went forth to all of
Israel, to each and every one in keeping with that person's particular capacity—to the elderly in keeping with
their capacity, to young men in keeping with their capacity, to the little ones in keeping with their capacity, and
to the women in keeping with their capacity.... It is like
the manna, which to young people tasted like bread,
to the elderly it tasted like wafers made with honey....
(Midrash, *Shemot Rabbah* 5:9)

A number of years ago, I had the opportunity to hear a great teacher,
Robert Coles, talk about a new book that he had just written.
Professor Coles was trying to figure out the role that religion played
in the lives of young people of all faiths. One way that he did this
was to ask kids this question: "What story in your scriptures is your
story?" Another way of putting this would have been: "What sacred
story has your name on it?"

In my years as a rabbi, I've spent a lot of time asking young people
like you that question. For many young Jews, when they become
bar or bat mitzvah, their Torah portion truly becomes *their story*.
At least temporarily, while they are preparing to become bar or bat
mitzvah, that passage from Genesis, Exodus, Leviticus, Numbers,

or Deuteronomy becomes the lens through which they view their world.

Sometimes, the results of looking at the world this way can be funny or ironic. At least five or six times in my career, a kid who had the Torah portion *Metzora*, which is about skin diseases, also happened to have a parent who was a dermatologist. Seriously. You can't make this stuff up.

Sometimes, in a very powerful and mysterious way, the Torah portion that was read during the week that you were born becomes *your story*. That was the way it was for me. The week that I was born, the Torah portion was *Vayishlach*, from the book of Genesis. It features the story of Jacob wrestling with the nameless stranger and getting a new name, Yisrael. By coincidence, my Hebrew name is Yaakov, which means Jacob, and I have always imagined myself to be someone who struggles. Or perhaps there are no real coincidences.

That's why I embarked on this exciting project, *Text Messages: A Torah Commentary for Teens*. Every passage in the Torah has the potential to be someone's personal story and teaching—and that definitely includes you as a teenager. If you read these stories, and if you really let these holy texts into your mind and into your soul, your life will be deeper and richer, and even happier.

I also believe that the more you as teens read these stories and think about these stories—not as little kids but as people who are becoming adults—the better our Jewish future will be. Let's face it: there aren't a whole lot of Jews out there in the world. (Maybe you've noticed that already.) But if we hold onto our stories and make them real for us and for others, together we can create a strong Jewish future.

Why is this book titled *Text Messages: A Torah Commentary for Teens*? Because if you are a "typical" teenager (whatever that means), you probably *text* almost as much as you *speak*. A recent study says that nearly one out of three teens between twelve and seventeen years old sends more than a hundred texts a day. Many teens are sending three thousand texts a month.[1] So, you know all about those kinds of text messages.

This book contains a different kind of text message. These are the messages that come out of the Torah—our sacred stories, laws, and teachings. Sometimes it is easy to "get" the messages that the Torah contains for us at each stage of our life. Sometimes it is not so easy. But for thousands of years people of all ages have discovered that it is truly worth the effort.

Second, the whole *technology* of texting is very Jewish—because it was developed in Israel. In fact, without Israel, there would not have been texting at all. The Israeli company Mirabilis first developed text-messaging technology in 1996. The program started its life with the name "ICQ," which means exactly how it sounds. "I seek you" is a good name for a messaging program, and it is a good way of understanding the meaning of Jewish life. "I seek you" could be what we "text" to God during prayer, and what God and our tradition "text" back to us, in the form of words of Torah and wisdom.

Like many things in our world, texting is a mixed blessing. It's fast and it's convenient, but if we communicate only in short messages that are filled with emoticons and abbreviations, we might lose something in the process. Imagine if Lincoln's Gettysburg Address had started as a text message: "4 scr + 20 yrs ago, our 4dads brought 4rth …" More than that: even though we have called this book *Text Messages*, the screen of an iPhone cannot contain anything remotely close to the true depth of Judaism. Just as you have to *scroll* through a text on your phone or computer screen, we find the real text messages when we go through the scroll—the Torah scroll.

In *Text Messages: A Torah Commentary for Teens*, we go through every Torah portion, and we ask, "What's in it for *you*?" What does this Torah portion have to do with you—your life, your concerns, your understanding of Judaism and the world? If you look at a single leaf, you can imagine the entire tree. If you look at a pebble, you can imagine a mountain. If you look at one character in the Torah, you can find every Jew, and if you read one story or one teaching in the Torah, you can find all of Judaism. Each Torah portion has every Jew's name on it.

The Torah is about your life. It's about how you deal with interpersonal relationships; social justice; sexuality and gender issues; personal ethics; responsibility to family, community, and the Jewish people; body image; tattoos; community service; the meaning of faith; authority and rebellion; the role of ritual; personal theology; prayer; civility; living safely; dealing with disabilities; the challenges of eating morally.

And that is just a short list.

To help you figure out these text messages, we assembled about a hundred people to write about the Torah portions. They are all North American Jews: congregational rabbis (of all or no denominations), cantors, musicians, educators, youth workers, Hillel rabbis, professors, writers, camp directors, social activists, community leaders, and philanthropists. We are grateful to them for giving their time and, even more important, for sharing their wisdom.

I am grateful to the publisher and editor-in-chief of Jewish Lights, Stuart M. Matlins, for his ever-present support and advice during the process of thinking about *Text Messages*. As always, Emily Wichland, vice president of Editorial and Production, has been extremely helpful and diligent in the editorial process, making sure that we have come up with a truly excellent book. Michael Bogdanow is an extraordinary artist whose cover art for *Text Messages* really captures the idea that the words of Torah are alive and always in motion. Thanks to my assistant, Debbie Anderson, for shepherding pieces of this project and seeing them through to fruition.

We are all grateful to Rabbi Michael Pincus of West Hartford, Connecticut, for originally noticing the need for this kind of book and suggesting the idea for it to us. I hope that the result lives up to his earliest vision.

I am grateful to my wife, Sheila Shuster, and our children, for their interest, support, and enthusiasm.

We also put together a teen editorial advisory board, consisting of teenagers from all over North America. They read each of the essays and told us whether they could understand them and whether the language and ideas were appropriate for teenagers.

They are Mikayla Blumenthal, Naomi Eisenberg, Sydney Fine, Shira Gottfried, Hannah Grover, Jadin James, Isaac Kenin, Ellie Largeman, Kobie Largeman, Ava Lubin, Remony Perlman, Dylan Rice, and Sid Tikalsky. We really appreciate their time and their efforts.

Finally, I have always loved one particular phrase in the prayer book. We ask that God will *tein chelkeinu b'toratecha*, "grant us our portion in Your [that is, God's] Torah." I think that this means that everyone has his or her own portion in the Torah—a story, a chapter, a verse that has his or her name on it. In my imagination, I would like to believe that when the Messiah comes, he or she will show each Jew the verse that was intended just for them.

Maybe you don't want to wait until the Messiah comes to find your verse. If that's the case, I can't blame you.

I hope that *Text Messages: A Torah Commentary for Teens* will point you toward the Torah text that, truly, has your name on it.

# Bereshit/Genesis

# בראשית
## *Bereshit*

## What If I Don't Like My Brother?
### Rabbi Sherre Z. Hirsch

**The Eternal said to Cain, "Where is your brother Abel?"**
**And he said, "I do not know. Am I my brother's keeper?"**
(Genesis 4:9)

What are the chances that God is going to ask you a question like that? Do you think that God doesn't know where Abel is? Or that Abel is dead?

So what are we supposed to learn from the story of Cain and Abel?

Let's recap the story. While they are out in the field, Cain, the son of Adam and Eve, kills his brother, Abel. God knows exactly what has happened to Abel—and yet, he still asks Cain, "Where is your brother?"

At first, Cain acts as if he doesn't know where Abel is. But in reality, he just wants to avoid God's questioning. He would also rather avoid any kind of responsibility for Abel, and so he adds, "Am I my brother's keeper?"

It does not work. God is *really angry*. Why did God ask Cain where his brother was? It was because God wanted Cain to take responsibility for his wrongdoing. Cain *was*, in fact, responsible for his brother. Cain *was*, in fact, Abel's keeper.

---

**Rabbi Sherre Z. Hirsch** is an author, a speaker, and a spiritual consultant for Canyon Ranch.

So what does it mean to be your brother's keeper? If you take the phrase literally and you're an only child or you only have a sister or sisters, then you might think that you are off the hook.

But that's not what "brother" means here. It's not just about blood relations, and it's not just about male "brothers."

A "brother" is the kid in the class you have never spoken to.

A "brother" is your ex-girlfriend.

A "brother" is your stepsibling.

A "brother" is the elderly neighbor next door.

You are responsible for your "brothers," and that responsibility goes way beyond not just killing them. You are not allowed to hurt a brother, physically or emotionally. Yes, that includes not forwarding the mean text message or pretending not to hear someone when she is talking to you.

But that's not enough. Being your brother's keeper means that if someone is trying to hurt that person, you do all you can to protect him or her from harm. In fact, in many countries, if you don't take active measures to help someone, the courts can hold you legally accountable *for doing nothing*.

Confronting your best friend, helping someone you don't know or like, or telling an adult that something wrong is going on— these can all be hard. And doing these things might have negative consequences for you. You might lose friends or status. You might feel like you were not a good friend.

But please understand: being an adult is not only about having your own car, your own money, and your freedom.

Being an adult means that you must think of the other person at least as much as you think of yourself. You have to act on behalf of others even if you know you will take a hit.

Of course, it is easy to do the right thing when there is no cost to you. On the other hand, when you are about to experience (or think you are going to experience) conflict or discomfort, it is much harder to intervene. To be your brother's keeper means that you protect another person even when it is hard. Even when there is nothing in it for you. Even when there is a price that you are going to have to pay.

But when you learn what it means to protect your brother (and when you figure out who your "brother" really is), *that* will be the moment that you become an adult.

In your eyes, in the eyes of others, and surely, in the eyes of God.

That will make you strong, and that strength will last for the rest of your life.

# Look in the Mirror; Now Look Again

Danny Maseng

**And God said, "Let us make humanity in our image, after our likeness...." And God created humanity in the divine image, in the image of God, God created them; male and female God created *them*.** (Genesis 1:26–27 [my emphasis—DM])

"Them"?

Why "them"?

Didn't God create one human?

In fact, yes—because God wants us to understand that we are all interconnected. Why are we on earth? Not to separate and to break apart, but to complete and to unite. We were created as twin reflections of each other—as human reflections of God.

When we read about the birth of Cain and Abel, we read in Genesis 4:2, "And again she [Eve] bore his brother Abel." The Hebrew text actually means "And she *continued* to give birth...." *Continued*—because Cain was not made alone, but rather as a reflection of his brother Abel. They completed each other.

What was Cain's sin? It was that he saw himself as separate and disconnected from his brother. He killed his brother, Abel, but in the process, his heart got broken.

**Danny Maseng** is chazzan and music director of Temple Israel, Hollywood, California.

We can still feel Cain's broken heart. Every time we disconnect from our brothers and sisters, we feel it; every time we say about other human beings' suffering, "It is not my problem; it is not my pain; it has nothing to do with me," we feel it.

The great Hasidic teacher known as the Kotzker Rebbe said, "If I am I because I am I, and you are you because you are you, then I am I and you are you. But if I am I because you are you, and you are you because I am I, then I am not I and you are not you!"[1]

There is a great lesson here: if I stand utterly alone and uncommitted to anything, then I am simply an abandoned creature. But if I find someone else to relate to, that's how I become human. Because only then are we a "we"; only then are we truly created in the image of God.

We each should look at our brothers and sisters, our fellow human beings, as though we are looking into a mirror and say: In the image and likeness of God *we* were created.

You need someone else to truly reflect the image of God.

# נח

# *Noach*

## Even Righteous People Make Mistakes

### Rabbi Aaron Bisno

**This is the line of Noah.—Noah was a righteous man;
he was blameless in his age; Noah walked with God.**
(Genesis 6:9)

A legend: At any given time, somewhere in the world, there are thirty-six righteous people whose very existence sustains all of creation. These are the *lamed vavnikim*, the thirty-six righteous people, *tzaddikim* (because *lamed* plus *vav* equals thirty-six). Their identities are a secret. Not even the thirty-six know they are in this privileged number.

What do we learn from this legend?

Anyone we encounter—even the face staring back at us from the mirror—could be a *lamed vavnik*, and the world's very existence could depend on that person.

The word *tzaddik* (righteous person) occurs more than two hundred times in the Hebrew Bible. And yet, only one person in the Hebrew Bible actually has that title. You might guess that it would be Abraham, or Moses, or Sarah, or Miriam, Moses's sister who led the Israelites through the parted waters of the Sea.

Actually, no. There is only one *tzaddik* in the entire Hebrew Bible—and it is Noah.

**Rabbi Aaron Bisno** holds the Frances F. and David R. Levin Senior Rabbinic Pulpit at the Rodef Shalom Congregation in Pittsburgh, Pennsylvania.

When you think about it, Noah seems like an unlikely choice. After all, the term *tzaddik* comes from the Hebrew root *tz-d-k*, which refers to the Jewish value of justice (as in *tzedakah*), and Noah was a gentile (a "pre-Jew," actually). That's not to say that gentiles or "pre-Jews" cannot be righteous people; of course they can. But shouldn't the Hebrew Bible reserve that *tzaddik* title for an Israelite?

Not only this: while Noah was the best of his generation (remember all his neighbors drowned for their lawlessness), perhaps this wasn't such a great honor. We might even say that Noah was only the *best* among the *worst*.

And, finally, when Noah learned that God planned to destroy the world in the Flood, what did he do? He remained silent.

So what makes Noah a *tzaddik*?

We all know how dangerous it can be to keep silent in the face of something that seems unjust. We know that it is a *mitzvah* to speak up in the face of evil; as Leviticus teaches, we cannot remain silent while our neighbor bleeds.

But just because Noah failed in this particular instance, this doesn't mean that it is his total identity. Do you think that it is really possible—always, at every moment—to live up to our fullest potential?

So we return to the legend of the thirty-six *lamed vavnikim* whose righteousness sustains the entire world. Let's remember: they might be *tzaddikim*, but they are still human beings. And because they are human beings, they surely make mistakes—just like Noah, and just like all of us.

Thus, in spite of our shortcomings and our own all-too-human failings, like the one alone whom the Bible calls a *tzaddik*, as long as we, too, are willing to take responsibility for our actions, and as long as we strive always to be the best "me" you and I can be, we might still be one of the persons upon whom the world depends.

Why Noah?

Why *not* Noah?

*Why not you?*

# Being the "Un-Noah"

### Rabbi Nina Beth Cardin

**The Eternal said to Noah, "Go into the ark, with all your household, for you alone have I found righteous before Me in this generation."** (Genesis 7:1)

There are times when things seem out of whack—when others think the world is just fine, and yet you look around and think, "That's just wrong."

The question is: what do you do about it?

What do you do when you know that "everyone else" cheats on their tests, or lies to their friends, or even pays someone to take the SATs for them?

What do we make of a society where bosses make many times the salaries of their administrative assistants? Or that Americans are only 5 percent of the world's population, but consume 25 percent of the earth's resources? Or that we buy many products that will contribute to the destruction of the earth and that were made by underpaid and ill-treated workers? How should we respond?

Once, when the world was full of things that were wrong, God said, "I have decided to put an end to all flesh, for the earth is filled with lawlessness ..." (Genesis 6:13). Noah had to figure out how to

---

**Rabbi Nina Beth Cardin** is a writer, an editor, a blogger, and founder of several organizations, including the Jewish Women's Resource Center, the National Center for Jewish Healing, the Baltimore Jewish Environmental Network, and the Baltimore Orchard Project.

respond. "I am about to bring the Flood," God added, and Noah was silent.

Noah was a good man. He saw the evil in the world around him and heard God's plan. Ten generations later, so did Abraham. But the two responded very differently. Noah didn't argue with God over the destruction of the earth; Abraham did—over the destruction of Sodom and Gomorrah (Genesis 18).

What if Noah had tried to save the world? What if God had allowed Noah to try and change the way people behaved?

What would Noah have done?

How do you tell people that things are wrong, that the ways they are behaving are wrong, that they and the world need to change? That if they don't, things will get very bad?

It is hard to speak to a friend or a family member and say, "Don't buy this" or "Don't do that." It is hard to say that what we did in the past will not work well tomorrow.

God didn't ask Noah to say that, and Noah chose not to say that. And the world was destroyed.

To increase honesty, kindness, and fairness; to save the world from runaway global warming; to create a marketplace of sustainable goods; to change the ways we build cities and grow food; to live lives that balance our desire to have things with a sense of contentment with what we already have—we need people to speak out.

For us, the silence of Noah is not an option. Because the destruction of the world is not an option.

Will you be the one who speaks up? What must you learn so that people will listen? How can you speak up so that others might hear? What can you say to help others understand?

# לֶךְ לְךָ

# *Lech Lecha*

## Get Going!

### Rabbi Carl M. Perkins

**Go forth ... from your father's house....** (Genesis 12:1)

Throughout my childhood, I always thought of religion as being a source of comfort. I had always heard my rabbi preach soothing words—words designed to support people during difficult times.

One day I was sitting in synagogue with my father when my rabbi started talking about *Lech Lecha*. Suddenly, I heard the opening words of the Torah portion as if I had never heard them before.

"*Go forth!* Get out of here! Get going! Go out on your own! Leave your parents' home!"—which I interpreted to mean: "Get out from under your parents' influence. Make sense of the world *as you see it.*"

I looked at my father. Suddenly, I realized that the message of the Torah portion had nothing to do with what I had always thought the purpose of religion to be. I realized why Judaism always viewed Abraham with approval. It was because, as the legend puts it, Abraham broke his father's idols—which means that Abraham rejected the wisdom of his parents' generation.

At that moment I realized that Judaism could not possibly want me to uncritically adopt my parents' way of relating to God. Not at all. The Torah wanted me to strike out on my own and to follow my conscience wherever it would take me. Yes, everywhere in the Jewish

---

**Rabbi Carl M. Perkins** is spiritual leader of Temple Aliyah in Needham, Massachusetts.

world, people talk about the need for one generation to continue the work of the previous generation. But that's not always how it works. Sometimes we shouldn't continue the work of our parents' generation. Sometimes we should do our own work.

This radical idea was exciting, but it also made me sad. I looked at my father again. Things could never be the same between us. My values, my perspective, my commitments would not be identical to his. Where was I to turn for wisdom and guidance, if not to my parents? How was I to figure it all out? I was, and am, no Abraham. It's one thing to have lived in a world in which (apparently) God spoke quite clearly to people. When did God ever speak to me? When *would* God ever speak to me?

The rabbi kept talking. I realized why the story of Abraham is in the Hebrew Bible. It teaches us that although every human being inherits much from the world he or she grew up in, each of us must eventually struggle with—pick your term: our conscience, the source of our sense of right and wrong, God—and create our own religious identity.

In figuring out who we are, *who we are called to be*, in this world, we have to start with ourselves. (That's not where we end, but that is where we start.)

And so, lo and behold, I realized that the words of this Torah portion are, indeed, soothing. The message is simple: *Go forth!* Go forth with courage and care and good sense. Don't forget the lessons of your parents and your rabbis, and don't stop listening to them or caring about them. But as you sometimes find yourself thinking differently and making different choices from theirs, realize that this, too, is the way that it is supposed to be.

"Go forth ... and be a blessing!"

# A GPS for Compassion

Rabbi Rami Shapiro, PhD

Now HaShem said to Abram, "Go from your country
and your kindred and your father's house to the land
that I will show you. [As a consequence of your going]
I will make of you a people vital to life, and I will bless
you, and spread your reputation [as a people devoted
to justice and compassion], so that you will be a
blessing. I will bless those who bless you, and the one
who curses you I will curse; [those who follow the way
of justice and compassion will be blessed with justice
and compassion, those who do not will be cursed with
injustice and cruelty;] and through you all the earth's
families [human and otherwise] shall be blessed."
(Genesis 12:1–3 [my translation—RS])

This is the mission statement of the Jewish people.

The Hebrew translated here as "go" is *lech lecha*. It means to go on a journey, to leave behind nationalism, tribalism, and your family "baggage." Judaism is not about conforming to the *past*; it's

---

**Rabbi Rami Shapiro** is adjunct professor of religion at Middle Tennessee State University and the director of Wisdom House, an interfaith center in Nashville, Tennessee.

about living God's command in the *present*. It isn't about fitting in; it's about moving on.

We do not (yet) know the destination. Yes, in one sense, it is, of course, the Land of Israel, but it's about something more. It's about creating a whole new *state of mind*. This journey is based on trust.

When will we know our destination?

Only when we get there.

Our importance as a people depends on our taking this journey into the unknown. We are called to be the boundary crossers (this may be the original meaning of *Habiru*/Hebrew); we are the ones who "boldly go where no one has gone before." But the purpose of the journey is not to become great; rather, it is to become a vehicle through which all of the earth's families will be blessed.

Our goal isn't to conquer or convert, but to bless and bring blessings to the entire world, every family, of every species. We do this by embodying compassion: engaging the world justly, lovingly, and humbly (based on Micah 6:8).

When someone asked him to sum up the Torah while standing on one foot, the ancient sage Hillel said, "What is hateful to you do not do to another. This is the whole of the Torah; all the rest is commentary. Now go and study it" (Talmud, *Shabbat* 32a).

I take Hillel literally. The entire Torah—all of Judaism—is a guide to compassion when we read and live it as such. If your reading of Torah and/or your living of Judaism doesn't make you more just, loving, and humble, then you are not only misreading Torah but you are also not living Judaism.

This is why I am a Jew. At its best, Judaism challenges you to drop the known and step into the unknown; to be a blessing and a vehicle for blessing so that all life benefits from your life; and to embody a specific level of consciousness that embraces the world with justice, love, and humility.

True, Judaism is often not at its best, but you can find enough examples, past and present, to keep you loyal to the mission.

# וירא

## *Vayera*

## Answering the World's Oldest Question

Rabbi Brad Hirschfield

**Some time afterward, God put Abraham to the test. God said to him, "Abraham," and he answered, "Here I am."**
(Genesis 22:1)

What is the world's oldest question?

How can answering it help you figure out your place in the world, and how to live the life you want to live, and what you need to do so?

First things first. What is the oldest question in the world?

According to the Hebrew Bible, it is a simple three-word question: "Where are you?" According to Genesis 3:9, that is what God says when looking for Adam and Eve, after they ate the fruit from the Tree of Knowledge in the Garden of Eden.

OK, I know that it seems a little ridiculous; God can't seem to find the humans that God created. But here's what's even more significant: *the humans never answer God's question.*

Instead, what does Adam do? He blames Eve, and then he makes a bunch of other excuses. But, he never gets around to answering God's simple question: "Where are you?"

---

**Rabbi Brad Hirschfield** is president of CLAL: The National Jewish Center for Learning and Leadership.

In fact, for the twenty generations that separate Adam from Abraham, that question just hangs in the air—that is, until this Torah portion. God calls out to Abraham, and Abraham answers by saying what might be the single most powerful word in the entire Hebrew Bible. *Hineini*, "Here I am."

Adam couldn't answer God's question, and neither could anyone else. And then Abraham comes along and figures out that the most important thing in the world is the ability to know where you stand. The issue isn't *who* you are; it's *where* you are.

Abraham answers that question, and so can you.

*Who* you are will probably keep changing over the course of your life; it does for most people. You have new experiences, you understand things in different ways, and your understanding of who you are shifts. That's actually a sign of growth.

But *where* you are is not simply about *who* you are, or who you *think* you are, or who people think you *should* be. *Where* you are actually depends on your relationship with other people, places, and things.

Abraham's life is pretty much like most of our lives. It has its twists and turns. But, unlike any character before him, he is willing to answer the oldest question in the world. He is willing to stand up with both a strong sense of *who* he is and the awareness that *who* anyone is also depends on *where* he finds himself.

We can all be Abrahams. In fact, we all need to be. We need to have great pride in who we are, draw strength from those around us, and pay attention to the needs of others.

I don't know if there "really" was an Abraham or not, but I know that we can all follow in his footsteps and that we can rise to the challenge of answering the world's oldest question.

And when we do, we live the best lives possible—lives of greatness beyond our wildest imaginations.

# Be Present

## Rabbi Judith Schindler

**And the two walked off together.... And the two of them walked on together.** (Genesis 22:6, 22:8)

It is actually very easy to connect with friends. We e-mail, text, and Skype. Even from a distance, we can figure out ways to relate to our friends.

Connecting with parents—not so easy. Even though we might be with them physically, it can be much more difficult to simply relate to them.

Abraham and Isaac are father and son, but they clearly are not on the same page. God calls to Abraham to travel to the distant site Mount Moriah (presently the Temple Mount in Jerusalem), to sacrifice his son. On the third day of the journey, after leaving the servants behind, Abraham and Isaac are alone. Abraham has the firestone and a knife in his hand, and Isaac is carrying the wood. "The two of them walked off together," the Torah tells us (Genesis 22:6).

Isaac has been more than a little concerned, and he finally gets up the courage to ask his father a very hard question: "Father, here are the firestone and the wood; but where is the sheep for the burnt offering?" (Genesis 22:7). Abraham answers, "God will see to the sheep for His burnt offering, my son" (Genesis 22:8).

---

**Rabbi Judith Schindler** is senior rabbi of Temple Beth El in Charlotte, North Carolina.

The Torah then tells us a second time, "And the two of them walked on together" (Genesis 22:8).

The first time Abraham and Isaac "walk together," they clearly aren't connecting with each other. Isaac has no idea what his father is doing. Rashi, the eleventh-century French sage and commentator, says that through their conversation, Abraham and Isaac come to understand each other better. At the end of their conversation, they walk closer together, because they are of a single mind and purpose. They both know: Isaac will be the sacrifice.

Many teens read this text in a different way. They understand that while Abraham is not exactly lying to Isaac about what is going on, he also is not being completely honest with him. Why? He probably wants to protect his son's innocence and not expose him to the terrible truth. At the end of the conversation, Isaac still has no idea that his father intends on sacrificing him.

It forces us to ask: when is it acceptable for parents not to tell their children the whole truth? Yes, they might want to shelter and protect them from life's harsh realities. But does that help the relationship, or does it just damage it?

It is not easy to "walk together" with our parents and to fully connect with them. We are all busy. With cell phones, text messages, homework, housework, and work, we all have things that distract us from each other. We find it difficult to listen to each other, to hear each other, and to be fully present for each other.

It's not just parents who have to commit to being there for and with their kids; teenagers have to do the same thing.

As you leave your teenage years and leave your childhood homes, I pray that you will be able to look back on your relationships with your parents and say, echoing the Hebrew Bible, "And the two of us walked on together."

This is the holiest relationship in the world; let's treat it that way.

# חיי שרה

# *Chayei Sarah*

## A Story of Prayer and Love

Rabbi Elie Kaunfer

**And Isaac went out walking in the field toward evening and, looking up, he saw camels approaching.** (Genesis 24:63)

As someone who does a lot of thinking and teaching about the meaning of prayer, I have learned the following over the years:

Some people pray when they are sad.

And some people—a lot of teenagers, I think—pray for love.

What does it mean to pray for love?

In this Torah portion, Isaac loses his "love"—his mother, Sarah—who, according to legend, he has not seen since his father, Abraham, almost sacrificed him.

Isaac cannot get over the death of his mother. He is simply heartbroken.

Isaac is depressed. Who wouldn't be? Maybe you have had a similar loss, or a friend has had a similar loss. But Isaac has a way of dealing with it. In the late afternoon, as the sun is setting and the shadows grow long, he goes out into the field, and he walks, and meditates.

What kind of a walk is it? It really isn't *walking*; it is more like *wandering* aimlessly. In his later years, Isaac would be famous for not being able to see so well, and he can't see too well here, either.

**Rabbi Elie Kaunfer** is cofounder and executive director of Mechon Hadar (www.mechonhadar.org), the first full-time egalitarian yeshiva program in North America, which includes a high school summer program.

Instead of walking purposefully or seeing clearly, he speaks. What does he say? The Talmud says that Isaac recites the words of Psalm 102: "My days have vanished like smoke.... My body is stricken and withered like grass.... I lie awake.... My days are like a lengthening shadow; I wither like grass."

At the precise moment when the sun is setting, at the precise moment that the sun seems to be setting in Isaac's life, when life seems to be getting dark, in the middle of his aimless wandering, what does Isaac do? He offers a prayer in the middle of his wandering. The Talmud tells us this is the first *Minchah*—the first twilight prayer—ever spoken (Talmud, *Berachot* 26b).

But things are about to change for Isaac. Yes, he has lost one "love," but now he is about to find another.

His father's servant has found Rebekah, the future love of his life, and he is returning home with her. Rebekah has the ability to see very clearly. In fact, when she approaches Isaac, his presence is so striking that she literally falls off her camel.

But, in that moment, what does Isaac see? He doesn't really see Rebekah; he can only see the camels that accompany her.

When does Isaac start to get the picture? When does he finally understand what is going on? It is only when the servant *tells* Isaac who this woman who fell off the camel is—the woman who is destined to be the true love of his life.

The Torah makes it very clear: Isaac loves Rebekah. This is only the second mention of the word *ahavah*, "love," in the Torah. The first time is when God tells Abraham to sacrifice the son whom he loves—Isaac.

The love has come full circle. Abraham's love for Isaac reemerges as Isaac's love for Rebekah.

And it was all because Isaac had the courage to pray at twilight, at the precise hour when the shadows grow long.

# Getting the Order Wrong—or Right

Rabbi Steven Z. Leder

**Isaac then brought her into the tent of his mother Sarah, and he took Rebekah as his wife. Isaac loved her, and thus found comfort after his mother's death.** (Genesis 24:67)

Rebekah offers water to Abraham's servant and his camels. What makes her a suitable wife for Isaac?

If you think that it's her beauty, guess again.

It's her *kindness*.

She returns with the servant to meet her soon-to-be husband and then, as the Torah simply says, "Isaac took Rebekah as his wife and he loved her."

If you stop to think about it, the Torah seems to have things backward. Shouldn't it say that Isaac loved Rebekah and then, afterward, that he took her as his wife? Isn't that the way it works—like that old song, "First comes love, then comes marriage, then comes Daddy with the baby carriage?"

Not for any of us who have been married for a while. We who have overcome the lack of time, money, and sleep; who have survived the pettiness, stubbornness, serious illnesses, and naive dreams tempered by reality. We who also know the secret laughter, the gentle touch, the quiet walk, the moments watching children

---

**Rabbi Steven Z. Leder** is senior rabbi of Wilshire Boulevard Temple in Los Angeles, California.

sleep silently in their beds. We know it takes a certain kind of love to start a marriage—but it takes a deeper love to make it last.

Whenever I meet a couple who has been married for more than fifty years, I always ask them how they managed to make it work. One woman who had been married for sixty years leaned over and said there were only three words necessary to stay married: "Get over it." Whatever it is that disturbs you, talk it through, say you are sorry, and get over it.

Just about every couple says pretty much the same thing in slightly different ways. It always comes down to putting the other person's needs before your own, to listening, to forgiving, to showing kindness as you go through life together—really together. It always comes down to the simple truth revealed in this Torah portion. First comes marriage—then comes love. Marriage isn't something that happens to us on a particular day or in a particular place. Weddings don't make people married. Weddings are beginnings. Marriages are *journeys*, and the best kind of love takes time.

Wait a second. Why am I giving *you* marital advice? You've got—who knows?—probably a decade or even more before you even think about marriage.

Because this isn't only about marriage. Every relationship that matters takes friendship, forgiveness, and time.

# תולדות

# *Toldot*

## The Most Serious Thing That Ever Happened to Me, by Esau Isaacson

### Rabbi Mordecai Finley, PhD

**When her time to give birth was at hand, there were twins in her womb. The first one emerged red, like a hairy mantle all over; so they named him Esau. Then his brother emerged, holding on to the heel of Esau; so they named him Jacob.** (Genesis 25:24–26)

### The Most Serious Thing That Ever Happened to Me, by Esau Isaacson

**Life Skills**
**Period 6**
**Mr. Washington**

I come from a very disturbed family. I think my father Isaac (he is pretty old, and blind) grew up in some kind of cult. My mother is his cousin or something. Very disgusting. Something very bad happened to my father when he was a kid. I know this will sound like I am crazy or something, but I think my grandfather Abraham tried to kill him in some weird religious

---

**Rabbi Mordecai Finley, PhD,** is spiritual leader and cofounder, with his wife Meirav, of Ohr HaTorah Synagogue in Mar Vista, California. He is also a professor of liturgy, mysticism, Jewish ethics, and professional skills at the Academy for Jewish Religion, California campus.

thing. You know that I have a twin brother Jacob (we are fraternal twins, not identical twins, obviously), who was in your second period class. He is a total dork and a nerd. He can't even throw a football—much less catch one.

In my family, there was this idea that I will get to be the leader of this cult when I grow up, because I was born a couple of minutes before Jake, and the firstborn son gets to be the leader. It actually sounded kind of cool, you know—get to boss people around. Like being the captain of the football team, but for a whole religion. Anyway, it seems that my mom, Rebekah (you met her at back-to-school night), thought I was not good enough. I really hated her for a while.

I was supposed to go to the store and get my dad some steaks and cook them up for him, and then he was going to give me this piece of paper that says that I get to inherit everything. While I was at the store, my mom cooked up some steaks that she already had in the refrigerator and had Jake bring them to my old blind dad and pretend that he was me. So he got the piece of paper.

Mr. Washington, you know that I am not a crybaby, but I really cried. I actually cry now when I think about it. It wasn't so much that I shouldn't be the leader of the religion. I actually am not that religious, and I didn't take it that seriously. But I used to look down on my family. My father, a religious nut; my mom helping him; my dorky brother. But now, I realize that they looked down on me. I suddenly realized that even though my dad acted like he liked me because I was all outdoorsy and all that, that he probably secretly preferred my brother. My mother and my brother totally hated me and betrayed me.

Now here is the part you can't tell anyone. You know that Jake transferred out to live with my uncle in Fresno. Well, it was because I really was going to kill him. I mean, really. It was as if I understood why I never felt I fit anywhere in life, and I was going to take it out on him. I felt that if he was alive, then I felt dead, and I would only feel alive if he was dead.

I have always tried to be the best at things, and if something did not come easy for me, I just avoided it. Sports came easy, so I did that. I act like I don't care about books, but it is really because my brother Jake is so smart, and I can't compete with him. I can't make my mother and father love me like they love him. I know that Jake thinks I am just a big dumb jock. And maybe I am. I actually don't know who I really am. I have been faking it my whole life.

So the most serious thing that ever happened to me is that I had to admit that I don't know who I am. I also realize what has really been happening in my family all these years. My soul feels dizzy. I feel sick.

This may surprise you, but now that my brother Jake is gone, it seems like my sneaky mom and blind dad are finally being honest with me and seeing me for the first time. We are talking all this through, so you don't have to call the police or anything.

# Esau's Tears

Rabbi Dana Saroken

**When Esau heard his father's words, he burst into wild and bitter sobbing, and said to his father, "Bless me too, Father!"** (Genesis 27:34)

Esau is sobbing. It is a wild and bitter cry that comes from deep down within his soul—a cry that no hug or words of comfort can ease. It's that feeling that you have when someone has just robbed you of your dignity, your pride, something that should have been yours. It's the wild and bitter cry of injustice.

Esau has been down this road before. Back then, he had been a teenager. He had just come in from outside, and he was famished. His brother, Jacob, had just made a red lentil stew, and at that moment, the only thing that mattered to Esau was getting that hot stew into his belly. He was living in the moment, and *only* in the moment. He ate the stew, had some bread, and then he got up and left the table. That was it.

Now, it's years later. Jacob has tricked Esau again—but this time, Esau understands the long-lasting value of the blessing that Jacob is about to receive. This time, his own mother, Rebekah, helps Jacob manipulate the situation, and that makes the injustice far greater. As Esau begs his father Isaac for the blessing that rightfully belongs to him as the firstborn son, Isaac begins to tremble violently, because

**Rabbi Dana Saroken** is associate rabbi at Beth El Congregation in Baltimore, Maryland.

he now understands what has happened, but it is too late. "Bless me, too, Father!" Esau begs—but what was done was done. The brothers' fates were sealed.

It's hard enough to forgive a sibling who has wronged you, but how do you forgive a parent who has so visibly and hurtfully favored your brother? What do you do with the sadness, the hurt, and the unfairness?

Esau's story reminds us: no matter how hard we try, we really can't change other people. No matter how hard Esau tried or how respectful he was toward his parents, he just couldn't make his mother love him more or convince her that he was worthy. He couldn't turn his brother, Jacob, into a trustworthy or loving brother. And he couldn't convince his father to reverse his blessing. Yet what Esau learned along his journey was that although he felt powerless at times, he really did have some control, after all. Like all of us, he couldn't control the choices that others made, but he could control his own actions and responses.

Esau eventually has the opportunity to seek the revenge for which he has yearned. After countless years of alienation, growth, and maturation, when the two brothers are finally reunited, instead of killing Jacob, Esau holds him tightly and kisses him. Instead of accepting the gifts and riches that Jacob offers, Esau declines, assuring Jacob that he has everything he needs. In this moment of reunification, it is clear that Esau has found his inner strength and integrity. Esau is not only content with all he has; he is also confident with who *he* is. For all of these reasons, he is able to forgive his brother and to accept him for the person that *he* is.

And so it is with all of us. No matter how hard we try to gain the respect, adoration, and friendship of others, we might never gain their acceptance or favor. And so, we realize that all we can be is ourselves. Ultimately, we will find our own true inner peace. And when we can like ourselves and find ourselves "good enough," regardless of what others think or feel, we will be able to live, to forgive, and to create for ourselves lives that are full and whole. Ultimately, Esau learns that all that we can control in life are our own actions and responses.

# וַיֵּצֵא

## *Vayetzei*

### Jacob's Stairway

Rabbi Sandy Eisenberg Sasso

**Jacob had a dream: a stairway was set on the ground and its top reached to the sky and angels of God were going up and down on it.** (Genesis 28:12)

In a midrash, the Rabbis ask, "Why didn't Jacob go up the ladder with the angels?"

This is how the midrash imagines Jacob answering:

> Jacob says, "I was afraid. Look, all those angels went up, but they also had to come down. I don't mind going up. But I don't want to have to come down. I don't want to fall."
>
> God responds, "Fear not, Jacob. If you go up the ladder, trust Me—you will not fall."
>
> But Jacob didn't believe, and he did not go up.
>
> (Midrash, *Vayikra Rabbah* 29:2)

All along the way, there will be people and circumstances that will try to prevent you from going up, from fulfilling your goals. Jacob's uncle, Laban, tried to keep him from realizing his dream. Jacob worked seven years for what he wanted, and he found that it still wasn't enough.

---

**Rabbi Sandy Eisenberg Sasso** is senior rabbi of Congregation Beth-El Zedeck in Indianapolis, Indiana.

As with Jacob, things may not work out exactly as you plan. You may say, "I worked hard, I gave it my best try, and I failed." Others may tell you—and you may tell yourself—that you are not good enough, strong enough, or smart enough to accomplish your dream. Jacob had initially fallen in love with Rachel, but his father-in-law, Laban, made him marry Rachel's sister, Leah, first. Maybe, like Leah, you will feel rejected, as if you are the second choice. You might be tempted to believe the worst about yourself, to settle for less.

*Don't.* Don't let disappointments stop you.

Sometimes, you might be afraid. Like Jacob who was invited to go up the stairway, you might think that it is too dangerous. After all, you have always been a winner. Why take a chance at losing? Why take the risk of falling?

Maybe you want to stand for something that is unpopular or do something that has never been done. Maybe you feel like you are all alone, like no one else understands. Others may tell you, or maybe you will even tell yourself, "Don't be a fool; it is better to fit in. Stay with what you know." You might be tempted to give up.

Don't. Don't let fear stop you.

Jacob made a bargain with God. If God watched over him and kept him safe, he would stay faithful. Maybe like Jacob, you, too, will want to strike a bargain. If someone—a parent, teacher, coach, or friend—promises to make it easier, to cushion your fall, to take the blame, then you will take a harder class, defend an unpopular position, stand up for a classmate, or accept a challenge. Without guarantees, you might be inclined to settle for less.

Don't.

If you want to achieve your dreams, you will have to go forward without any assurances, except the promise of the love of those who care for you, no matter what.

That is what Jacob did. He struggled. He made mistakes. He worked hard and took a risk. He changed. He became "Israel."

You can do the same.

# Jacob's Life Is Our Own

Rabbi David J. Wolpe

**Jacob had a dream....** (Genesis 28:12)

Jacob has another name—"Israel." As Israel, Jacob symbolizes the entire Jewish people. There are many reasons why Jacob is called Israel. One of those reasons is wrapped up in a dream. Jacob has fled from his home, away from his brother's murderous threats. That's one of the ways in which he becomes his own person.

In one simple but mysterious moment of dreaming, some powerful things happen.

A rabbi in the Talmud said that ever since the end of creation, God has been building ladders. Some people go up; others go down. We are always—each of us—in spiritual motion. And that's what Jacob's dream teaches us.

A ladder can teach us important lessons:

Jacob dreams that he sees a ladder, "and angels of God were going up and down on it" (Genesis 28:12). We would think that angels would originally come from heaven, but in fact, they begin their journey here on earth.

What does this teach us? People can act as angels, right here in our lives. And when we do, when we have angelic moments of goodness, it is as if we are going up, spiritually, to heaven. On our worst and most boring days, the idea that we can be angel-like can truly inspire us.

---

**Rabbi David J. Wolpe** is rabbi of Sinai Temple in Los Angeles, California.

Jacob wakes up, saying, "Surely God is present in this place, and I did not know it" (Genesis 28:16). For the first time, Jacob learns that God is not only in the expected places—his father's house or his place of prayer.

Rather, every place he will go is a place of prayer and a treasure-house of dreams. This is what gives Jacob the strength to continue his journey. Suddenly, he realizes that no place is simply empty. Suddenly, he realizes that the world is filled with the magic of holiness.

At first, the text says that Jacob gathered *stones* for his pillow, but when he sleeps, the Torah changes the plural form of "stones" to the singular "stone"—to only one stone. In an ancient legend, the Rabbis imagine that all the stones quarreled about who would get to be the one upon which Jacob would lay his head. But when the time came, they acted together as one.

When we pull together for a larger cause or purpose, we discover that ego no longer matters. In sports, it is about the team; in our best moments, it is about the family; and when we need each other, it is all of Israel—the entire Jewish people.

From angels to prayer to unity: Jacob's dream teaches us some central lessons about being a Jew. He is called Israel because the lessons of Jacob's life are lessons in our own lives, and those lessons belong to *am Yisrael*, the people of Israel, as well.

# וישלח

## *Vayishlach*

---

## How to Become *Yisrael*

### Rabbi Vernon Kurtz

**And a man wrestled with him until the break of dawn.**
(Genesis 32:25)

It is the middle of the night, and you are alone with your thoughts. Surely, this has happened to you. It might be on the eve of a great decision, an important event, a crucial exam, or a significant interview. You know what it is like: tossing and turning in your bed, worrying about what will happen in the morning.

As our patriarch Jacob prepares to meet his brother, Esau, after twenty years of separation, he has one of those sleepless nights. Who could blame him? After he stole the blessing of the firstborn from Esau, his brother threatened to kill him. Now that Jacob is about to return home to Canaan, he must face his older brother. No doubt about it: he must be terrified.

Jacob has taken his family across the Jabbok River, and he has returned to the other side for some last-minute arrangements. It is the middle of the night, and Jacob is alone. "And a man wrestled with him until the break of dawn" (Genesis 32:25).

Who is Jacob's wrestling partner?

Take your pick.

Perhaps the angel is a reflection of God.

---

**Rabbi Vernon Kurtz** is rabbi of North Suburban Synagogue Beth El in Highland Park, Illinois.

Perhaps it is, as a midrash suggests, the angel of Esau. The angel of Esau represents all of Jacob's fears and worries about the vengeance that he might rightfully expect from his brother.

Perhaps it is Jacob himself. Jacob has to wrestle with his own self-doubts.

Perhaps it is the darker parts of himself. To overcome his brother's hatred and his concern for his own welfare, Jacob has to fight the evil inclination that is part of his very essence.

The Torah tells us that the struggle continues throughout the night. When the dawn is breaking, the "man" wants Jacob to let him go, but Jacob answers: "I will not let you go, unless you bless me" (Genesis 32:27).

At that point, Jacob, a name meaning "heel" or "deceiver," becomes "Yisrael"—for "you have striven with beings divine and human and have prevailed" (Genesis 32:29).

Whoever you think the wrestling partner is, one thing is certain: Jacob is no longer the same Jacob that he was before the wrestling match. For the first time in his life, Jacob has refused to run away from his responsibilities. He is ready to confront his own weaknesses and to face a future in which he will be able to rely on his strengths.

We are *benei Yisrael*, the children of Israel—those who continue that struggle our patriarch ultimately won. You may have doubts about yourself, your future, or even what will happen to you tomorrow morning. However, as *benei Yisrael*, we must have faith in ourselves, in our mission, and in our God that we will prevail.

In reality, each of us is both Jacob—capable of deception—and Yisrael—capable of struggle. It is your choice. Challenge yourself to be a member of *benei Yisrael*, so that with strength, insight, and wisdom you can engage in the battles that are before you, secure in the faith that you will be successful in your endeavors.

# Each of Us Has a Name

### Rabbi Amy Joy Small

**They set out from Bethel; but when they were still some distance short of Ephrath, Rachel was in childbirth, and she had hard labor.... But as she breathed her last—for she was dying—she named him Ben-oni; but his father called him Benjamin. Thus Rachel died.** (Genesis 35:16–19)

Do you have a nickname?

In high school, my friends dubbed me "Joyful," because of my middle name, Joy. It is now decades later, and I still smile just remembering the sound of my friends calling for "Joyful" down the hall.

Some people also called me "Animal's Sister," because my older brother Hal (*zichrono l'vracha*, may his memory be a blessing) was known in our school as "Animal"—for his wild reputation. I didn't enjoy hearing, "Hey, Animal's Sister!" shouted through the hall.

But, when I heard, "Animal's Sister," it meant that my brother's friends accepted me and that we were connected.

To give another person a name is a very powerful thing. The guys who called my brother "The Animal" were not only describing who they saw him to be, but also the man that he might become. Those boys helped shape my brother, Hal, and because of that, they

---

**Rabbi Amy Joy Small** is rabbi of Reconstructionist Congregation Beth Hatikvah in Summit, New Jersey.

had a remarkable connection. The friends who called me "Joyful" did that for me, too.

Do you have nicknames given to you by friends or family? Have you nicknamed anyone? How has that name changed you or them or your connection?

Names are such a funny thing; they can describe and shape us. Our ancestors would have agreed, because in ancient times, people believed that your name could actually shape your soul.

For better or worse, our parents give us our first set of names. In Ashkenazic Jewish tradition, we are named in memory of deceased family members. Do you know why your parents chose your name? Do you know the story of the person or people for whom you were named? Does it describe who you are?

In our portion, there is a powerful story about naming. We read: "They set out from Bethel; but when they were still some distance short of Ephrath, Rachel was in childbirth, and she had hard labor.... But as she breathed her last—for she was dying—she named him Ben-oni; but his father called him Benjamin. Thus Rachel died" (Genesis 35:16–19).

This sad story tells us a lot about naming. Ben-oni means "son of my sorrow." Rachel imprints her child with the sorrow she was feeling, but Jacob could not tolerate this. He changes the infant's name to Benjamin, "son of the right hand," meaning that he would be the source of his father's strength. And with that new name, Benjamin receives the blessing of a promising future.

Once, my three kids and I went hiking on part of the Appalachian Trail. We met many "thru-hikers" who were journeying up the entire trail. They all had "trail names." We spent a stormy night at a shelter with "Yoga Boy," "Achilles," "Bootleg," and "Cricket." We were left to imagine how they got these names and who these people really were. Later, we talked about what we would name ourselves. It was not as easy as we thought it would be. We each tried offering names for each other, but none of us accepted the suggestions. We wanted to own the power of naming for ourselves, and yet we were hesitant and uncertain. Maybe the power of naming really should rest in the hands of others.

Sometimes the names that we choose become our masks—like the screen names that we give ourselves in cyberspace. But, later we might become uncomfortable with the public face that we have perhaps too carelessly created for ourselves. Here, again, we learn the lesson of how a name can be very powerful.

Imagine, now, that you have the chance to choose your name or your nickname. What would it be?

That's what the Israeli poet Zelda was thinking about:

> Each of us has a name
> given by God
> and given by our parents
>
> Each of us has a name
> given by our stature and our smile
> and given by what we wear ...

The truth is, when I consider what I'd like my nickname to be, I'll stick with "Joyful." My parents and my high school friends gave me my true names. And that is what Jacob did for his youngest son, Benjamin, as well.

# וישב

# *Vayeshev*

## Not Your Plans—God's

Rabbi Lawrence Kushner

**Even while he was there in prison, the Eternal was with Joseph....** (Genesis 39:20–21)

You ever get the feeling something is coming down? No matter how hard you push in one direction, things seem to be moving in another. After a while, you look back on what's happened, and you begin to suspect that maybe there's some bigger plan. This isn't a topic they usually talk to you about, because everyone assumes that you are having too much fun enjoying the pleasures of (finally) being in charge of your own life. There's even an old piece of wisdom: The younger you are and the closer you are to an event, the more you think you're running it. But the older you are and the farther you get from an event, the more you suspect you haven't been running anything.

Well, that's what *Vayeshev* is all about. It's the story of how a bunch of people (would you believe—all the Jews in the world, and a few Egyptians, too) thought they could run things the way they wanted.

This is even more curious because, unlike everything we've read in the Torah up until now, and what we'll read after the Joseph story and the end of the book of Genesis, God doesn't say or do anything!

**Rabbi Lawrence Kushner** is Emanu-El Scholar at Congregation Emanu-El of San Francisco.

Everyone else in the story is convinced that he or she is running things. And, often, they seem to be: Joseph's brothers sell him into slavery; Ms. Potiphar frames Joseph; Joseph tries to get out of jail.

But once we look back over the whole story, we realize that God has had a plan from the get-go: by the end of the book of Genesis, God has got to get the Jews living in the land of Egypt. Even though it sounds funny, here's why: if there were no Jews living in Egypt at the end of Genesis, it would be a pretty dumb book of Exodus. "A new king arose over Egypt" (Exodus 1:8). But if there had been no Jews there, who would have cared?

This was God's plan. Before God could make a deal with us at Mount Sinai, we first had to personally experience slavery—four hundred years of it—just so we would never forget. And it worked! Three thousand years later, and we're still having Seders!

Joseph's brothers decide to sell him into slavery; Jacob believes his favorite son is dead; Joseph thinks he's dead meat; Ms. Potiphar thinks she's framed Joseph forever; Pharaoh thinks he's, well, a god.

Indeed, it's not until a few more Torah portions that finally one person gets it—only one guy in the whole saga. Joseph explains to his brothers, "Relax, it wasn't you who sent me down here to Egypt; it was God all along" (Genesis 45:8 [my translation—LK]).

And, wouldn't you know it? They don't believe him.

But now we do.

# That Man Is You

### Rabbi Jack Moline

**When he reached Shechem, a man came upon him wandering in the fields. The man asked him, "What are you looking for?" He answered, "I am looking for my brothers."** (Genesis 37:14–15)

You are walking through the mall, down the street, across campus and a stranger—obviously a tourist—has that panicked look of being completely lost.

Would it surprise you to discover that you could literally change the course of this person's life with a few kind words?

I can prove the point from the story of Joseph in chapter 37 of Genesis—look it up. Jacob has sent his son Joseph to find his brothers, and Joseph gets lost. Along comes a nameless man who finds him wandering around in the field, and he asks Joseph, "What are you looking for?" Joseph tells him he is looking for his brothers, and to paraphrase the man's response, he says, "They went that-a-way."

Think about it for a minute. If this mystery man had given the wrong directions, or if he had said "I don't know," or if he had sent Joseph home, the rest of the Bible wouldn't have happened—no Moses, no Exodus, no Torah, no Promised Land, no King David, no Akiva, no Maimonides, no Einstein, no Andy Samberg, no you.

**Rabbi Jack Moline** is rabbi of Agudas Achim Congregation in Alexandria, Virginia.

And so it is worth asking, "Who was that man?"

I like to tell people that there is no such thing as a coincidence. They credit me with great faith in God's plan for humanity, that the Holy One has put everything in motion for a purpose. And I do not apologize for that sleight of hand.

But the fact is, I am not quite that pious. When I say that there is no such thing as a coincidence, I mean that there is an explanation for everything in this world—good, bad, or indifferent. The football bounced into the hands of the defense because of the trajectory of the throw and the angle of the receiver's fingers. You got a particular grade because of how well (or how not so well) you prepared. Your beloved relative contracted a terminal illness not as punishment, but because the combination of genetics and marriage choices and the environment conspired to make him susceptible to it. Like the butterfly that flaps its wings and becomes the main actor in chaos theory, nothing is incidental, and therefore nothing is coincidental. Everything counts.

So when I tell you that Joseph's encountering that guy in the field was no coincidence, what do I mean?

I mean that the Bible deliberately leaves the man's name out. This small act—reaching out to help a confused teenager find his way—is the small act of kindness that I hope any one of us might perform in similar circumstances. We hold the door for the people entering a building behind us. We provide some change for the homeless man on the street. We give a lost tourist directions.

The first person who is reported to have asked that question changed the course of history. His name isn't mentioned and his origin is unknown, but he offers, perhaps, the most elevating lesson in the entire Bible: there is no person, no act, no kindness, and no outreach that is incidental. Each human being can determine the course of history.

Wow—what a responsibility.

I hope it makes you consider the consequence of every action you make in your life. I hope that it offers you a sense of humility, the ability to see that the big picture of this world that is God's domain might depend on your simplest decision. You can change the course of a person's life with a simple act.

Do you want to know the answer to my question? Do you want to know, "Who's that man?"

It is you.

# Miketz

## Truth or Consequences

### Rabbi Cherie Koller-Fox

The plan pleased Pharaoh and all his courtiers. And
Pharaoh said to his courtiers, "Could we find another
like him, a man in whom is the spirit of God?"
(Genesis 41:37–38)

How do you know whom to trust and what is true? In *Miketz*,
Pharaoh faces that problem.

One night, Pharaoh dreams that there are seven large, healthy
cows grazing in the pasture. Behind them are seven thin and ill-
looking cows. Suddenly, the thin cows eat the fatter ones. The dream
startles him.

Pharaoh falls asleep again, and this time, he dreams about seven
good ears of corn going up a stalk. Springing up after them are seven
lean and scorched ears. The lean ears swallow up the good ears.

Pharaoh is disturbed by his dreams, and he needs to know
what they mean. None of his wise men can tell him, so Pharaoh's
cupbearer tells him about a Hebrew named Joseph who correctly
interpreted a dream for him in prison.

Pharaoh summons Joseph from prison. Joseph tells Pharaoh that
what seems like two dreams is really one, that the dream and its

---

**Rabbi Cherie Koller-Fox** is president of NewCAJE, a national organization
that advocates for Jewish educators and Jewish education, and serves as
rabbi of the Chapel Havurah in the Boston area.

interpretation come from God, and that the dream is a message to Pharaoh. The dream means that there will be seven good harvests followed by seven terrible years of famine. To save Egypt, Pharaoh needs to appoint someone to gather and store food during the good years and organize distribution during the bad ones.

When Pharaoh and his servants hear this, they know Joseph is telling the truth. "The plan pleased Pharaoh and all his courtiers. And Pharaoh said to his courtiers, 'Could we find another like him, a man in whom is the spirit of God?'" (Genesis 41:37–38).

Why do they believe Joseph? Pharaoh trusts Joseph because he has a good reputation as a dream interpreter. More than that: Pharaoh believes that these dreams come from his own mind. He knows that when he hears the true meaning of the dreams, his heart will know it.

Pharaoh understands that the dreams are serving as an important warning, and he wants to use this information to help his people. Only Joseph understands enough to be able to warn him about a famine and to give him a plan for the future.

In your own life, how can you know what is true? How can you know whom to believe? Nowadays, teens can find this to be very difficult, especially because the Internet has basically drowned us in *information*. The Hasidic teacher Menachem Mendel of Kotzk taught that every day we should search for truth as if we had never seen it before. He believed the key to finding truth was to be a freethinking person. To recognize truth, you can't be biased or give in to outside pressure to conform. There is an interesting coincidence here: we read *Miketz* during Hanukkah, when we remember that the Maccabees fought against Antiochus, who wanted everyone to conform to *his* truth.

You can learn to judge people by their character, and not by what they wear or how they look. In this way, it is OK to imitate Pharaoh. Pharaoh didn't dwell on Joseph's prison attire or on the fact that he was a Hebrew. He judged him by listening closely to the words Joseph spoke.

It is very important in life to trust your judgment and to listen to your heart. Prejudice can stand in your way. So can peer pressure. Don't give in to those who would put pressure on you so that they can control the way you think and how you act.

# The Tests of Adulthood

Rabbi Kerry M. Olitzky

**When Joseph saw his brothers, he recognized them; but he acted like a stranger toward them and spoke harshly to them.** (Genesis 42:7)

The "Joseph saga" takes up about one-quarter of the book of Genesis, and for those who have read this far, you would have some expectations. You would have expected to learn that Joseph has matured and that he is now ready to confront his brothers openly. After all, Joseph has been through a great deal since his "sibling rivalry" days of childhood. Even though Joseph's brothers disliked him (and there were probably others who disliked him as well), his father Jacob favored him. That's really what the so-called coat of many colors was all about. It might even have reflected the fact that he would get a majority stake in the inheritance. No wonder his brothers were jealous and angry—enough to want to kill him.

In Egypt, first Joseph was a slave, and then he was a prisoner—and then Pharaoh made him his prime minister. Nevertheless, when Joseph reunites with his brothers, he goes back to the same manipulative games that he used to play when he was a young boy. Not pretty. Here's something to look forward to: sometimes when grown kids get together, they go back to their "default settings,"

---

**Rabbi Kerry M. Olitzky** is executive director of the Jewish Outreach Institute.

the way they were when they were kids. It is as if their relationship script never changes.

That's the way it is for Joseph. We would have expected that Joseph's experiences would have pushed him toward greater maturity. But it doesn't work out that way—at least, not in the way that he relates to his brothers. Joseph still feels like he is the outsider, trying hard for his brothers to accept him. But his behaviors actually make them despise him more.

In what seems to be a short time, Joseph has achieved an unbelievable level of authority in Egypt. He accomplished his rise in authority with the very same dream-interpretation skills that got him in trouble with his brothers in the first place. As is the case for most of us, the bright side of Joseph also casts a shadow. In this Torah portion, Joseph lauds his authority over his brothers, even if they have yet to learn his identity.

Asserting authority works with young kids. It helps them establish a moral direction. That's why they like people in uniform and pay attention to parents and teachers.

But as we start to get older, we think for ourselves, as well as being influenced by what our peers think. Joseph must have skipped that page in the "Prime Minister Manual." Instead, he forces his brothers to beg him for food—something no brother should ever do. He takes advantage of their bad situation. They are hungry, and they are seeking refuge and support.

And what is Joseph's response? To put it bluntly: Joseph messes with their heads. He toys with his brothers by hiding his personal cup in his younger brother Benjamin's sack—his only full brother, and the one who seems to have taken Joseph's own place for his father's affection. We have to wait for the next Torah reading before we know what happens to the brothers and Joseph's reaction to the "theft."

What is the Torah trying to teach us here?

Joseph is just like many adults we know; he hasn't really grown up. He is still the kid he was when his brothers last knew him, before they sold him into slavery. We would have hoped that he would have grown up. We might expect the same of ourselves; as we grow older, we hope that we will become better.

But this kind of growth doesn't happen on its own. We have all sorts of drives in us that pull us in different directions. The Rabbis call these drives the *yetzer ha-ra* (the inclination to do evil) and the *yetzer tov* (the inclination for goodness). Our job, as we get older, is to balance them.

Will this happen with Joseph? Yes. People can change, and Joseph does—by engaging in *teshuvah*, "repentance" or "return." Joseph has to make peace with his competing drives. That's what helps him right his behaviors and repair his relationship with the Divine.

We might even say that Joseph returns to his "real" or essential self—and that, too, is the essential goal of *teshuvah*.

# וַיִּגַּשׁ
# *Vayigash*

## Joseph Comes Out of the Closet
### Rabbi Eve Rudin

**Joseph could no longer control himself before all his attendants, and he cried out, "Have everyone withdraw from me!" So there was no one else about when Joseph made himself known to his brothers. His sobs were so loud that the Egyptians could hear, and so the news reached Pharaoh's palace. Joseph said to his brothers, "I am Joseph. Is my father still well?" But his brothers could not answer him, so dumbfounded were they on account of him.** (Genesis 45:1–3)

If you could choose a little brother, would you choose Joseph? He was a bratty, bragging show-off. Joseph's brothers responded pretty dramatically to their little brother's obnoxious behavior; they threw Joseph into a pit and sold him into slavery.

To put it mildly, this is a story in which no one was acting his or her best.

---

**Rabbi Eve Rudin** is director of the Congregational School at the Park Avenue Synagogue in New York City. She previously served as the North American director of the North American Federation of Temple Youth (NFTY) and as the director of the Union for Reform Judaism (URJ) Kutz Camp for Reform Jewish teens.

Fast-forward twenty-two years. Joseph is now the prime minister of Egypt, and he is a big success. He is rich and powerful, and he seems to have it all.

When Joseph's brothers come to Egypt, he recognizes them, but they do not recognize Joseph. And so it is that Joseph left one prison only to enter another, for he keeps his true identity in the closet from those surrounding him and, perhaps, even from himself.

When Joseph meets his brothers, he experiences deep inner pain. After a dramatic set of games, the brothers plead for help and try to tug at the powerful stranger's heartstrings with sob stories of their father. Then, Joseph experiences Judah's true act of *teshuvah* (repentance); when faced with a familiar choice to discard a brother, Judah, instead, offers to be punished in Benjamin's place—and this moves Joseph more than anything else.

At that precise moment, Joseph can "no longer control himself" and sends out all his Egyptian attendants "so that there was no one else about when Joseph made himself known to his brothers. His sobs were so loud that the Egyptians could hear, and so the news reached Pharaoh's palace." The time has come for Joseph to dramatically come out of his closet and to be honest about who he really is. And at that moment, Joseph proclaims to his brothers, "I am Joseph" (Genesis 45:1–3).

Today, many people spend their lives in the anguish of similar closets and prisons. Whether you hide your love of the arts from presumably disapproving high-pressure parents or hide your homosexuality, not being true to yourself can create extraordinary anguish with tragic results.

As you can see in the many testimonial videos in the *It Gets Better Project*, when people free themselves from those closets, the darkness and the anguish lift, and that paves the way for a new life of truthfulness, confidence, and wholeness.

David Deschamps, who produced Hebrew Union College–Jewish Institute of Religion's *It Gets Better* video, describes his anguish growing up and the acceptance he received when he came out as a gay man: "I hated myself as a teenager because I was gay. And, when

I came out and told the best friends in my life, it made no difference to them. They completely accepted me."

Coming out of the closet allows Joseph to rise above the situation, to do the right thing, and to pave the way for a new chapter in his family. Joseph's brothers are "dumbfounded" by Joseph's admission. Why? The medieval commentator Rashi explains that they are embarrassed. But they might also be frightened that Joseph will take revenge on them. That is not what happens; Joseph urges them to come closer to him and says, "Do not be distressed or reproach yourselves because you sold me hither" (Genesis 45:5).

Yes, Joseph is ready to forgive his brothers. But that forgiveness is complicated, painful, and risky. Judah has to show that he has changed. Joseph has to accept that change is possible. Only then can Joseph take the ultimate risk and come out of his closet and be honest—not only with others, but also with himself.

Only then can the brothers truly make peace.

# Joseph or Moses: Who Do You Want to Be?

Barry Shrage

"Let us not perish before your eyes, both we and our land. Take us and our land in exchange for bread, and we with our land will be serfs to Pharaoh; provide the seed, that we may live and not die, and that the land may not become a waste." So Joseph gained possession of all the farm land of Egypt for Pharaoh, every Egyptian having sold his field because the famine was too much for them; thus the land passed over to Pharaoh. And he removed the population town by town, from one end of Egypt's border to the other. (Genesis 47:19–21)

Our Rabbis call Joseph "*ha-tzaddik*, the righteous one"; we therefore consider him a role model, both as a leader and as a human being. Because you might be learning how to be a leader, or you might already be a leader, or you will grow up to be a leader (maybe even, I hope, a Jewish leader), let me teach you what the story of Joseph can teach us about leadership.

Or let me put it this way: let me teach you what the story of Joseph has to teach us about how *not* to be a leader.

**Barry Shrage** is president of Combined Jewish Philanthropies, Boston's Jewish Federation.

Most of us think of Joseph as a powerful, talented leader. After all, he rose from prisoner, to prison administrator, to overseer in Potiphar's house, to the prime minister of Egypt. Everything Joseph touched became successful.

But was he someone you'd want to have leading you or the kind of leader you'd want to be?

A great scholar, Aaron Wildavsky, compared Joseph to Moses, and he suggests that the story of Joseph appears in the Torah for one reason: precisely to teach us what a true leader is *not. Joseph was the anti-Moses.*[2]

What do I mean by this?

Joseph was the Hebrew who became an Egyptian. Moses was the Egyptian who became a Hebrew.

Joseph was the slave who became an overseer. Moses was the prince who identified with slaves.

Joseph was the overseer who enslaved the Egyptians. Moses was the prince who freed the slaves.

Joseph strengthened Pharaoh's dictatorship, and he helped produce an Egyptian system that rejected foreigners and strangers. Moses weakened Pharaoh, liberated the slaves, and commanded his people to welcome strangers and protect the oppressed, "because you were strangers in the land of Egypt" (Exodus 22:20).

Joseph believed he was God's instrument. Moses, the most humble of men, did not want to accept his role as God's messenger.

Yes, Joseph had many good qualities. He had a strong ethical core, which we saw when he resisted Potiphar's wife. But let's be honest—Joseph was loyal to whomever could best serve his personal interests, and he showed very little responsibility to the greater society. Joseph was a great worker and a great manager, but that's about it.

By contrast, Moses was a *leader*. How did he lead? He showed us a vision. He taught us to care for the oppressed and to build a society around that value.

Yes, Joseph was competent, and he was successful. But competence and success are not the only measures of leadership.

Rather, it is the strength and beauty of the vision we seek to serve and our commitment to our people's history and destiny.

So as you grow older, and as you prepare to become a leader, ask yourself: do you want to be Joseph, or do you want to be Moses?

# ויחי

## *Vayechi*

### Both Kindness to Others and Loyalty to Ourselves

Rabbi John Moscowitz

**And when the time approached for Israel to die, he summoned his son Joseph and said to him, "Do me this favor, place your hand under my thigh as a pledge of your steadfast loyalty [*chesed ve'emet*]: please do not bury me in Egypt."** (Genesis 47:29)

There are few biblical phrases as beautiful as *chesed ve'emet*, which we usually translate as "steadfast loyalty," but which literally means "kindness and loyalty." *Chesed* refers to acts of kindness; *emet* means that a Jew would be loyal to the Jewish people and to the Jewish land—*Eretz Yisrael*, the Land of Israel.

For centuries, those two words—*chesed ve'emet*, "kindness and loyalty"—always went together. You could not separate *chesed*, doing acts of kindness, from *emet*, being loyal to the covenant with one's people.

But today, many Jews prefer *chesed*, acts of kindness, to *emet*, being faithful to the covenant.

But, you ask, what could possibly be wrong with *chesed*, doing acts of kindness, especially for non-Jews? The homeless, the hungry,

---

**Rabbi John Moscowitz** is senior rabbi at Holy Blossom Temple, Toronto, Canada.

the marginal beyond our ranks—sometimes, the further away the better: that's where our *chesed* goes. Isn't that what Judaism is all about?

There's nothing wrong with *chesed*, acts of kindness. Could you imagine being Jewish without it?

But being Jewish hardly stops there; it can't, otherwise we forget ourselves. That's why we still need *emet*: being loyal to our covenant with God and the Jewish people. We cannot simply help others without showing loyalty to our own Jewish people. That's exactly why, in the Bible, you had to mention *chesed* (kindness) and *emet* (loyalty to the Jewish people) in the same breath. That's why we must keep them together today. For the sake of others—and for our sake, too.

Fortunately, we are living in a time when we have come to realize the importance of maintaining the strength of the Jewish people, and not just caring for everyone else in the world. Among all Jews, and certainly among those Jews who are not Orthodox, we are experiencing a renewed sense of Jewish peoplehood and loyalty. This doesn't mean that we shouldn't do for others. But it does mean that we don't forget who we are; we do for our own as well as for others.

And now, a word about the State of Israel, and what's at stake.

When Israel is threatened, we must express ourselves through acts of loyalty and support for our Land. Israel and Jerusalem are central to Jews and Judaism; they have sustained us. Now it is our turn and responsibility to help Israel—with the same strength that we have often used in helping others.

# *Sababa!*

Rabbi Avi Weiss

**Assemble and hearken, O sons of Jacob; hearken to
Israel your father.** (Genesis 49:2)

*Vayechi* completes the circle of the story of Joseph. It ends in a very
different place than where it began.

When the story starts, Joseph and his brothers are fierce rivals.
Joseph dreams of bundles of wheat and stars bowing down to him.
The bundles of wheat represent the promise of land, while the
stars symbolize the promise of children. In dreaming about these
symbols, Joseph is saying that the covenant, which revolves around
the promise of land and children, will be his—and *only* his.

As you can imagine, this creates great disagreement among the
brothers.

In our Torah portion, at the very end of the story of Joseph and
the book of Genesis, Jacob gathers all of his sons and offers them
blessings: "Assemble and hearken, O sons of Jacob; hearken to Israel
your father" (Genesis 49:2).

This is a very big deal, because for the first time in the book of
Genesis, *no one is excluded.* Everyone receives a blessing. Everyone

**Rabbi Avraham (Avi) Weiss** is senior rabbi of the Hebrew Institute of
Riverdale, Bronx, New York. He is also the founder and president of YCT,
the Modern and Open Orthodox Rabbinical School in New York, and
cofounder of the International Rabbinic Fellowship (IRF). Most recently,
he founded Yeshivat Maharat, a school training women to become Jewish
spiritual leaders.

seems to be on the same page. What started out as sibling *rivalry* has turned into sibling *unity*.

Not only this: even though we are already at the end of Genesis, for the first time in the Bible, we meet a grandfather—and that is Jacob. While there were certainly grandparents and grandchildren in Genesis before this, we have no record of grandparents and grandchildren actually relating to each other, actually having a conversation. That's why when Jacob meets his grandchildren, Ephraim and Manasseh, it is an important moment in human and biblical history. When Jacob meets his grandchildren, he blesses them by saying that they are as important to him as his own children: "Ephraim and Manasseh shall be mine no less than Reuben and Simeon" (Genesis 48:5).

Today, too often, Jews fight with each other. We now need a spirit of unity. But, please understand: unity does not mean *uniformity*. It doesn't mean that we have to erase all of our differences. Unity means that we can live together as one Jewish community—*despite* our differences.

So, here's some "homework": find a Jew in your community with whom you disagree. Maybe you disagree about which rituals are important. Maybe you disagree about what Israel should be doing. It doesn't matter—just connect with that person, and learn to listen to that person. Feel the unity of the Jewish people—*despite* our differences. That's how Jacob could bless *all* his sons, even though they didn't always agree.

Let's also remember how Jacob blessed his grandsons. Grandparents have much to gain from grandchildren, and grandchildren have much to learn from grandparents. What can you do to help create places where people of all generations, young and old, can be with each other—at worship services or through social and Jewish activism?

Nowadays, there is a lot of serious tension in Israel. But, despite that, the way that people talk tells a different story. Young people use an interesting word to greet each other: *achi*, "my sibling, my brother, my sister." And young people open and close phone conversations with the word *sababa*, a slang term that means "great, cool, awesome, no worries."

A little piece of slang has a lot to teach us. Because, what is *sababa*? We can imagine that it is a combination of the words *saba* and *aba*—"grandfather" and "father," though it could just as easily be "grandmother" and "mother"—words that link the generations together.

This is the real message of the Joseph story. It begins with real, painful family breakdown, but it ends with repair—a repair of relationships between siblings, and a repair of relationships between the generations.

*Sababa*!

Shemot/
Exodus

# שמות

# *Shemot*

## No Such Thing as an Innocent Bystander

### Rabbi William G. Hamilton

**The midwives, fearing God, did not do as the king of Egypt had told them; they let the boys live.** (Exodus 1:17)

You see someone being teased in the cafeteria. What do you do? Do you stand by and do nothing? Or do you stand up for the person being bullied, not worrying how it makes you look?

The opening portion of the Torah's second book, *Shemot*, teaches some good lessons about the ways we can do the right thing. When we see cruelty, we need to think about *when*, *to whom*, and *how* we react—so that we can be more than bystanders.

Exodus begins with Pharaoh's order to murder all the male Hebrew infants. But the midwives Shiphrah and Puah do not obey. They believe in God, which means they know that murder is wrong. Their willingness to ignore unjust laws will inspire leaders like Martin Luther King and Gandhi.

When Pharaoh challenges the midwives, they quickly reply, "Before the midwife can come to them, they have given birth" (Exodus 1:19). When it comes to preventing murder, *timing is everything*. Act quickly!

But, how about when you see someone being bullied? When is the right time to act?

**Rabbi William G. Hamilton** is rabbi at Congregation Kehillath Israel in Brookline, Massachusetts.

You're at a party, and someone is making fun of your friend. In that moment, what do you actually do?

Shiphrah and Puah's courage shows us that when someone is being hurt, we all expect (and hope) that someone will step up.

But the lesson of *Shemot* is that even the most unlikely person can challenge cruelty. Later in this story, that unlikely person is Pharaoh's daughter. Her father has a *hard heart* and has ordered the murder of the Hebrew babies. Her *open heart* insists on saving the baby in the basket.

What is the Torah's reward for this act of bravery—of a daughter going against not just a father, but also a king? She names the baby Moses, the name he has throughout his life.

The other heroes in the Bible like Abraham, Sarah, and Jacob get their names changed. Not Moses. In fact, he must have had an earlier name, a birth name that his "biological" parents had given him. We don't know what that name was. The only name we know him by is Moses—the name that was given to him by a noble woman who was willing to act courageously.

Even if the time is right and you are the one to challenge a bully, *how* do you do it? *Shemot* gives its answer through yet another brave woman—Moses's sister, Miriam. Her resourceful thinking sets an example. She makes sure that the baby's mother will still be able to feed him (Exodus 2:7).

The lesson: go with your instincts. Even if you risk embarrassing yourself, it is never wrong to do the right thing. And helping someone else will make you feel better—longer than anything else you can imagine. When your heart tells you that it's your moment to step up, chances are that you're right, and you'll know what to do, just as Miriam did.

The path to go from being a *bystander* to an *upstander* (thanks to Facing History and Ourselves for this term) may not be easy, but it will be right.

Bystanders are invisible.

But like the heroines in Moses's infancy who stood up for him, *upstanders* can change the world.[1]

# So, When Do You Really Grow Up?

Rabbi Jeffrey K. Salkin

**Some time after that, when Moses had grown up, he went out to his kinsfolk and witnessed their labors. He saw an Egyptian beating a Hebrew, one of his kinsmen. He turned this way and that and, seeing no one about, he struck down the Egyptian and hid him in the sand.**
(Exodus 2:11–12)

I could not wait to become a teenager.

I was so impatient that from the time I was ten, I counted the days—actually, the years. When I was eleven, I proudly proclaimed to my parents that I was, in fact, a teenager. My reasoning (and my mathematical sense, which was never my strong suit) was clear: eleven is one more than ten; therefore, it is a number that is in the teens.

My parents disagreed. To them, the word "eleven" did not have the "teen" element in it. Neither, they informed me a year later, did "twelve." (Why aren't those numbers different? Why aren't they, say, "one-teen" and "two-teen"?)

In those days, they had not yet invented the term "tweens." I would have to wait until I reached an age that had "teen" in it—which meant, of course, thirteen.

**Rabbi Jeffrey K. Salkin** is the editor of this volume. He has been a congregational rabbi and is the author or editor of many books, published by Jewish Lights Publishing, as well as a regular contributor to online and print Jewish journals.

So, apparently, that's when you become a teenager.

But, when do you become a grown-up?

I invite you to look at Moses's early life as an answer to that question.

The first, and the most essential, step on Moses's journey to maturity is that he must recognize his people, which is the Jewish people. And when he *does* recognize his people, that recognition goes from his eyes to his brain to his soul—and directly to his hands. Moses sees an Egyptian torturing a Hebrew slave, and he kills the Egyptian.

It would have been nice if Moses did not have to do that. When the text tells us that Moses "turned this way and that" before killing the Egyptian, maybe he wasn't looking to see whether there were any witnesses around. Maybe he was looking to see whether there were any other people around who could help. But no—Moses was totally alone, and he had to act with courage and with speed.

We all need role models who can teach us about standing up for others, and being decisive, and acting with force. For us as Jews, Moses is that role model.

The truth is, I was never particularly good with "force." I never liked using my fists. I relied on a second way that Moses acted— using my words.

The next day, Moses sees two Hebrews fighting, and this time he doesn't respond with force. Rather than letting his fists do the talking, he asks a question. Like all good Jewish questions, it starts with "Why?" "Why do you strike your fellow?" (Exodus 2:13).

As you journey through your teenaged years, and as you approach adulthood, you will figure out that a major part of growing up is learning to ask good questions.

That has always been the Jewish way: to act decisively when necessary, and to ask questions whenever possible.

That's your legacy. Love it and live it.

# וארא

## *Va'era*

---

# Conviction, Yes; Stubbornness, No

### Rabbi Howard L. Jaffe

**But when Pharaoh saw that there was relief, he became stubborn and would not heed them, as the Eternal had spoken.** (Exodus 8:11)

I think that we can all agree: it is good to be self-confident.

It is also good to have strong convictions.

But it is not good to be stubborn.

In fact, when you refuse to accept powerful evidence that you are wrong, it can be dangerous. When that refusal to admit wrong affects other people, it can be worse than dangerous; it can also be evil.

Pharaoh is a ruler, but he is much more than a ruler. To his people and to himself, he is a god on earth, and no one is as powerful (and certainly, more powerful) than him. Of course, we know better—and Pharaoh is about to find out. But despite the most overwhelming evidence, he just cannot accept the fact that there is one more powerful than him.

God gives Pharaoh every opportunity to say "I give up." God starts out simply enough, by having Aaron's rod turn into a serpent,

---

**Rabbi Howard L. Jaffe** is senior rabbi of Temple Isaiah in Lexington, Massachusetts. He is a past vice chair of the Union of Reform Judaism Youth Commission, and he has spent many years as a staff member of Reform movement camps, including sixteen summers as a camp rabbi at the URJ Harlam and Eisner Camps.

but because Pharaoh has his magicians do the same thing with their rods, he remains unimpressed—even as Aaron's rod swallows up the other rods.

No, it is clear that Pharaoh is not going to give up that quickly or easily. So God brings on those famous (or infamous) plagues: blood, frogs, lice, insects, pestilence, boils, and hail (the final three plagues come in the next Torah portion). Pharaoh is still not ready to give in. God turns the Nile River into blood, so Pharaoh has his magicians do the same thing. In short, Pharaoh is not impressed.

So God brings a plague of frogs. This is a feat that Pharaoh's magicians cannot replicate, and it gets his attention. He agrees to let the Israelites go to worship their God. But as soon as the frogs disappear, Pharaoh changes his mind.

And that becomes the pattern: God keeps upping the ante, bringing plagues that are progressively more destructive and more damaging. Each time, Pharaoh agrees to let the Israelites go, until that particular plague ends. Then, once again, Pharaoh reneges.

So here's the question: if God keeps hardening or stiffening, or even *strengthening* Pharaoh's heart, then how can Pharaoh be responsible for what he is doing?

Read the text closely. After each of the first five plagues, Pharaoh hardens, or stiffens, or strengthens his own heart. In short, he becomes stubborn.

It is only after God gives him five opportunities to respond properly that God helps Pharaoh, as God helps all of us, become who Pharoah has determined he is going to be.

So why does the Torah need three different words to describe what happens to Pharaoh's heart? When Pharaoh is stubborn, his resolve is strengthened. When Pharaoh' s heart is stiffened, he gives no thought to the impact that the plagues will have on the Egyptians.

But when his heart is hardened, what happens to the Israelites? It is something that we have all experienced. Perhaps the worst thing Pharaoh does is to raise the hopes of the Israelites, only to dash them over and over again—and maybe that kind of stubbornness is the worst and most evil of all.

Conviction is important. We all need to believe in our ideals and ourselves. But when, in the face of mounting and sometimes overwhelming evidence, we refuse to accept reality, then not only we but also those around us suffer the consequences of our stubbornness.

Worse yet, when, like Pharaoh, our stubbornness is only temporarily suppressed, because we temporarily find that we cannot deny the truth, we can wind up saying "yes" one moment and "no" the next, and that can cause even more damage.

As you grow into adulthood, you will discover that there is a difference between believing in your ideals and yourself and being so committed to them that you refuse to let evidence and truth get in the way.

# Hard Hearts—For Real

Dr. Ron Wolfson

**You shall repeat all that I command you, and your brother Aaron shall speak to Pharaoh to let the Israelites depart from his land. But I will harden Pharaoh's heart, that I may multiply My signs and marvels in the land of Egypt.** (Exodus 7:2–3)

I was thirteen years old when I first learned that the human heart can be really hard. I was convinced that my father was slowly killing himself.

He worked crazy long hours in a high-pressure business, his diet consisted mostly of fatty meats and fried foods, and worst of all, he smoked four packs of cigarettes a day. In school, the health education teacher had taught me that a substance called cholesterol could build up in the arteries of the body, forming a hard plaque that would eventually block blood flow. If the plaque got so thick and hard in the arteries of the heart, it would cause a complete stoppage of blood, resulting in a heart attack that could kill you.

And what are the main sources of cholesterol? Fatty meats, fried food, and smoking cigarettes—or, to be precise, my father's official diet.

---

**Dr. Ron Wolfson** is Fingerhut Professor of Education at American Jewish University in Los Angeles, California, and cofounder of Synagogue 3000.

So I launched a campaign to get Dad to get healthy. I recruited my brothers to help me make warning signs that we placed around the house while he was at work. Most of the signs featured skull and crossbones, along with various messages: "Smoking kills," "You're eating your heart out," "You're too young to die." One sign was more sympathetic: "We love you, Dad. We need you."

When Dad came home that night and saw what we had done, he was furious and tore the signs down.

That was when I learned a different way that the heart can be hardened. Dad was stubborn—refusing to listen to us, to Mom, and to his doctors. He kept smoking, eating, and working like crazy. Sure enough, ten years later, he suffered a major heart attack. He was only fifty-three years old.

In *Va'era*, we learn about the consequences of a hardened heart. Conditions for the Israelite slaves were unbearable. At the end of last week's portion, *Shemot*, God sent Moses to demand that the Pharaoh free "My people," but that only made matters worse.

So at the beginning of our Torah portion, God tells Moses to try again—only this time, God has a plan to make sure Pharaoh will let the people go: "You shall repeat all that I command you, and your brother Aaron shall speak to Pharaoh to let the Israelites depart from his land. But I will harden Pharaoh's heart, that I may multiply My signs and marvels in the land of Egypt" (Exodus 7:2–3).

The "signs and marvels" promised by God are the famous ten plagues of the Exodus story. We recall them during the Passover Seder: blood, frogs, vermin, beasts, cattle plague, boils, hail, locusts, darkness, and the death of the firstborn Egyptian. Only the first seven plagues are in our *parashah*, but they set the stage for the final catastrophic disasters to come.

Although God promises, "I will harden Pharaoh's heart," the text describing the first five plagues tells a different story. First, we read that Pharaoh *hardened his own heart*. In other words, Pharaoh was stubborn; literally, "his heart was heavy." During the last five plagues, however, the text reads, "God hardened the heart of Pharaoh."

What is the text message? Being stubborn can back you into a corner. Pharaoh had five chances to grasp what he was up against, but he was unmoved and arrogant. With each plague, his heart got harder, heavier. It is as if God said, "OK, you hardened your heart. You ignored Me. Let Me add to your burden; even if you wanted to give in now, no way. I gave you chances; now, I will harden your heart."

My father had a hard heart—which is to say, he was stubborn—and that stubbornness was, in fact, contributing to the actual hardening of his real, physical heart. He wouldn't listen, even to the pleas of his children.

But his heart attack was a wake-up call. He stopped smoking. He changed his diet. He took time off from work. He softened his heart. On Valentine's Day 1977, the day when people send each other hearts, he underwent a successful open-heart surgery.

Soon, God willing, he will celebrate his ninetieth birthday.

Judaism teaches that you can change.

Don't be stubborn. Don't be a Pharaoh.

Open your heart and live.

בא

# *Bo*

## Being a Global Team Player

Lisa Exler and Ruth W. Messinger

**In the middle of the night, the Eternal struck down all the firstborn in the land of Egypt, from the firstborn of Pharaoh who sat on the throne to the firstborn of the captive who was in the dungeon, and all the firstborn of the cattle.** (Exodus 12:29)

Imagine: You're in gym class playing soccer, when one of your teammates, Sam, trips a member of the other team. Blowing the whistle loudly, your teacher stops the game and tells your whole team to do twenty-five push-ups before resuming the game.

"That's not fair," one of your teammates calls out. "Sam committed the foul. Why do we *all* have to do push-ups?"

The ancient Egyptians could have asked a similar question about the ten plagues in the Torah. Even though only a handful of Egyptians served as brutal taskmasters, and it was only Pharaoh who refused to free the Israelites, *all* the Egyptians together suffered the

---

**Lisa Exler** is a senior program officer in the education and community engagement department at American Jewish World Service (AJWS).

**Ruth W. Messinger** is president of American Jewish World Service (AJWS), an organization that promotes the human rights of marginalized people in the developing world. She is a national leader in the movement to end the genocide in Sudan, and she has served on the Obama administration's Task Force on Global Poverty and Development.

devastation of the plagues. In fact, our portion describes the final plague—the death of the firstborn—as afflicting everyone, from "the firstborn of Pharaoh who sat on the throne to the firstborn of the captive who was in the dungeon" (Exodus 12:29).

We can understand why Pharaoh had to suffer this punishment; after all, he enslaved and oppressed the Israelites.

But why should the firstborn of an Egyptian *prisoner*—someone who certainly wasn't in a position to harm anyone—also deserve punishment?

What can we learn from this collective punishment?

Perhaps the average Egyptian was not as innocent as we might have thought.

For example: an Egyptian who did not physically beat an Israelite slave might have failed to speak up or take action against the injustice of slavery that was happening all around him.

The collective punishment of the Egyptians reminds us of our collective responsibility to fight oppression and to pursue justice. Just as every Egyptian was ultimately responsible for the injustice that existed in his or her society, we, too, are responsible for the injustice in our world if we fail to protect the rights and well-being of our fellow human beings.

If we know that there is poverty and war in the world and we do nothing about it, then poverty and war will inevitably continue. If our world's "team culture" is to look the other way when governments or individuals "foul," then we are passively helping to shape a world where violence and human rights abuses go unpunished.

While we may not be as powerful as Pharaoh, there are many things we can do to influence local and world events.

We can raise money for, give *tzedakah* to, and volunteer with organizations that fight poverty and protect human rights.

We can learn about injustice happening around the world and teach others about it, so that they, too, will be informed and be inspired to take action.

We can stop buying products from companies that oppress their workers.

We can tell our elected officials to vote for laws that promote equality.

As long as people in the world suffer, all of us—as individuals and as a collective—are responsible for doing what we can to stop that suffering.

The world is one big soccer team, and it is on all of our shoulders to make sure that everyone plays fair.[2]

# Does God Fight Fair?

Rabbi Avi S. Olitzky

**Now the Eternal had said to Moses, "Pharaoh will not heed you, in order that My marvels may be multiplied in the land of Egypt."** (Exodus 11:9)

Imagine two kids standing on the sidewalk, beating the heck out of each other, going punch for punch. Eventually, one of the kids starts to feel a bit light-headed and uneasy on his feet. Nevertheless, the steady-footed fighter continues to pound the dizzy one. In fact, as the soon-to-be "loser" begins to fall to the ground, the "winner" continues to steady him, raises him up, and knocks him down again.

Our parents would never approve of us taking part in such a fight. If any of us ever witnessed such a scene, we would probably intervene. We would eventually pull the kid who was dealing the relentless blows off the weaker kid.

So how do we deal with the fact that in this Torah portion, the uncompromising "butt-kicker" is, well, God?

Just before the Exodus from Egypt, God plays the role of relentless fighter, and Pharaoh (and the Egyptians) essentially get beaten to a pulp. By the time we reach our Torah portion, Pharaoh and the Egyptians are unsteady on their feet. But God continues to pick them up (hardening Pharaoh's heart) just to beat them down again with the final three plagues—locusts, darkness, and the death of the firstborn.

---

**Rabbi Avi S. Olitzky** is assistant rabbi at Beth El Synagogue in Saint Louis Park, Minnesota.

With locusts, God takes out the Egyptians' food.

With darkness, God takes out the Egyptians' ability to see and, according to the midrash, relieves them of their wealth.

With the death of the firstborn, God attacks the Egyptians' very existence—both their emotional ability to continue living and their future—destroying an entire generation.

What is more unnerving than God's continued assault on the Egyptians? It is how Moses acts. God hardens Pharaoh's heart, and just before Moses "tells off" Pharaoh, warning him of the death of the firstborn (Exodus 11:4–7), the great leader of the Jewish people becomes enraged. In fierce anger, Moses marches away (Exodus 11:8).

According to a Rabbinic tradition, the sage Resh Lakish taught that Moses actually slapped Pharaoh silly before he stormed off (Talmud, *Zevachim* 102a).

And there we see the most difficult part of this story. The problem does not only belong to the ancient text; it belongs to all of us.

God might have been trying to show the Egyptians (and the world) how awesome and how tough and powerful God is, but today, we need to question such brazen "grandstanding." Further, when Moses tries to imitate God, the great leader embraces this violent form of competition and one-upmanship. Anger gives way to anger; violence just produces more violence.

As slaves in Egypt, we turned to Moses for leadership and inspiration, and Moses turned to God. Future generations will no doubt turn to us. If such fighting is in our blood and our history, just as Moses learned from God, then we must steer clear of this particular piece of our inheritance. We simply cannot get into the same kind of fight that God got into with Pharaoh.

With that in mind, surprisingly, in this and surrounding Torah portions, we should *not* be imitating God.

Rather, we should be doing the exact opposite. It is our duty to create a new tradition of peace as liberated people, as opposed to a tradition of hostilities as people enslaved by history.

# בשלח
# *Beshalach*

## Finding Our Voice

### Cantor Benjie Ellen Schiller

**I will sing to God who has triumphed gloriously.**
(Exodus 15:1)

We Jews did not start as a nation, but as a random collection of tribal clans. In fact, all we had in common with other Jews was that we remembered that we had been slaves in Egypt. We had no ability to fend for ourselves. We had no voice of our own. And, frankly, we had lived so long this way that this was the only way of life that we knew.

As our ancestors saw it, their Egyptian masters solely determined their fate. If they attempted to change their destiny, their all-too-powerful oppressors probably would have destroyed them. Or, perhaps not. But that's the way it felt to them.

The truth was that they could not even *imagine* what it would be like *not* to be slaves. They lived a "slave mentality," a way of thinking that was so powerful that they did not even know that freedom was a possibility.

Let's be clear: being a young person is not the same as being a slave (even though it might feel that way at times). But just as the slaves in Egypt—your ancestors—"passed over" from being slaves to

---

**Cantor Benjie Ellen Schiller** is professor of cantorial arts at the Hebrew Union College–Jewish Institute of Religion, Debbie Friedman School of Sacred Music, in New York. She serves as cantor of Bet Am Shalom Synagogue of White Plains, New York.

being free, your teenage years are a time of moving between being a kid and being an adult. And that can sometimes be as scary as getting out of Egypt and not knowing what comes next.

In *Beshalach*, we crossed the parted waters of the Sea. It was a great miracle. It marked the moment when we truly became a people.

In truth, however, our escape from Egypt was only the beginning of a long and hard process of becoming a nation. Getting out of slavery was the easy part; becoming a free people is a bit harder. It requires "finding your voice"—figuring out what you truly need to sing out to the world.

Back then, we trudged on, and soon we reached the Sea. Looking back, we saw the Egyptian army coming toward us. Maybe leaving Egypt wasn't such a great idea in the first place. "Was it for want of graves in Egypt that you brought us to die in the wilderness? What have you done to us, taking us out of Egypt?" (Exodus 14:11). Moses cried back, "Don't be afraid! Stand by and see how God will deliver you!" (Exodus 14:13 [my translation—BES]).

At this point, we entered the Sea—and at that moment, we were no longer slaves, but independent people. We felt God's love. At that moment, we suddenly had a sense of destiny, of dignity, and of hope for the future. At that moment, we could finally sing and dance to God in song and praise: "I will sing to God who has triumphed gloriously" (Exodus 15:1).

At last, we found our voice.

When you go from childhood to being a teenager, that's when you find your voice.

# That Nachshon Moment

Rabbi Sid Schwarz

**Why do you cry out to Me? Tell the Israelites to go forward.** (Exodus 14:15)

Think about something that you really want to do. It is challenging, but it is also very important to you. There is a voice in your head that tells you that you just can't pull it off. But another voice in your head says something very different: "Go for it!"

How often have you played out this scene? Maybe it is trying out for a sports team. Maybe you hope to qualify for the school band or to get a big part in the school play. Maybe you have an idea to start a club, but if you take the initiative and no one joins it, you will feel like an idiot. Maybe there is this one kid in your school who always bullies other kids, including you. You think about standing up to that bully once and for all. But you are not sure that you can look the bully in the eye and not flinch.

You are not the first person to find that fear of taking a risk can paralyze you. The former president of South Africa, Nelson Mandela, writes in his autobiography, "The brave man is not he who does not feel afraid, but he who conquers that fear."[3]

**Rabbi Sid Schwarz** is a senior fellow at CLAL: The National Jewish Center for Learning and Leadership and a consultant to Jewish organizations. He founded and led PANIM: The Institute for Jewish Leadership and Values and is also the founding rabbi of Adat Shalom Reconstructionist Congregation in Bethesda, Maryland, where he continues to teach and lead services.

One of the most dramatic moments in the Bible is when the children of Israel reach the Red Sea. Pharaoh, having reconsidered his decision to let the Israelites go, is now pursuing them in the desert—with the full force of his horses and chariots. We can almost imagine six hundred thousand Israelites, men, women, and children carrying as many of their possessions as is humanly possible, hearing the oncoming Egyptian army, and imagining either massacre or a return to slavery. In front of them is a leader who is yet untested—Moses. The Israelites are anxious and second-guessing their leader and his foolish dream to take them out of Egypt to some "promised land."

Moses prays to God for direction. God responds, "Why do you cry out to Me? Tell the Israelites to go forward" (Exodus 14:15). The midrash goes further. It puts a face and name on the first person to take a leap of faith into the raging sea. His name was Nachshon, the head of the tribe of Judah. And once he jumped into the water, it parted—and the rest of the Israelites were able to cross in safety.

Maybe you don't believe that the miracle happened as the midrash suggests it did. But you don't have to. Every great moment in history, every person who achieves greatness, every person who conquers the fears that may have paralyzed him or her has that Nachshon moment.

In *Pirkei Avot* (the ethical teachings of the early Sages), we read, "In a place where there is no one of moral courage, strive to be courageous" (*Mishnah Avot* 2:5). The world calls out for you to stand up where no one else does.

Can you summon up the Nachshon in you?

## Rules Are Jewish Love

### Rabbi Angela Warnick Buchdahl

**All the people answered as one, saying, "All that the
Eternal has spoken we will do!"** (Exodus 19:8)

How often have your parents responded to a challenge of their rules
or orders by saying, "Because I said so"? It can be an infuriating
response, because it gives you no room for argument, no means for
reconsideration. But generally speaking, you obey them—perhaps
because you have no choice, but maybe also because deep down you
have faith that your parents have your well-being and best interests
at heart.

Sometimes, parental orders are easy to understand: "Eat your
green beans and drink your milk" (so you can be strong and
healthy). But others might seem like total nonsense: "Say 'tooie
tooie' when someone says something nice about you." In these cases,
sometimes even our parents cannot say why this action is important,
but they have a strong sense that these rules will keep you safe and
help you be the best person you can be.

And that is Jewish love.

Love—*ahavah*—appears in two prayers that surround the *Shema*.
The prayer before the *Shema* is *Ahavah Rabbah*, and the *V'ahavta*
comes after. The *Ahavah Rabbah* says that God had such a great love

**Rabbi Angela Warnick Buchdahl** is senior cantor of Central Synagogue
in New York.

for us that God gave us Torah, our "rule book" for how we are to walk in this world.

The *V'ahavta*, in turn, talks of how we show love to God, by following these rules and teaching them to our children, "in our home and on our way." These prayers remind us that we show our love through actions, not just through our words, and that God loved us enough to teach us how to live in this world.

Our Torah portion teaches us ten of those most important and most famous rules, known as the Ten Commandments. Some of these rules are self-evident, such as "You shall not murder" and "You shall not steal" (so that society does not descend into chaos; Exodus 20:13).

But others are harder to figure out, such as "You shall not make for yourself a sculptured image" (Exodus 20:4).

But when God gave our ancestors all of these rules, what did they say? "All that the Eternal has spoken we will do!" (Exodus 19:8). While they did not know all that was in the Torah, and sometimes they did not understand why they had to follow some of these rules, they were willing to take it on faith that God had the Jewish people's best interests at heart.

As teenagers, you often don't get much choice about following your parents' rules, even the ones you do not fully understand. But often, as time passes (and maybe only when you become parents yourselves), you can understand that when your parents put various boundaries on your life, it was because of their wisdom and their love: the curfews that kept you safe at night, or learning the life lesson of what would happen if you broke a trust.

That's the way it was with our ancestors. They accepted the mitzvot and they followed them—and often, it took a bit of time for them to understand their meaning. For example, keeping the Sabbath has preserved our identity through a life of exile for two thousand years, and leaving the corners of our fields for the poor has made our people understand how to care for the most vulnerable in our communities. We know that these rules were given in love. *Na'aseh v'nishma*—"We will do and then we will understand" (Exodus 24:7 [my translation—AWB]).

# What Kind of Leader Do You Want to Be?

Rabbi Jonah Pesner

**But Moses's father-in-law said to him, "The thing you are doing is not right; you will surely wear yourself out, and these people as well. For the task is too heavy for you; you cannot do it alone."** (Exodus 18:17–18)

What kind of leader are you?

What kind of leader do you *want* to be?

Do you simply figure out what needs to be done and then do it? Or do you turn to others and work together to make things happen?

In the story of Moses and his father-in-law Jethro, we see the classic tension between doing it yourself as opposed to turning to others for help. Moses successfully leads the Hebrew slaves in an uprising against Pharaoh and the Egyptians. He guides them out of bondage, across the Sea of Reeds (sometimes called the Red Sea), and toward Mount Sinai, where they will receive the Torah.

But they get stuck—because Moses was stuck.

The text tells us that Moses "sat as magistrate among the people; the people stood about Moses from morning until evening" (Exodus

**Rabbi Jonah Pesner** is senior vice president of the Union for Reform Judaism. He teaches on all four campuses of the Hebrew Union College–Jewish Institute of Religion. He is the founding director of Just Congregations, the community organizing effort of the URJ.

18:13). Picture the scene: every time an Israelite had a dispute with another person, they had to wait in line for Moses to resolve it. Imagine how frustrated the people must have been—standing in line all day, waiting for a chance to get a decision from the only leader who had the power to issue a ruling. Consider, also, how overwhelmed Moses must have been. No wonder they were all worn out and unable to move forward.

Jethro gives Moses advice—and if you want to become a leader, then you will have to take this advice to heart. He tells him to "seek out from among all the people capable men who fear God, trustworthy men who spurn ill-gotten gain. Set these over them as chiefs of thousands, hundreds, fifties, and tens and let them judge the people at all times" (Exodus 18:21–22).

Of course, today we wouldn't say "capable *men*," but rather "capable *people*." Even so, this story is telling us much more than the importance of having a strong legal system with smart, impartial judges; it is even telling us a truth more profound than the importance of "delegating authority" (though it is saying both of those things).

I believe the deeper meaning of this story is that real leaders are effective *because they can identify other potential leaders*, support them, and trust them to lead. The Israelites could resume their journey toward Sinai and the Promised Land because thousands and thousands of them would now be able to make decisions for the community and help lead the people forward.

Moses realizes that he cannot possibly build a community alone; he needs a vast network of other talented, creative leaders whom he trusts to extend his reach. In fact, God's teachings would be irrelevant to the Israelites without a corps of wise people to engage them. Torah only comes to life when God and Moses trust the people to make it work.

So, what kind of leader are you? Will you turn to others who are smart, talented, and creative and work collectively for the future you believe in?

# משפטים
## Mishpatim

### "... And Another Thing!"
Rabbi Lester Bronstein

**You shall not wrong or oppress a stranger, for you were strangers in the land of Egypt.** (Exodus 22:20)

How do you feel when an adult tells you to act "responsibly"? Or, more specifically, when that adult tells you to "take responsibility for your own actions"?

When I was young, whenever I got that lecture, I hated it. My mind would start sorting through everything that I had done in the past seventy-two hours, trying to figure out what was so "irresponsible" about my behavior. Why else would my dad, or my Scoutmaster, or my coach, or my math teacher be pushing me to take responsibility if they weren't *mad* at me—or at least *disappointed* in me?

If we read the Torah portion *Mishpatim* (what I call "rules for responsible behavior") with a guilty conscience, we are bound to feel as if someone is yelling at us. "Don't do this, and don't do that. And, oh yeah, another thing ..." More or less, that's what it says, and that's how it *could* make us feel if we let it. This portion has more than fifty commandments, and many of them begin with "don't."

But, we do not have to be guilty of something to get what could be a loving lecture on growing up responsibly. This Torah reading could be giving us a chance to inherit a really beautiful gift: a

**Rabbi Lester Bronstein** is rabbi of Bet Am Shalom Synagogue, a Reconstructionist congregation in White Plains, New York.

guideline for being responsible for ourselves, our community—our whole world, really—and to feel *great about ourselves as adults.*

My favorite "don't" in *Mishpatim* is "You shall not wrong or oppress a stranger, for you were strangers in the land of Egypt" (Exodus 22:20). In shorthand, "Don't oppress."

To me, this commandment feels a bit like being told to be nice to my younger brother because I know how it feels to be dumped on. And even if I *don't* know, I'm old enough to *imagine* how it feels.

What could this Torah portion mean for a person who bullies other kids in school or even in cyberspace? Or how about a kid who picks on minority kids, or gay kids, or disabled kids? In other words, someone who picks on anyone who is a "stranger"?

To that person, the Torah might be saying, "Hey! You should know better! You should be old enough to know how it feels to be picked on! *Don't oppress!*" (In fact, most bullies were themselves victims of abuse or persecution when they were younger, and now they are taking it out on a defenseless victim.)

So much for the bully. But, *you* are not a bully! What, then, can this verse say to *you?*

You may not have intentionally done anything wrong to a stranger, but at some point in your life, you might feel inclined—or pressured—to do so. So now, while you're young and still forming yourself into a mensch, a good and decent person, take this lesson to heart and remember it. Don't oppress the stranger *in the future.*

And remember why. Remember the pain you yourself *would* have felt *if* someone had oppressed or bullied you. Or discriminated against you. Or disgraced you publicly. Or, God forbid, acted violently against you. Learn this special way of being responsible (some call it being "holy") and you will come to learn all the other ways of growing into the mensch you need to become.

Oh, and another thing: while you're at it, stand up straight and don't slouch!

(Just kidding!)

# God Sweats the Small Stuff

### Rabbi Debra Newman Kamin

**If you take your neighbor's garment in pledge, you must return it to him before the sun sets.** (Exodus 22:25)

When we think about the Torah, we often think of big ideas: the creation of the world, freedom from slavery, the giving of the Ten Commandments.

But here is what I love most about the Torah: its smallest details. Sometimes the Torah will offer us a verse that is so specific that it is easy to overlook. That is when we really need to focus and find the greatest meaning in the smallest detail.

We find such verses in *Mishpatim*. Exodus 22:25 reads, "If you take your neighbor's garment in pledge, you must return it to him before the sun sets." In ancient times, there were no banks. If you needed a loan, you had to borrow from someone you knew. The lender has a right to take something from you as a pledge that you will pay back the loan. If you don't repay the loan, the lender can keep the object that you have pledged.

Back then, this was common business practice. Usually the lender would keep the pledge until the borrower repaid the loan.

But what if all you have to pledge is the clothing that you wear? The lender cannot keep the clothing. He or she must return it to the borrower every night.

---

**Rabbi Debra Newman Kamin** is spiritual leader of Am Yisrael Congregation in Northfield, Illinois.

To quote the famous line from the Passover Haggadah: Why is this pledge different from all other pledges?

The next verse tells us.

"It is his only clothing, the sole covering for his skin. In what else shall he sleep?" (Exodus 22:26).

This person is so poor that he has to use his cloak or his coat as a pledge. It's the only thing that he has to sleep in, because he doesn't own a bed or even a blanket.

God worries: how is this man going to be able to sleep at night? If he has no coat to sleep in, he is going to be cold. There will be nothing between him and the hard floor. God does not want the lender to let that happen. Imagine that you are a businessperson who is accustomed to dealing with all kinds of people every day, but at the end of your busy day, you must give this guy back his garment. You must remember every evening what life is really like for this person.

Here's the great thing: *God worries about stuff like this.*

So, why don't you just go and *give* him the money? Because he did not ask you for *tzedakah*! He came to you, just like any other person who was doing business. By day, you treat him just like everyone else, preserving his dignity—but at night, you show him compassion.

Isn't that precisely what we all hope for from the world—to be treated with dignity and compassion? The Torah could have just said, in rather old-fashioned language, "Thou shalt treat every person with dignity and compassion." But, instead, it tells us about this poor man and encourages us to remember his plight.

You've probably heard of Marie Antoinette, the queen of France prior to the French Revolution. Remember her infamous quotation? After she heard that the French peasants had no bread to eat, she replied, "Let them eat cake." She could not imagine a world where people were really starving.

Our portion tells us that even though you go to bed every night in a comfortable bed with fluffy pillows and a warm blanket, you need to remember that there are people who do not have that privilege.

We all need to have the imagination, sensitivity, and compassion to ask the question, "In what else shall he sleep?"

# תרומה

## *Terumah*

---

## What Kind of Sanctuary Are You Building?

Rabbi Amy Schwartzman

**And let them make Me a sanctuary that I may dwell among them.** (Exodus 25:8)

Have you seen this quotation somewhere in your synagogue?

It might be above the doors to the sanctuary or on the ark, or it might even be running across the bottom of the giant computer screen that might be in your synagogue lobby.

This famous line appears in *Terumah*, a Torah portion that describes how our ancestors built the Ark of the Covenant and the tabernacle during the time they wandered in the desert. It makes sense that this sentence about building a sanctuary would be found in this section, but the real meaning of the verse is about a lot more than nails and wood.

Look at this line carefully, and you will find a wonderful and relevant message within it.

The text says, "Make Me a sanctuary and God will dwell *among you*" [my translation—AS]. We might expect the text to say, "Make Me a sanctuary and I will dwell *in it*." But it doesn't. It says something

---

**Rabbi Amy Schwartzman** is a rabbi at Temple Rodef Shalom in Falls Church, Virginia. She serves the Reform movement in leadership capacities through the Union for Reform Judaism (URJ), Central Conference of American Rabbis, and Hebrew Union College–Jewish Institute of Religion.

much better: work together to build holiness, and God will dwell *with you*. When we engage in sacred work, God is in our midst. God wants to dwell not in a physical place, but with all of us.

You may understand what this text is trying to suggest. You may have even experienced it yourself.

Have you ever been involved in something truly meaningful—something you know is holy work?

Perhaps you volunteered to read to seniors or play soccer with children with disabilities; perhaps you helped a friend who was having a tough time at school or even at home. You knew that what you were doing really mattered. You felt a strong connection to the person sitting next to you. Your time and energy and compassion were appreciated. Through your kindness and your good deed, you created a sacred space, a sanctuary of a sort, and God was right there with you.

This Torah portion teaches us that building a sanctuary is not only about a room with chairs and a bimah and an ark. Although sacred activities can happen in our sanctuaries, just because we build and decorate these places doesn't guarantee that God will be there. Surely, we all have walked into a sanctuary and felt nothing special.

*Terumah* makes it clear that God will dwell among us, hang out with us, and be with us. But that will happen only as a result of what we choose to do when we are with others—our friends, classmates, and family—in any space. Each of us can build holiness and kindness and help create love and fairness. Each one of us can choose to turn an everyday gathering into something that is sacred. We can make good decisions about our activities; we can model considerate language; we can include those who are left out; we can turn a bad event into a good one. Every day you can make your gatherings into sanctuaries, and God will be right there with you.

# Inside Out

### Dr. Ira H. Schweitzer, RJE

**They shall make an ark of acacia wood, two and a half cubits long, a cubit and a half wide, and a cubit and a half high. Overlay it with pure gold—overlay it inside and out—and make upon it a gold molding round about.** (Exodus 25:10–11)

How do we look at ourselves?

In fact, it's "what's inside" that counts.

The ark in our synagogues is a unique part of the sanctuary. In our wanderings in the desert, the Ark was a unique feature of the *mishkan* (portable dwelling place for God and the tablets in the desert) as well. Rabbis have described it as "a model of balance, honesty, and integrity."[4]

Let's take a closer look at the actual construction of the Ark. It was made of acacia wood, surrounded by an overlay of pure gold. Had the Ark been made of pure gold, we may have thought that it symbolized a community that had, at the core of its value system, a veneration of wealth.

Rather, its construction models the fact that the external beauty has to reflect its internal beauty and "spirit." In ancient times, the tablets of the Ten Commandments were inside the Ark; in the arks in our contemporary synagogue, the Torah scrolls dwell within.

**Dr. Ira H. Schweitzer, RJE,** is director of education at Temple Sinai in Toronto, Canada.

What is even more perplexing is the command to also put the "gold overlay" on the inside, where the texts are housed. The Talmud offers us a good explanation, as well as a challenge: "Let your character be like the *aron kodesh* [the holy Ark that contained the tablets of the covenant], which is gold both on the inside and on the outside" (Talmud, *Berachot* 28a).

There is a Hebrew expression that describes the ideal nature of someone's character: *tocho kevaro*, "the inside and the outside should be the same." As you develop your own personality, this is the real challenge in life. You need to strive to be "pure and true" with intentions and actions both within your heart as well as with your words and actions. Your inner thoughts and motivations should be as important to you as how you look to others.

When you spend time to make sure your clothes and hair are just right, take a few moments to make sure your intentions and actions also match. If you are tempted to do things that are not healthy to yourself or to others, remember this other piece of Talmud: "Every day, a person is obligated to see him/herself as if he/she went out of Egypt" (Talmud, *Pesachim* 109a).

How liberating! Each day, you have a chance to see yourself as a free person, one who can choose to be golden both on the outside and on the inside.

Take the time to nurture both. It may not be easy, but you will get a good feeling from doing so. Not only that—people will notice that your inner beauty has grown in a positive way, just like your outer beauty.

# תצוה
# *Tetzaveh*

## Dress Code
### Rabbi Sue Levi Elwell, PhD

**Make sacral vestments for your brother Aaron, for dignity and adornment.** (Exodus 28:2)

Our clothing speaks.

What we wear can shout or whisper, invite or repel. Our clothing is rarely silent.

Clothing makes a statement. Are the items you wear mass-produced or made by hand? Are the laborers who make the garments paid a fair wage? Are you intentionally advertising a company, a brand, a designer, or an attitude? Are you declaring your connection to a school, a camp, a community, or a philosophy? Are you showing off your prosperity, or are you proclaiming your modesty?

*Tetzaveh* describes the clothing of a specific group of individuals: the priests who serve the Israelite people. After the spectacular fireworks on Mount Sinai and the Jewish people's acceptance of the Ten Commandments, the work of establishing a holy community begins. Our Torah portion continues God's instructions to Moses and directs him to appoint Aaron and Aaron's sons as priests: "Make sacral vestments for your brother Aaron, for dignity and adornment" (Exodus 28:2).

We might rephrase this: "Make sacred, special outfits for Aaron, clothing that will reflect the dignity of his position. And make

---

**Rabbi Sue Levi Elwell, PhD,** serves as Union Rabbi, East District, for the Union for Reform Judaism.

94

them beautiful!" God continues, telling Moses to find "all who are skillful" to design and construct these garments, providing detailed instructions to ensure that these elaborate and unique costumes will be made according to God's exacting plan.

The priestly garb includes one item that functions both as decoration and as ritual object. God instructs the construction of a priestly breastpiece that includes four rows of semiprecious stones, twelve in all, each "engraved like seals, each with its name, for the twelve tribes" (Exodus 28:21). This piece of fabric, bound in gold rings, chains, and cords, is fashioned of "gold, blue, purple and crimson yarns" (Exodus 28:15). Aaron wears this heavy, glittering breastpiece across his chest—more precisely, over his heart. This ritual garment is a sign, and a reminder, of Aaron's priestly position.

As priest, Aaron serves God. And as priest, he also serves the Israelite people. In the *V'ahavta* prayer, each Jew is challenged to love God with "all your heart," *b'chol l'vavcha*. The word for "heart" is often spelled with two letters: *lamed* and *bet*. In this prayer, the word appears with three letters—with not one but two *bets*.

Perhaps, for Aaron, this is the message of the *V'ahavta*: this double *bet* reflects the double layer of fabric that rests on Aaron's heart. Aaron is challenged to love and serve both God and the Jewish people. Aaron's clothing speaks, both to Aaron, who wears these special garments, and to all who encounter him.

Could it be that the *V'ahavta* prayer reminds all of us that love for God and service to God are incomplete without a love for and service to other people? Perhaps the two *bets* in *l'vavcha* remind us of the importance of clothing ourselves in meaning, dressing ourselves with intention, and realizing that what we wear always has something very loud to say.

# Someone Is Always Watching

### Rabbi Michael Pincus

**You shall further instruct the Israelites to bring you
clear oil of beaten olives for lighting, for kindling lamps
regularly. Aaron and his sons shall set them up in the
Tent of Meeting, outside the curtain which is over [the
Ark of] the Pact, [to burn] from evening to morning
before the Eternal. It shall be a due from the Israelites
for all time, throughout the ages.** (Exodus 27:20–21)

Imagine: One day a teacher leaves her classroom, and pandemonium breaks out. The students, freed from their teacher's eyes, act out. But one of the students in the class notices the teacher looking through the window in the door, and order is quickly restored. It is amazing how quickly order can return. When we sense that others are watching us, we become more aware of the things that are happening around us, and we often act as best as we can.

A story: One day, a young boy was walking along the road, when a wagon, traveling in the same direction, slowed down. The wagon driver offered him a ride, and the boy accepted. After a short while, the driver saw a pile of wheat stalks standing in a field. He wanted to steal the wheat from the fields, but he was afraid that someone would come along and see his act of theft.

---

**Rabbi Michael Pincus** is senior rabbi of Congregation Beth Israel in West Hartford, Connecticut.

So he said to the boy, "I am going to take some of that wheat. You stand guard, and let me know if anybody is watching." The boy heard but said nothing.

The driver hurried over to the pile of wheat, grabbed a large armful, and hurried back. "Somebody is watching, somebody is watching!" the boy shouted. The frightened wagon driver tossed the wheat to the ground, jumped on the wagon and whipped up the horses. When they had put some distance between themselves and the field, the driver looked around, but he saw no one following.

He said to the boy, "You deceived me! No one saw me taking the wheat!" The boy pointed upward to the heavens, and he answered, "God saw you. God sees everything, and nothing is hidden from God's sight."

In *Tetzaveh*, we read about the *ner tamid*, the eternal light—a symbol that, even today, hangs in our synagogues, reminding us that God is always present. The Talmud (*Shabbat* 21a) comments that the priests had to light it only until the flame would rise by itself. In other words, the light had no function other than to remind us of how we should act. Later in the Torah portion, we find a detailed description of the priests' wardrobe. Again, according to our tradition, each item of clothing served primarily as a reminder for the priest, and those who looked at him, of his holy duties.

No matter how old we are, it is easy to forget how to be on our best behavior. When we are out in the world, it can feel liberating to think that no one is watching us. But, if we live our lives *as if* someone (or Someone) is watching us, that knowledge can help ensure that we will be proud of our actions. Live life as if someone is watching.

# כי תשא
## *Ki Tisa*

## Our Duty to One Another
### Rabbi Julie Schonfeld

**The Eternal spoke to Moses, saying: When you take a census of the Israelite people according to their enrollment ...** (Exodus 30:11)

*Ki Tisa* begins with a count of the Israelite males over twenty years old, who put half a shekel into the communal budget, acknowledging their status as ready to serve their people. When fellow soldiers surround him, the soldier is part of a community, a collective. When he has been captured and separated, he is alone and in need of his nation's protection.

Perhaps the most important and exciting event in recent Jewish history occurred when the captured Israeli soldier Gilad Shalit finally came home after having been a prisoner of the terrorist group Hamas for five years.

In the months leading up to Shalit's exchange and release, Israel made the decision to trade a thousand Palestinian prisoners for this one soldier—one thousand lives for one. Among the prisoners whom Israel released were the murderers of innocent Israelis. While the risk of more violence from these released terrorists weighed on the minds of Jews around the world, everyone celebrated the moment

---

**Rabbi Julie Schonfeld** is executive vice president of the Rabbinical Assembly (RA), the international association of Conservative/Masorti rabbis.

when this young soldier finally returned to his family and to his people.

What was the basic principle underlying Shalit's exchange, and how is it a major principle of Jewish responsibility? It is the covenant—the collective agreement—that a country makes with its soldiers: *you defend us, and in turn, we defend you.* This covenantal relationship that a soldier has with his country echoes the sacred covenant that the Jews have with God. We keep the covenant with God, and what do we get in exchange? The sense of being part of a sacred community, engaged in a way of life that gives meaning and purpose to our existence by furthering God's plan for a holy community.

Our Torah portion focuses on this covenant. We learn, "You must keep My Sabbaths, for this is a sign between Me and you throughout the ages" (Exodus 31:12)—and again, in verse 16, "The Israelite people shall keep the Sabbath, observing it throughout the ages as a covenant for all time: it shall be a sign for all time between Me and the people of Israel." You may have heard this before. It is the V'shamru prayer that we recite every Shabbat.

You simply cannot imagine the Jewish tradition without imagining the infinite value of every human life. The Sabbath is a cornerstone of Jewish practice, and yet, if we have to save a life, then we *must* violate the Sabbath. In the Jewish tradition, the holiness of a human life is so important that if there is a chance that we can save that life, then we must even break one of the essential pieces of our covenant with God.

Every day, young men and women in Israel leave their homes to become soldiers to protect the Jewish people. The return of Gilad Shalit was one example out of many, reminding us that we are all connected to each other and that were are all obligated to protect one another.

# No Free Lunch

Rabbi Daniel G. Zemel

**Carve two tablets of stone like the first, and I will inscribe upon the tablets the words that were on the first tablets, which you shattered.** (Exodus 34:1)

One of the best books I read for a college course was *Tanstaafl (There Ain't No Such Thing as a Free Lunch): A Libertarian Perspective on Environmental Policy*. The title of the book tells you everything you need to know. There is no free lunch—in the end, someone, somewhere, pays for everything somehow.

When I read *Ki Tisa*, I think of that book title. The text of this Torah portion states it clearly: "The tablets were God's work, and the writing was God's writing, incised [written] upon the tablets" (Exodus 32:16). It was the Sinai equivalent of the free lunch. All Moses had to do was go for a nice hike up the mountain, encounter God, pick up the covenant, and march down a hero—until it all backfires with a Golden Calf and some serious punishing, deadly retribution, and the forced swallowing of that divine brew (the melted-down calf mixed with water) in Exodus 32:20.

God gets Moses back up the mountain for round two—but the free lunch is now over, and this time, Moses has some work to do.

First, God tells him, "Carve two tablets of stone like the first, and I will inscribe upon the tablets the words that were on the first tablets, which you shattered" (Exodus 34:1). God is telling Moses,

---

**Rabbi Daniel G. Zemel** is rabbi of Temple Micah in Washington, DC.

"This time, we will split the work. You carve, I'll write." Then comes that low-blow reminder to Moses about that unfortunate tablet breakup and thus this necessary repeat performance.

Moses cooperates—carving the tablets (Exodus 34:4)—but apparently, God wants more from him, because by verse 28 we read that for forty days Moses "ate no bread and drank no water; and he wrote down on the tablets the terms of the covenant, the Ten Commandments." This time around, Moses is doing all of the work.

Not only that: the commandments have changed! Last time we got a pretty straightforward "big ten": I am God; no other gods; keep the Sabbath; honor your parents; no murder; no adultery; and all the others.

Now, we have a radically different set of commandments, including drive all those Canaanites and others out of the land, and then destroy their shrines; God gets the first of everything you have; observe the Feast of Unleavened Bread for seven days; observe the Feast of Weeks (Shavuot) and the Feast of Ingathering (Sukkot); and no boiling a kid in its mother's milk.

Whenever I read this part of *Ki Tisa*, I always take away the same lessons.

*Lesson one*: God has learned a lot about us humans. Give us a freebie, and it's toast. Make us work for something, and it might last. The first set of tablets that came to Moses so easily—well, we know what happened. The second set of tablets lasted through forty years of wilderness wanderings—and then, through the period of Joshua, the judges, Samuel, all the way to Solomon's Temple.

*Lesson two*: Rules need reminders; good ethics require good ritual as a way of reminding, reinforcing, and transmitting. We learn through stories, not through lectures. The first set of commandments was beautiful, but they lacked a ritual structure through which to teach and cajole, remind and reward. With the second set—the one in which Moses shared in the work—we have holidays and eating rules as a way of showing us what our ethical strivings should be about.

There may be no such thing as a free lunch, but from matzah to cheesecake, we have a great menu.

# וַיַּקְהֵל
# *Vayakhel*

## Finding Your Life's Purpose
### Rabbi Spike Anderson

**And everyone who excelled in ability and everyone
whose spirit moved him came, bringing to the Eternal
his offering for the work of the Tent of Meeting....**
(Exodus 35:21)

Who am I? What is my place in the universe? What does God expect of me?

We might say that the purpose of Judaism is to help us ask these questions and to begin to answer them in a way that gives each Jewish life both meaning and purpose.

Now, right away, let's point out that when it comes to these big questions, Judaism holds certain assumptions: you matter, even on a cosmic level; your place in the universe is important, and God does expect certain things from you that will help you realize your potential as a human being. This is a major statement! And Judaism makes these truths clear to us through our sacred stories.

*Vayakhel* takes place when our ancestors were not feeling good about themselves, because they had made some pretty major mistakes. Mainly, they had really offended God by worshipping the Golden Calf, despite all that God had done for them to free them from Egyptian slavery.

---

**Rabbi Spike Anderson** serves as a rabbi at Stephen S. Wise Temple in Los Angeles, California.

Even more than this: our ancestors were feeling really lost. They were having a crisis of identity and purpose because they did not know who they really were or what they were supposed to do with their collective lives. Until recently, all they had known was slavery and how to be a slave. With every crack of a whip and harsh word, they relearned that they were worthless and that their life's purpose was to benefit their slave masters.

Once they were free, all of those delusions fell away, but what should take their place?

And so, God gave our ancestors a task. Its purpose was to redeem their sense of self-worth and confidence. It would help them understand who they really were and what God wanted from each and every one of them.

The task was to construct a portable sanctuary (the *mishkan*), where our people could come together to worship God. If and when the Israelites completed the *mishkan* exactly as God instructed, then God promised to "dwell among them" (Exodus 25:8). God gave them exact instructions of how to build the *mishkan*, right down to the blueprints and materials.

God made it clear that to be successful, everyone needed to work together, and each person would have to think hard about what he or she could do to help make this project a success.

People used the skills that they already had, and they brought the best of those skills to their work. For example: if you were a carpenter, then you could bring the best of your skills to carving the doorways; if you were a weaver, you could donate your best works for the curtains; and if you were a laborer, then you could commit to carrying the sanctuary from place to place.

By working together, each one bringing the best of who he or she was to the effort, they were able to build the *mishkan*, and God came to dwell among them.

So here are the questions you need to ponder:

- What might be our modern equivalent of our ancestors' *mishkan*—the place where people could come together and where

God would dwell? Hint: it could be your community, your synagogue, or your family home.

- If God asks that we each bring the very best of who we are to this modern *mishkan*, then what will you bring? What is really special about you? How can you use that for a higher purpose?

Those are the big questions.

Now, go find the big answers.

# Who Else Is Coming?

Rabbi Pamela Jay Gottfried

**But when these [people] continued to bring freewill offerings to him morning after morning, all the artisans who were engaged in the tasks of the sanctuary came ... and said to Moses, "The people are bringing more than is needed for the tasks entailed in the work that the Eternal has commanded to be done."**
(Exodus 36:3–5)

I don't know about you, but when I'm invited to a party, I'm always curious about who else is going to be there.

Even though I know in my heart that I should accept or decline the invitation for the right reasons—because I want to attend and not because I want to be seen by the right people—I just can't help myself. Of course, I never ask the host outright, "Who else is invited?" That question might be considered rude or insulting. It's also unnecessary, because Evite and Facebook make guest lists visible to everyone. Technology presents me with a challenge; I have to suppress my curiosity and make a choice without being influenced by peer pressure.

---

**Rabbi Pamela Jay Gottfried** teaches students of all ages in churches, colleges, community centers, schools, and synagogues. She spends her summers teaching ceramics to teenagers at Camp Ramah Darom.

*Vayakhel* offers a solution to this dilemma, because it describes how the people of Israel bring gifts to Moses for the construction of the sanctuary in the wilderness:

> But when these [people] continued to bring freewill offerings to him morning after morning, all the artisans who were engaged in the tasks of the sanctuary came ... and said to Moses, "The people are bringing more than is needed for the tasks entailed in the work that the Eternal has commanded to be done."
>
> (Exodus 36:3–5)

Why is the word "morning" repeated? Perhaps because the people bring their gifts early in the morning—even before it is light enough to see who is coming. They are eager to demonstrate their dedication to God—not because they want to be seen at the construction site.

In fact, they may be trying to avoid being seen because they don't want to get caught up in a popularity contest. Or perhaps they just don't care who else is going to be around when they arrive. Their deep commitment to God and their desire to participate in building a place where they can feel close to God inspire them to show up every morning before dawn—regardless of who else will be there—bringing as many gifts as they can carry. The text implies that the people simply want to do the right thing.

When faced with a choice—whether it is a difficult decision about an ethical issue or a relatively mundane one—can I follow the example of my ancestors in the wilderness and do the right thing for the right reasons?

Honestly, when I get an Evite or a Facebook invitation, I am still curious about who else received it. But first I ask myself whether I want to attend; I decide whether I am willing to wake up early in the morning. Then I click on the RSVP button *before* I scroll through the guest list to see who else is inspired to join me in celebration.

# פְקוּדֵי
## *Pekudei*

## Are You Accountable?

Rabbi Jill Jacobs

**These are the records of the Tabernacle....** (Exodus 38:21)

Can we trust our leaders?

Too often, the answer is *no*. Over and over, we hear about governors, senators, and various politicians and public officials who lie, accept favors, and put their own financial and emotional desires over the well-being of the people they serve.

As a result, many of us expect little from those who represent us. We hear over and over: "You can't trust politicians." "There's no point in voting—they're all the same." "Why bother trying to change anything?"

The Torah offers a different model.

When Moses puts out the call for donations to the *mishkan* (the ancient desert tabernacle), the Israelites respond in droves. They bring all of their gold, silver, precious jewels, and fine linens to the cause. In fact, there are so many donations that Moses has to call a stop to the flow of gifts!

According to the midrash *Tanchuma Pekudei* 7, some of the people begin to wonder whether they can really trust Moses with their valuables. After all, it would be easy for him to pocket a few diamonds or to assume that no one would notice a missing bar

---

**Rabbi Jill Jacobs** is executive director of Rabbis for Human Rights–North America.

of gold. Moses hears this talk in the camp and calls for a public accounting of the materials.

This midrash begins by wondering why *Pekudei* repeats the list of donated materials recorded earlier in the Torah. By way of explanation, the midrash suggests that the first words of this portion, "These are the records of the Tabernacle," introduce a public accounting. Moses, the midrash continues, lists every single gemstone, piece of gold, and scrap of cloth and shows that each has its place in the *mishkan*.

This is what we should expect from our leaders: a full accounting of every penny, every political interest, and every personal consideration that compromises the public good.

But this midrash also makes clear what our elected officials should expect from us. The midrash does not criticize or punish the people who question Moses's honesty. Instead, they receive an immediate and public response from their leader. Perhaps Moses even welcomes the opportunity to clear up doubts.

Perhaps this is why this accountability episode comes at the end of the book of Exodus. Moses had to grow into being accountable. It's not only Moses who needed to be accountable. And it's not only politicians who need to be accountable. This is an essential part of the growing-up process: being accountable to your parents, and to your teachers, and to your friends.

In fact, as you grow older, your "circle of accountability" just grows larger. Start practicing now.

# No Boat

### Rabbi Paul Yedwab

**When Moses had finished the work, the cloud [of God's Presence] covered the Tent of Meeting, and the Presence of the Eternal filled the Tabernacle.** (Exodus 40:33–34)

I have a friend who lived for a time on a beautiful Greek isle. His father, a successful executive, happened to be flying to Athens on business, and he decided to take a rare weekend off to visit his son. They had a nice time together, but at the appointed time for his dad to catch the boat back, there was some sort of disturbance out in the Aegean Sea. So there they were waiting at the dock, but there was no boat!

The father made furious phone calls, but in the end—no boat. The next day, they came down to the pier, but once again, there was no boat. Since it seemed that no means of transportation would be on the horizon, father and son sat out on the porch overlooking the sea, and they talked in a way that they had rarely done.

My friend remembers that day as the best time he had ever spent with his dad.

And it was all because there was no boat.

Ever since I first heard this story from my friend, my personal mantra has become "no boat." The traffic is unbearable; *no boat.* Someone is late to a meeting; *no boat.* My teenager wrecks the family car; *no boat.* When the people you love disappoint you; *no boat.*

---

**Rabbi Paul Yedwab** serves Temple Israel of West Bloomfield, Michigan.

The honor you didn't receive, the gift you should have gotten, the call you were waiting for; *no boat*. Just accept the situation as it is, even embrace it as it is. Who knows what opportunity will arise as a result?

At first glance, the Torah portions leading up to *Pekudei* seem baffling. The Israelites have just escaped from the hands of the Egyptians. They are scratching out a meager existence, and what do they do? They build a tabernacle. And for the past several weeks, we have read the very specific and exacting details of this building project. Every material is listed, the clothing of the priesthood outlined, the fund-raising plan revealed, and then the Torah goes back over it all again and again. Really, who cares what color thread they used in the ephod (part of the priestly garments)?

Then, suddenly, in our portion, we read, "When Moses had finished the work, the cloud [of God's Presence] covered the Tent of Meeting, and the Presence of the Eternal filled the Tabernacle" (Exodus 40:33–34). Pages and pages about the building of this fancy box, and then suddenly it all becomes worthwhile. There is meaning: the Presence of the Eternal fills the Tabernacle.

To me, the Tabernacle symbolizes the rituals that we perform. We sing the ancient melodies; we bend our knees and bow our heads; we light the candles and plan the Passover Seder; we take the time to build our tabernacles—and then, suddenly, if we are lucky, it happens: the Presence of God enters our homes and our hearts. We find ourselves in the harbor of no expectations, and wouldn't you know it—there is no boat, which really is just another way of saying *Shabbat Shalom*.

# Vayikra/
# Leviticus

# ויקרא

# *Vayikra*

## Who's Calling, Please?

### Rabbi Elyse Frishman

_____ **called to Moses and the Eternal spoke to him....**

(Leviticus 1:1 [my translation—EF])

The opening verse of *Vayikra*, the first portion in Leviticus, reveals the secret of Moses's relationship with God, and how we might draw closer to God, too: "_____ *called to Moses and the Eternal spoke to him ...*" (Leviticus 1:1).

The word *vayikra* gives a verb but no clear subject: "_____ called to Moses." We assume that it was God who called. If so, then this seems unnecessarily repetitive, because the verse continues, "God called to Moses *and then God spoke to him.*" Calling is a form of speech, so if God called, why does it add "God spoke"?

The Hebrew unveils the mystery. The first word, *vayikra*, is written with a small *aleph*, so that it's sort of like this: *vayikr*ℵ (with that small ℵ hovering slightly above the line. This separates the ℵ from the rest of the word, creating two words: *vayakar*ℵ. *Vayakar*ℵ can be translated as "ℵ was precious to Moses."

Who is ℵ? The thirteenth-century mystical Torah commentary, the *Zohar*, reveals that small Hebrew letters in the Torah signify the lower world that God inhabits.[1]

---

**Rabbi Elyse Frishman** is senior rabbi of The Barnert Temple in Franklin Lakes, New Jersey. She is the editor of *Mishkan T'filah*, a prayer book for the Reform movement.

This lower world is *ours*. The small letter א, in particular, represents the *Shechinah*—the so-called feminine Presence of God. It's the way we experience God in the details of daily life and the physical world. The *Shechinah* represents our joy and our pain, our triumphs and our losses, the totality of our experiences. The *Shechinah* is our life.

But, the *Shechinah* isn't just my life, or yours alone; it is all of our lives, all Jews, all people, all the world. To hear the call of the *Shechinah* is not just to hear one's own heart; it is to hear the heart of the stranger, to look into her eyes, to touch his soul.

Now, let's try our new translation of the verse: "Because the *Shechinah* was precious to Moses, so God spoke to him."

Another insight: perhaps *Vayikr*א begins with a small א to whisper: *get over yourself.* Moses made himself smaller. As it says in Numbers 12:3, Moses was humbler than any other person. With humility, he overcame his fear of failure. Because he was humble, he was able to make room for God in his life, and he evolved from being the "prince of Egypt" to being a "servant of God's people."

Rabbi Abraham Isaac Kook, one of the great mystical teachers of our time, taught that there is only one good way to love God—and that's to love people.[2]

If we feel distant from God, it might be because we are actually distant from those around us. We might be so focused on ourselves that there is no room for anyone else—even God. From Moses we learn: to be close to God is to care for those around us, even the stranger.

We all know what it feels like to be a stranger. We each have lonely moments, lonely days, and lonely weeks. Sometimes we wonder: who is there for us?

God is always calling. If we find it hard to hear God, perhaps it is because we are listening only for the voice within us and we need to make room for other people. When you do, then you can look up and out into the eyes and hearts of others. Then, you will hear God's call.

# Sacrifice Play

Rabbi Stuart Weinblatt

**When any of you presents an offering of cattle to the Eternal, he shall choose his offering from the herd or from the flock.** (Leviticus 1:2)

The Torah is a book unlike any other. It is not like any history book, novel, science book, or textbook you have ever read.

Genesis and Exodus, the first two books of the Bible, focus on stories about the beginning of the world and the origins of our people, how we came to be slaves and then how we went free from Egypt. We read about the giving of the Torah at Mount Sinai (especially those teachings that came to be known as the Ten Commandments) and how our people agreed to accept the covenant with God. Finally, Exodus ends with instructions about the building of a tabernacle, a portable place of worship.

But now, as we start the book of Leviticus, we turn away from stories—to a totally different style altogether.

*Vayikra* is the first Torah portion of the third book of the Bible. In English, we call it Leviticus, because it contains the laws of the Levites, the tribe that served in the Temple. It serves as a manual for

**Rabbi Stuart Weinblatt** is founding rabbi of Congregation B'nai Tzedek in Potomac, Maryland. He is also the director of Israel Policy and Advocacy for the Rabbinical Assembly and the chairman of the Rabbinic Cabinet of the Jewish Federations of North America.

the priests and the Levites who helped them, and it explains in great detail the types of sacrifices that the people were to bring as offerings to the tabernacle and then to the ancient Temple in Jerusalem. Ever since the Romans destroyed the Temple nearly two thousand years ago, we no longer have a place to perform these rituals. As a result, it can be very difficult for us to understand the customs and practices that this Torah portion describes.

Here comes an understatement: our modern religious schools don't exactly focus on these difficult passages.

But, believe it or not, at one time, this Torah portion is *precisely* where young children would begin their study of the Torah. Our ancestors believed that because children are pure and innocent, they should start their Jewish education by learning about the things that would help people become pure and innocent. For them, that meant the laws of Leviticus—especially the laws about sacrifices.

The Hebrew word for "sacrifice" is *korban*, which comes from the Hebrew word *l'kareiv*, "to draw near." One of the reasons for making a sacrifice is to feel closer to God. You might wonder how giving up something you own brings you closer to God. The act of bringing a sacrifice, of giving up something of value, shows that you are willing to think not only about yourself and your own needs, but also about others.

One of the most famous comments about this Torah portion is about its title, *Vayikra*, which means "God called." God called Moses to come into the Tent of Meeting, to hear the instructions about the procedures for the sacrifices. It is as if Moses is just standing around and God had to call him to come hear what God had to say.

Our ancient Rabbis had many explanations for this, especially because they noticed that the first letter has a small *aleph* at the end of it. Despite all that Moses had done, and despite how great a leader he was, he still was very humble, and he did not want to assume that God was calling him. He was a little bit embarrassed to be singled out, and so he was reluctant to come forth.

This Torah portion teaches us a valuable lesson: the importance of not thinking just about ourselves or of how great we may be. By having some humility, and by being willing to share and give up certain things, we make God proud, and thereby we can associate ourselves with how God wants us to act, even if we cannot offer sacrifices anymore.

# צַו

# *Tzav*

## A Perpetual Fire

### Rabbi Jeremy Kalmanofsky

**A fire on the altar must be kept burning within.... Keep fire burning constantly on the altar; do not let it go out.**
(Leviticus 6:2, 6:6 [my translation—JK])

For many people, the least popular book in the Torah is Leviticus, with all its strange rituals like animal sacrifices and its fascination with skin diseases and ritual impurity. But I love this book, and you can discover all kinds of poetic spiritual insights in its details. The commandment in the verses above is a great example, with its requirement to keep stoking a constant fire within—*something*.

What fire is this verse talking about? And what is it burning within?

On one simple level, the Torah describes how priests should take care of the sacrificial altar in the ancient tabernacle (and later, the ancient Temple in Jerusalem): there always had to be some kind of sacrifice simmering all the time, with some kind of fuel added regularly, even on Shabbat, when burning fire was otherwise forbidden.

On a more poetic level, the commandment to keep the "constant fire" burning symbolizes how we should nurture our own inner spirits, our passion and enthusiasm. After all, where does the fire

---

**Rabbi Jeremy Kalmanofsky** serves as rabbi of Congregation Ansche Chesed in New York City.

burn? Not *on* the altar, but *within*—within the heart of the *person* who brings the offering.

As I'm sure you've already learned, life can run you down. It can disappoint you, and it can frustrate you. Sometimes you may want to give up. Sometimes you may find things boring or unimportant.

But you should also know that you have a fire within your heart. You've got emotional depth, empathy for other people, and moral courage. You have the wisdom to discover what is meaningful and beautiful in the world, and the capacity to be sensitive to God's presence. You are a spirit, not just a body.

All those precious qualities require protection. If you want the fire to keep burning, you have to tend it and restock it with fuel. Stoking the fire means you have to devote time to spiritual activities, like prayer and study. You have to do good deeds that connect you to others and build your enthusiasm for more ethical action. You have to pay attention not only to the physical dimension of life but also to the spiritual dimension—the fire *within*. And when you start to feel the fire going out, that is when it is most important of all to add fuel.

The *Zohar*, the central work of Jewish mysticism written in thirteenth-century Spain, offers a wonderful teaching about the fire within us. I paraphrase: "A wise person should open his or her eyes and see a flame burning above his or her head, and realize that the flame needs fuel. The human body is a wick, and the Divine Presence is a flame. What is the fuel? Good deeds" (*Zohar* 3:187a).

So keep the fire burning.

# Time for a God Upgrade

## Rabbi Jamie Korngold

**The Eternal spoke to Moses....** (Leviticus 6:1)

A mere five words into the Torah portion, and already I am lost.

"The Eternal spoke to Moses."

What am I supposed to do with that?

(Warning: If you have no difficulty with the concept of God speaking to Moses, or to anyone, for that matter, do us both a favor and skip to a different essay. You will not like this one, and I have no desire to offend you, which, if you keep reading, will most certainly happen.)

The Torah is our most sacred text, yet in chapter after chapter, these five challenging words confront me—"The Eternal spoke to Moses."

Despite our modern interpretations, in verse after verse, the Torah talks about God as if God is a man who has the power to make it rain if we follow the commandments, and if we don't—well, no rain.

The Torah comes from a time when people understood the world differently than we do today. They thought that demons caused people to have strokes, that comets were signs of God's anger, and that infected shopping cart handles could spread the common cold.

But our understanding of the world has changed. Those things that we used to think God caused—now we know that they have nothing to do with God. For example, we used to assume that

---

**Rabbi Jamie Korngold,** "The Adventure Rabbi," is senior rabbi of the Adventure Program based in Boulder, Colorado.

violating the Sabbath could cause droughts. Now we know that droughts are a result of climate change.

The idea of a biblical God who punishes and rewards us based on our behavior just doesn't fit with the world as we experience it. We all know wonderful people who suffer and nasty people who thrive.

So what do you do about that?

When you have an old computer, or an old operating system, or old software, what do you do? You *upgrade*. And that's precisely what great Jewish thinkers throughout time have done with the idea of God: as they learned more about the world, they *upgraded* their ideas about God. Practically as soon as someone wrote, "The Eternal spoke to Moses," someone else came along and asked, "What does 'the Eternal spoke' mean?"

Unfortunately, not enough Jews are familiar with the variety of available Jewish ways of thinking about God. They still think that the only "official" Jewish God concept is of a person-like deity who commands and criticizes.

Many of us do not know about these great thinkers who offered us upgrades of our God ideas: Baruch Spinoza, of seventeenth-century Amsterdam, who suggested that we can best experience God through nature and that God cannot affect the daily workings of the world; or Martin Buber, a twentieth-century thinker, who suggested that we can experience God through our relationships.

Jews often avoid God conversations by arguing that it is impossible to describe what God is. It might be impossible, and yet it is still important to talk about God, wonder about the nature of God, and try to wrap our heads around what it means to say, "The Eternal spoke to Moses."

If you are still reading this essay and I have not offended you, perhaps you would like to learn more about other great Jewish thinkers. Maybe you will even add your own thoughts to theirs, and something that you think about and teach will become part of someone else's "God upgrade."

# שמיני
# *Shemini*

## The Gold Standard for Kashrut
### Rabbi Morris J. Allen

**These are the creatures that you may eat from among all
the land animals: any animal that has true hoofs, with
clefts through the hoofs, and that chews the cud—such
you may eat ... and the swine—although it has true
hoofs, with the hoofs cleft through, it does not chew the
cud: it is unclean for you.** (Leviticus 11:2–3, 11:7)

In discussing the construction of the ancient desert tabernacle, the
Torah declares that it must be overlaid with gold "inside and out"
(Exodus 25:11). When the early Sages read that verse, they interpreted
it to mean that external appearances must be matched by internal
consistency. They said that if a Torah scholar's private behavior
differed from his/her public teaching, then that scholar wasn't *really*
a true scholar. We are a people that sees public practice as being truly
meaningful, but only when it is matched by inner belief.

This teaching is quite clear when we look at the idea of kashrut
(the Jewish food laws), which has a starring role in this week's
Torah portion. Leviticus 11 defines which animals are fit or unfit for
consumption. To be kosher, an animal must have split hooves and
chew its cud—in other words, there must be a consistency between
external signs (the hooves) and the internal function (chewing cud).

---

**Rabbi Morris J. Allen** is spiritual leader of the Beth Jacob Congregation
in Mendota Heights, Minnesota.

That is how the pig became the classic example of a *treif* (nonkosher) animal, unfit for kashrut-observing Jews to eat. On the surface, a pig meets the criteria for being kosher; it has split hooves. However, on the inside, it fails the "chewing its cud" test. If you go only by external appearance, a pig would appear to be kosher.

But, there is an internal test as well—and this is where the pig fails.

As Jews, we care deeply about external and internal agreement. When we don't have that external and internal agreement, there is a Jewish "disconnect," and that disconnect borders on phoniness.

That is why we need an additional test for whether something is kosher.

Several years ago, there was a scandal at an American kosher meat-producing plant. The ritual act of slaughter that was happening at that plant might have been *technically* acceptable. But only technically, because the owners of the plant paid no attention to the safety of the workers, the environment, and the welfare of the animal prior to the slaughter itself.

And, *these* concerns are *also* Jewish concerns.

Both the Torah and the Rabbinic literature contain laws regarding the appropriate treatment of workers, the need for safeguarding the earth on which we live, and the importance of not inflicting pain to animals under our care. Suddenly, the Jewish community understood that while the "visible" signs in the production of kosher food were acceptable (although there were also concerns expressed by many about the use of hoisting and shackling the animals), the "hidden" aspects of its production were, from a Jewish point of view, unethical.

As a result of this, a group of activists began to work on something absolutely crucial. We actually expanded the whole notion of what it means to "keep kosher." Kosher customers deserve to know that the people who are producing ritually kosher food are doing so in a way consistent with the norms, values, and laws of Jewish ethics. When kashrut-observing Jews sit down to a meal, they need to respond to the "higher authority" that kashrut demands.

And then, it won't be only the ancient Ark that would have gold both on the inside and on the outside. It would be our observance of kashrut as well.

That's a *real* seal of approval.

# A Time for Silence

Rabbi Zoë Klein

**And Aaron was silent.** (Leviticus 10:3)

One of the hallmarks of being a teenager is a tendency to hold feelings inside in simmering, smoldering silence. The desire to work things out independently combined with a general mistrust of anyone who has lived longer than Jim Morrison, James Dean, Janis Joplin, Kurt Cobain, River Phoenix, Jimi Hendrix, or Tupac often creates an impenetrable curtain that adults like to misread as sullen.

Many times in the Torah, people are silent. What, exactly, did Cain say to Abel before slaying him? What did Sarah say when she saw Abraham take Isaac up the mountain? The Torah doesn't tell us. This is where the Rabbinic imagination truly flourishes, and to fill in the blanks, it creates its own set of stories, including midrash.

But, in Leviticus 10:3, we find: *Vayidom Aharon*, "Aaron was silent." This is the only time that the Torah tells us *specifically* that someone is silent. Aaron's voice is not missing. It is purposely withheld, for Aaron is a man who has just witnessed a fiery terror.

*Shemini* begins with the ordination of Aaron and his four sons. It should have been a day of great celebration. Aaron's two youngest sons, Nadab and Abihu, "each took his fire pan, put fire in it, and laid incense on it; and they offered before the Eternal alien fire, which God had not enjoined upon them. And fire came forth from the Eternal and consumed them; thus they died" (Leviticus 10:1–2).

---

**Rabbi Zoë Klein** is senior rabbi of Temple Isaiah in Los Angeles, California.

Aaron stands before the burnt bodies of his sons. He is silent.

Moses isn't silent. He says, "This is what the Eternal meant when He said, 'Through those near to Me I show Myself holy'" (Leviticus 10:3).

Perhaps Aaron's wife is screaming. Perhaps Aaron's other sons are howling with rage.

But Aaron's response is *silence*.

Some ancient Rabbis said that Nadab and Abihu died because they had drunk wine, because right after the fatal incident, the Torah says, "Drink no wine or other intoxicant ... that you may not die" (Leviticus 10:9).

Rabbi Levi said that they were arrogant and that they thought that they were too good to marry.

Rabbi Judah, in the name of Rabbi Aibu, said that they could not wait for Moses and Aaron to die so that they could take over.

Others thought that they died because they actually caught glimpses of God.[3]

Some believed that they died because their father, Aaron, made the Golden Calf.[4]

But through it all, and no matter what the reason for the death of his sons, Aaron is *silent*.

A midrash says that Aaron got a special blessing specifically because he chose not to scream against God. But what kind of blessing could possibly have made up for the massive pain he was feeling?

In Aaron's silence, he is not questioning God's existence. He cannot say, "There is no God," for he has just witnessed God.

There are moments in which words can only cheapen. Silence and empty space can create things of beauty. Music is not only notes; it is also silences.

Aaron is silent. His silence is the ingredient of all art.

You may at times find yourself unable to find the words to express the turbulent kaleidoscope of ideas, emotions, and feelings you are experiencing in your body, mind, and soul.

In those times, you are not alone. Aaron stands beside you, steadying you, until you are ready, at last, to begin to speak.

# תזריע

## *Tazria*

### Deep and Looking Up: How a Weird Story of Skin Disease Can Tell Us about Life over Death and Seeking Inner Peace

Rabbi Peretz Wolf-Prusan and Rabbi Asher Lopatin

On the seventh day the priest shall examine the scall [the blemish]. If the scall has not spread on the skin, and does not appear to go deeper than the skin, the priest shall pronounce him clean; he shall wash his clothes, and he shall be clean. (Leviticus 13:34)

**To: Asher Lopatin**
**From: Peretz Wolf-Prusan**

Dear Asher:

I am so happy to be in contact with you again. It has been too many years since we were together in Jerusalem.

However, now that we will be discussing *Tazria*, I want to share a story with you.

---

**Rabbi Peretz Wolf-Prusan** is rabbi and senior educator for Lehrhaus Judaica in San Francisco, California.

**Rabbi Asher Lopatin** is rabbi of Anshe Sholom B'nai Israel Congregation, a modern Orthodox synagogue in Chicago, Illinois.

When I was a rabbinic student at the Hebrew Union College–Jewish Institute of Religion in Cincinnati, I was asked to give the *devar Torah* during a Teen Leadership Kallah at college.

"Great," I replied. "What is the Torah portion?"

"*Tazria.*"

Skin disease and a bunch of teenagers.

Terrific.

That's when I thought of the death of Sean. He had been a college student and a weekend counselor for me when I was directing youth retreats at a Jewish camp. Sean helped run a successful weekend; we hugged and said goodbye; he returned to his campus, walked to a bridge, and jumped to his death. Only at his funeral did I learn that he had been suffering from depression.

At the Teen Leadership Kallah, I shared Sean's story. I connected it to Leviticus 13:1–28. I noted that the person who was suffering from a blotch on the skin is not immediately thrown out, but, instead, that person is brought to Aaron or any other *kohen* (biblical priest) and that person is examined. If the blotch has not penetrated the skin, then you wait, examine again, and wait, and you examine again and wait, and so on and so on until that person's health returns.

I held up the note that Sean had left for me. In it, he apologized for being somber. He revealed his sadness, and he declared to me that he could not go on living feeling so depressed.

I was so angry that I didn't have the opportunity to tell Sean that he would not always feel this way. I would have wanted to tell him that, with help and care, this, too, would pass. I told them all to tell what the *kohen* might have said to a frightened teen with a blotch: This is not fatal; this will fade; you will get better; you will not always feel this bad. This is why you must intervene. This is why, even if someone you know makes you vow not to tell anyone that he is going to kill himself, you must break that oath. Even if we make friends angry by breaking a promise not to reveal their suicidal thoughts, they will not always feel that way. It may take some time, but they will be alive.

## To: Peretz Wolf-Prusan
## From: Asher Lopatin

Peretz, that's an incredible insight into a tragic story. That's exactly what I think *Tazria* is all about—it's all about going beyond the superficial.

This is a portion about everything going wrong with the way we look. Our skin breaks out in weird ways, we lose some hairs, or they start showing up in a different color. The Torah even speaks about our clothing getting messed up with some strange "gunk" that makes them look like they've been bleached!

But, instead of just reacting to external problems in an external way, the Torah wants us to use them as an opportunity for some deeper thinking—which means real reflection.

Actually, when it comes to *tzara'at*—that skin affliction that has a starring role in this Torah portion—we are not allowed to just rip off the nasty blemish. The midrash on the verse "The person with the scall [blemish] shall shave himself, but without shaving the scall" (Leviticus 13:33) says that the verse means: Hey, you've got a serious problem, and it needs some attention. Just snipping off the outward signs of the problem and moving on will not solve anything.

If we are getting into an argument with a friend all the time, just being phony and smiling and ignoring her won't get to the root of the problem. We need to find out where the tension lies. The same is true with our families, and it's even and especially true with ourselves. If we find ourselves frustrated, or bored, or unhappy, then the superficial solutions—eating, drinking, partying, and doing something wild—are not the *real* solutions.

Sitting down and thinking about what is upsetting us—talking to a friend about all this stuff—*that's* what the Torah is getting at. When we have a problem, we need to turn to someone we can trust to be our *kohen*—our priest—to see our blotches and to help us work our way through them.

As you said, Peretz, this will pass—and we have the strength within us to reach inside and to work it out through deep changes in our lives.

# מצרע

## *Metzora*

---

# When Words Become Contagious

### Rabbi Norman M. Cohen

**If, when he examines the plague, the plague in the walls of the house is found to consist of greenish or reddish streaks that appear to go deep into the wall ...**
(Leviticus 14:37)

This Torah portion, *Metzora*, is mostly about leprosy—or to be more accurate, a variety of uncomfortable skin diseases (a little worse than acne), mildew, and disgusting rot that gets into the walls of houses.

Or is that really what the text is talking about? *Metzora* is really a metaphor for something else—gossip. In Numbers 12, Miriam makes unkind comments about her brother Moses's choice of a dark-skinned wife, calling her a Cushite (an Ethiopian), which was the "n" word of its day. Her punishment is that weird skin disease in which her skin starts to turn white and flake off her body. (Get it? She doesn't like that Moses has a black wife, and her skin turns even whiter!)

Modern technology has only magnified our ancestors' concerns about gossip. After all, have you ever been slammed on the Internet? Insulted on Facebook? Has someone tweeted something mean and cruel about you? Surely someone you know has suffered because of

---

**Rabbi Norman M. Cohen** is founding rabbi of Bet Shalom Congregation in Minnetonka, Minnesota. He spends part of his summer each year at OSRUI, the oldest of the Reform movement's summer camps.

thoughtless texting. In fact, there have been people who have been so hurt by gossip that they have become isolated or depressed, and some even die by suicide. Long ago, the Sages compared spreading gossip to the spilling of blood.

Our Torah portion, although written in biblical times, is relevant to this phenomenon when it describes a fast-spreading contagion in Leviticus 15:34. It changes the colors of the walls of a house to a sickly green—sort of like how we feel when someone spreads rumors about us or those we care about.

And what about our modern walls? How about our "Facebook walls," which are smeared with ugly comments? "Viral" used to mean a sickness; now it refers to information—and once that information is out there, it is impossible to prevent it from "going viral."

Gossip spreads like *metzora*. The word *metzora* is a combination of the words *motzi* and *ra*, meaning "one who brings out the bad." That bad is slander and gossip—what we call today slamming and insulting through speech and rumors.

The Rabbis called gossip *lashon ha-ra*—literally, "the evil tongue." The Talmud says that the human body was constructed to help a person refrain from *lashon ha-ra*. The teeth and lips serve as "gates" to regulate what emerges from our mouth, while the tongue lies in a horizontal resting position. Furthermore, while humans have two eyes, two ears, and two nostrils, we have only one mouth—to remind us to minimize our chatter. And, says the Talmud, for what purpose did God create earlobes? So that if we find ourselves in a situation where *lashon ha-ra* is being spoken, we can conveniently turn the lobes upward as earplugs!

Yes, sure—but who can prevent gossiping? Isn't it just part of human nature? Yes, and the ancient Rabbis knew it. That's why they said that you should not even repeat things that are true if there is a chance that it will damage another's reputation. It is therefore a Jewish value to demonstrate dignity and respect even when dealing with someone who has done wrong.

*Metzora* teaches us the power of words. Yes, we can do irrevocable harm by spreading gossip, but we can also do amazing good when we use caring words. We know how it feels to be appreciated and told something good. We have the power to do that for others. Technology has heightened the power of words. With power comes responsibility—and as teenagers, it's time to take precisely that kind of responsibility.

# Sacred Graffiti

Rabbi Shira Stern

**When you enter the land of Canaan that I give you as a possession, and I inflict an eruptive plague upon a house in the land you possess, the owner of the house shall come and tell the priest, saying, "Something like a plague has appeared upon my house."** (Leviticus 14:34–35)

Hands down, this is one of the most difficult portions to figure out in the entire Torah. It begins with leprosy, continues with rules for houses that develop plaguelike symptoms, and ends with bodily discharges—listed in painful and explicit detail.

Yuck factor: *high.*

*Wait—how can a house develop a plague?*

I really didn't have a clue about this—until I spent a week in New Orleans, six years after Hurricane Katrina, the worst national disaster in our nation's history. While I knew that there was still work to be done to restore this part of Louisiana to its former glory, I wasn't prepared for what I saw.

Our bus tour first took us through neighborhoods where entire square blocks were bare, still empty after millions of dollars were allocated to rebuild. And then there was the urban graffiti

---

**Rabbi Shira Stern** is in private practice, specializing in individual and family therapy, bereavement, and living with chronic pain, and serves as director of education at Temple Rodeph Torah in Marlboro, New Jersey.

spray-painted on the walls and doors of every house that hadn't been swept away—great big neon Xs, creating a special code for search and rescue workers who recorded what they discovered in every building. The first line, diagonal from right to left, meant a rescuer had entered the house; the opposite diagonal line that formed the X meant the rescuer had left. On top was the time and date(s) of the search, on the left was identified those who could help save what they could, on the right was a list of any potential hazards (mold, rats, rotten floorboards), and below was the number of survivors or the dead found on-site. The *New Orleans Times-Picayune* journalist Michael Perlstein described what he saw as "For Tales of Life and Death, the Writing's on the Walls."[5]

When they were able to come home and rebuild, some people painted over that writing on the wall. Others will never come back, because they either died or moved away. But, years later, the paint on the doors is still there.

So, who's responsible for plagues on houses?

In this particular portion, the priest goes in, identifies the problem, waits a period of time, and then reexamines the walls. At that point, he either declares the house "impure," which means that the house must be taken apart stone by stone, or if the plague recedes after scraping the walls, declares the house "pure" so that it is fit for people to live there once again.

Then the priest makes a ritual sacrifice: *Zot torat ha-tzara'at*, "Such is the ritual concerning eruptions [of plaguelike symptoms]" (Leviticus 14:57).

The key to this portion is that the plague has to be dealt with quickly, so that the homeowner can return with the family or find another place to live.

That's just *one* house.

But, a whole *city*—still so badly damaged, six years after the catastrophe?

Who are the modern-day priests whose role it is to diagnose and heal?

We are. You are. Your friends are. Anyone who can look and see what has happened, and what still has to happen, and can make a difference. We can volunteer to help rebuild, we can encourage the government to fund the city, wherever there is devastation, until people can come back and live their lives.

You are the priests of generations to come. Go out and make a difference.

# אחרי מות
# *Acharei Mot*

## The Physical Is Also Spiritual

Rabbi Dr. Bradley Shavit Artson

**The Eternal spoke to Moses after the death of the two sons of Aaron who died when they drew too close to the presence of the Eternal.** (Leviticus 16:1)

This Torah portion is, well, a *mess*.

From the opening passages that describe the ritual of selecting two goats and pushing one of them off a cliff as a symbol of releasing Israel of its accumulated sins; to the commandment to sacrifice an animal before eating any meat from it; to the laws of holiness that seem to be a lengthy set of sexual prohibitions and restrictions, which closes with the (in)famous passage that prohibits a male from "lying with a male as with a woman" (Leviticus 18:22), and labeling that act an abomination—every step of the way through this portion is bloody, physical, messy, and dangerous.

What are we to make of such an outmoded and apparently offensive text? Why would Judaism force us to read this kind of barbaric material? Shouldn't religion be uplifting and spiritual? Shouldn't it help us transcend our physical urges to achieve a more angelic state?

**Rabbi Dr. Bradley Shavit Artson** is Abner and Roslyn Goldstine Dean's Chair of the Ziegler School of Rabbinic Studies and vice president of American Jewish University in Los Angeles, California. He supervises the Miller Introduction to Judaism Program and mentors Camp Ramah in California.

An ancient midrash (Rabbinic legend) portrays the angels in heaven arguing that God should not give the Torah to human beings. "They lie!" the angels say of us. "They cheat. They steal. They commit adultery. They don't deserve the Torah!"

Moses responds by saying that God clearly intended the laws of the Torah *not* for angels, but rather for imperfect human beings: you shall not bear false witness; you shall not steal. A community of perfect saints does not need the Torah. The Torah is for *us*— struggling with our urges, trying to make meaning and justice in a world that is far from perfect.

But our Torah portion goes even beyond the idea of redeeming imperfection. Our portion teaches us that the spiritual and the physical are not opposites. Rather, the path to holiness means that we have to take our physical urges and elevate them so that they can reflect the Divine.

Can we learn to use every aspect of our humanity—our thoughts, passions, actions, and limbs—and help them rise to an expression of gratitude, joy, and service? Can we recognize our friends for who they are, not pretend they are something they are not (which is how I understand the prohibition of a man lying with another man as though he were a woman)? Can we live our lives and explore our relationships in ways that make it clear that God's image is physical and very much entails loving our bodies and loving this world?

Here's the important thing: you are probably not an angel. But that's OK, because the purpose of Torah is to make real people— people like you—into better, holier beings.

# Never Stand Idly By

Rabbi Steven Greenberg

**Do not lie with a male as one lies with a woman; it is an abhorrence.** (Leviticus 18:22)

*Acharei Mot* was my bar mitzvah portion. I prepared only the first few *aliyot*, the sections of the Torah portion—the part that deals with the service of the High Priest on Yom Kippur. The part I didn't read was chapter 18, which lists the rules of sexual morality. I knew that there were laws prohibiting adultery and incest, but that's about it. I really don't remember taking note of the particular verse that criminalizes same-sex relations between men. "Do not lie with a male as one lies with a woman; it is an abhorrence" (Leviticus 18:22). At the time, had I read it, it would have meant nothing to me.

Later, in my early teens, I vaguely recall my head turning sharply toward athletic boys. At Pesach Seders, my little brother would stare at a stunning female cousin, while I could not take my eyes off her equally beautiful brother. I had no idea what it meant to be homosexual. There were no categories for my experience; no way to explain the jerking around of my head, the warm sensation on my

**Rabbi Steven Greenberg** is a senior teaching fellow at CLAL, the National Jewish Center for Learning and Leadership, and director of the CLAL Diversity Project. He works with a new organization, Eshel, which supports Orthodox LGBT Jews and works toward their fuller inclusion in Orthodox communities (www.eshelonline.org).

face, or the flutter in my chest. What I did know is that if others were to read those feelings on my face or body, they could be dangerous. I spent much of high school focused on schoolwork and hiding from social situations that might reveal me.

It took years for me to accept that I was truly attracted to men. Once I was aware, in my mid-twenties, I felt tormented by this verse. It is read not only in the middle of spring during the regular Torah reading cycle, but also during the afternoon service in traditional synagogues on Yom Kippur. On many Yom Kippurs in my young adulthood, I would sit in shul (synagogue), put my *tallit* over my head, and when I heard that verse, I would weep.

Out of deference to gay people, some congregations have stopped reading that verse on Yom Kippur, but I think that just gives it more power. (Things you deny get bigger, not smaller.)

Instead, I think that we should read the verse aloud and ask our communities to take responsibility for how it has been interpreted (and misinterpreted) in the past. Simplistic readings of this passage have ruined thousands, if not millions, of people's lives. For their sake, we must face the text squarely and honestly.

In my view, the most reasonable reading of this verse is that it prohibits the violent and demeaning ways people can engage in sexual relations. This may seem like a stretch, but it isn't hard to find evidence for this in the Torah.

The first mention of homosexual relations in the book of Genesis is about violence. Lot, Abraham's nephew, lived in Sodom, a lovely "gated community" on the shores of the Dead Sea. He notices a couple of poor vagrants (who later turn out to be angels) and invites them to take shelter in his home.

Sodom's inhabitants were selfish and cruel. They were afraid that beggars, vagrants, travelers, and immigrants would take what was theirs. The midrash actually says that they made it a rule to punish anyone who helped people in need, and because Lot invited the poor travelers in, the people gather at his door to punish him. Gang rape was a common form of communal violence in the ancient world. Sodom is all about mob violence, fear, and cruelty.

If so, then the verse in Leviticus "Do not lie with a male as one lies with a woman; it is an abhorrence" would not be about the loving relationship between men. Rather, it would be about the kind of forced sex that happens in prisons or the kind of rape that soldiers use in wartime to humiliate the defeated enemy.

This makes sense because most of the other sexual laws in chapter 18 of Leviticus are about violence and abuse. Adultery inspires violence, and incest threatens the safety of families. Sexual intercourse with a menstruating woman looks like a bloody act of violence.

The only nonsexual law in the list is one that prohibits the worship of the Canaanite deity, Molech. How was this ancient god worshipped? According to the medieval sage Maimonides, by passing a child through fire. According to another medieval sage, Nachmanides, this was not mere coal walking or fire jumping, but actual child sacrifice. No one knows exactly why this law about child sacrifice is located here, but one thing is sure: if the key to this chapter is violence, then surely this practice of child sacrifice is the height of violence in the name of religion.

The relevance of all this came home to me recently, when I learned that the Michigan Senate passed a bullying law called "Matt's Safe Schools Law." The law is named for Matt Epping, a fifteen-year-old who committed suicide in 2002, after being tormented by students at his high school. The statistics are shocking. One in six LGBT (lesbian, gay, bisexual, transgender) young people contemplate suicide, and one in twenty makes an attempt.

However, the most shocking piece of the story is that after Matt's parents worked for years to get the law passed, conservative senators added a paragraph to the law at the last minute that excluded bullying "motivated by sincerely held religious belief or moral conviction." Translation: if you have a religious or moral rationale for bullying, then you've got a green light.

The law asks bystanders to act in defense of the harassed students—unless, of course, they also have religious reasons to turn a blind eye. Can there be good reasons to bully anyone? Should bullies be able to defend themselves by claiming to be motivated by a verse in scripture? Moreover, what sort of religious system would encourage a person who witnesses a great wrong to stand idly by and remain silent?

Every Jewish youth organization in America has signed a pledge that promises their members will commit to stopping homophobic bullying—even the youth leadership of the Orthodox community's National Council of Synagogue Youth (NCSY). Of course, there will be differences of opinion in different Jewish communities, but on one thing we can all agree: no one should have to be afraid to go to school. In whatever way we interpret Leviticus 18:22, we cannot do so in a way that supports or even drives some people to emotional and physical violence and convinces others that life is not worth living.

I was trying to find a more upbeat way to end to this essay, and the phone rang. A junior at an Orthodox yeshiva high school on the East Coast called me for advice. A straight friend had arranged to meet with the school principal to request the establishment of a gay–straight alliance (GSA), and she wanted him to join her. He wanted to know whether I thought he should join her.

I first wanted to make sure that he felt ready for this. He said "yes." I asked if he felt that this might eventually "out" him to the entire school. He said "yes." Was he ready if that happened? He was nervous about it, but it was OK. I asked him why he was doing it. While his parents were supportive, he knew that there were other gay teens at the school who were not out at home, many of whom were very scared and needed a safe place to talk about things. I told him that it was an enormous mitzvah, a courageous and holy thing to do.

You can do it, too. If your school doesn't have a GSA, consider what it might take to start one. There are organizations that can help. Keshet (www.keshetonline.org) can help you get started, and the GSA Network (www.gsanetwork.org) can connect you to other teens who are working to make schools safe. And if you just don't feel up to taking on such activism, at the very least, do this: commit in your gut to never stand idly by.

## Tattoo, Taboo, and the Jew: Can I Be Buried in a Jewish Cemetery?

Rabbi Peter Berg

**You shall not make gashes in your flesh for the dead, or incise any marks on yourselves: I am the Eternal.**
(Leviticus 19:28)

For Generation M, tattoos are becoming the norm rather than the exception—even in the Jewish community.

A college student I know who recovered from a devastating illness recently etched the Hebrew word *koach* (strength) into his left shoulder blade. For him, this was not an act of rebellion, but rather a bona fide Jewish ritual experience.

In contrast, baby boomers and Generation Xers tend to be uncomfortable with Jews who have tattoos on their skin, be it a skull and crossbones or a Star of David. Other than the fact that their parents or grandparents would become angry, few are able to explain the nature of their discomfort.

Perhaps it is the result of the greatest Jewish fear tactic of all time: the widespread notion that Jews with tattoos can't be buried in Jewish cemeteries!

Another source of confusion is that the information that we do have about tattoos (from both the Bible and contemporary

---

**Rabbi Peter Berg** is senior rabbi of The Temple in Atlanta, Georgia.

Jewish law) is limited, if not slippery. In Leviticus 19:28, we find the following verse: "You shall not make gashes in your flesh for the dead, or incise any marks on yourselves: I am the Eternal." The great Torah commentators even debate whether this is a *chok* (a commandment that we must obey—not only because God said so but also because the human mind could never possibly understand it) or whether we should even try to explain why this law exists in the first place.

What's the classic reason for this law against tattoos? *You're not allowed to destroy your body.* The human body is God's creation, and human beings are not allowed to mutilate God's handiwork. God is the greatest of all artists. God formed each person in a unique and fitting way, and we must not change this form. Changing one's body (except for medical reasons) is the same as insulting God's handiwork. This is a clear case for the biblical law, "Thou shalt not get a tattoo!" In a similar way, excessive use of alcohol, overeating, or smoking is also a violation of Jewish law, because you are endangering your body, which is God's supreme act of artistry.

In the Talmud (*Makkot* 21a), Rabbi Shimon decided to look very closely at the Torah's phrase, "I am the Eternal." He concluded that tattooing is forbidden only when it is *connected to idolatry*. In ancient times, as a sign of commitment to their deity, idol worshippers would tattoo themselves in the same way that sometimes the owner of a cow will brand the animal. The brand says, "I own this animal," and the tattoo says, "This god owns *me*." The Torah constantly rejects those practices that have pagan origins—because if you follow pagan practices, the next step is that you might actually believe in those false gods.

When Leviticus was written, the purpose of tattooing was to mark slaves and even to show devotion to Pharaoh. You could argue that such a law is outdated today. Not only that: just because many people don't happen to find tattoos to be particularly attractive doesn't mean that they should be against the law.

For many years, tattooed Jews could not be buried in Jewish cemeteries, because people assumed that a tattoo represented evil—either in the form of pagan practices or, in modern times, engaging in criminal activity.

But most Jews who tattoo themselves today are not taking on pagan practices; neither are they engaging in criminal activity. Rather, they are simply attempting to adorn their bodies. Therefore, most Jewish cemeteries today will allow the deceased with a tattoo to have a proper Jewish burial, even as it is inconsistent with strict Jewish law. Of course, Jewish grandparents won't tell you that, because they still want to discourage you from getting a tattoo.

(Incidentally, the only crime that will *truly* get you excluded from a Jewish cemetery is apostasy—the absolute rejection of Jewish faith. If you aren't planning on doing that—and we hope you aren't—then you're safe!)

And yet, before you might decide to get a tattoo, you should think about some very important considerations.

> **First:** *the tattoo is pretty much permanent.* As hard as it might be, try to think ahead to when you are seventy years old—or even, say, thirty years old. A tattoo is pretty much a permanent commitment. Are you *really* sure that you will still want that tattoo in ten, twenty, or fifty years? *Really?*
>
> **Second:** *honor your parents.* Will permanent ink on your body simply push them over the edge?
>
> **Third:** *be careful about your health and safety.* Do you trust the person who works with the needles? Do you *really* trust that the needles are going to be completely sterile? And if you are going to put your body in danger, should it really be for this kind of reason?

Before you make the (basically irreversible) decision to alter your body in any way, you should be considering those questions, among many others.

Now, here's something really interesting: the Hebrew term that is associated with tattoos—*ketovet ka'aka* (incised or etched mark)—appears only in this one biblical verse. However, the verb *k-t-v*, which means "to write," more accurately means to "incise or to engrave," and that verb appears both in Exodus and Deuteronomy. But in those contexts, what does that verb mean? It describes how God wrote the Ten Commandments on the tablets.

In other words, *etching or writing is what God does—on the tablets. It's not what you do—on your body.*

Come to think of it, much of the book of Leviticus is about the sanctity of the body. For example, we learn what to eat and not eat (the laws of kashrut). We also learn about the proper concern for what comes out of the body, in the form of fluid discharge or skin conditions. From a biblical perspective, then, it is only logical that the Bible would prohibit the permanent etching of an ink mark on one's body.

But, isn't it true that we all want to leave our mark on the world?

Judaism teaches us that we do leave a mark on the world—but it's not one that we etch into our skin. Rather, we should strive to inscribe marks on the hearts and souls of other people.

That's what *Kedoshim* is all about: our ethical behavior toward our fellow neighbors. God etched commandments into stone tablets, and through our own actions, we etch them upon others.

# Sacred Sexuality

## Rabbi Danya Ruttenberg

**You shall sanctify yourselves and be holy....** (Leviticus 20:7)

*Parashat Kedoshim* is part of the "Holiness Code," referring to its opening words: "You shall be holy, for I, the Eternal your God, am holy" (Leviticus 19:2).

It's a powerful setup. But how do we do that? How do we mortals become sanctified? How do we behave in a godlike way?

You might assume that the commandments that follow this statement are going to be about ritual—prayer, or the complicated animal sacrifices that our ancestors offered at the ancient Temple in Jerusalem. But instead, this Torah portion concerns itself almost entirely with interpersonal commandments—how humans deal with each other.

This Torah portion tells us that how you become holy includes doing things like honoring your parents, leaving some of the harvest for the needy, not holding grudges, paying your workers on time, caring for the stranger in your midst, and respecting the elderly. These are all crucial mitzvot that are worthy of discussion in their own right.

It's very Jewish—this idea that we honor the Divine when we treat our family, peers, and coworkers with respect, and when we

---

**Rabbi Danya Ruttenberg** is the author of *Surprised By God: How I Learned to Stop Worrying and Love Religion*, and editor of *The Passionate Torah: Sex and Judaism* and *Yentl's Revenge: The Next Wave of Jewish Feminism*.

take steps to care for the most vulnerable members of our society, whether poor, elderly, or strangers.

But this portion also deals with sexual prohibitions—against adultery, incest, bestiality, prostitution, and other forms of sexual exploitation.

Being holy is about more than what we do with our money or our time. We begin living a life in tune with the sacred, with our highest selves, with the great, pulsing stream of existence itself, in the ways we handle our most intimate relationships. How we use our body, and to what ends, is a matter of ultimate consequence.

All of the sex-related prohibitions here are forms of betrayal, exploitation, and imbalance of power in relationships. None of them depicts a fully present relationship between two loving equals.

Jewish texts don't generally describe sex as a terrible thing to be feared or as an evil to be endured only for the sake of reproduction. Rather, our texts view sex as a wonderful, healthy, exciting part of being human. Countless Jewish texts affirm the value of sexual pleasure in its own right. The Jewish tradition honors intimacy for its own sake.

But our portion teaches us that becoming holy means using our sexuality carefully, with an awareness that our actions can bring us closer to, or further from, the Divine, other people, and ourselves. When we take all the kindness, caring, and respect demanded elsewhere in the Torah portion, and we put that kindness, caring, and respect into our most intimate relationships, when we understand that sexuality is a serious thing that requires a great deal of care and thought—then we can, like God, become holy, and that's how we sanctify our lives.

# אֱמֹר

## *Emor*

## Animals: What's Cruel, and What's Not So Cruel?

Stan J. Beiner

**The Eternal spoke to Moses, saying: When an ox or a sheep or a goat is born, it shall stay seven days with its mother, and from the eighth day on it shall be acceptable as an offering by fire to the Eternal. However, no animal from the herd or from the flock shall be slaughtered on the same day with its young.**
(Leviticus 22:26–28)

At some point in time, you (or one of your friends) are going to announce that you have decided to become a vegetarian.

Most people who settle on this path do so because of their concern over animal cruelty. In some cases, people are very understanding and even respect this dietary choice; others simply do not get it. "What's the big deal?" they say. "Why would anyone ever want to give up the taste of a juicy burger or not participate in those fun wing-eating contests at camp?"

True, the Torah teaches us to be kind to animals.

But, it does not prohibit us from hunting or eating them.

Isn't that a double standard?

---

**Stan J. Beiner** is head of school at the Epstein School in Atlanta, Georgia.

Leviticus 22:26–28 addresses this problem: "The Eternal spoke to Moses, saying: When an ox or a sheep or a goat is born, it shall stay seven days with its mother, and from the eighth day on it shall be acceptable as an offering by fire to the Eternal. However, no animal from the herd or from the flock shall be slaughtered on the same day with its young."

So, you can kill an animal in the name of God, but you have to do it *nicely*.

"Huh? I don't get it," you're saying to yourself. "If the Torah teaches us to treat animals kindly, why is it alright to sacrifice them in the name of God?"

Well, it's complicated.

Should we tell Eskimos that they can't hunt elk or the endangered polar bear for food and clothing? There are some animal rights groups that would do that. But, then, what would those Eskimos eat?

In a 1999 movie, *Drive Me Crazy*, an activist girl gets angry with her boyfriend because he does not want to protest laboratory experiments on animals. She learns that the boy's mom died of cancer and that he supported the research being done on lab rats to find a cure. Who was right—the anti-animal-experiment girl or her boyfriend, whose dying mother might have benefitted from the results of animal experiments?

Consider a Japanese fishing village. For hundreds of years, its economy has depended on whaling. Yes, we want to protect endangered species. But does that mean that we simply end that village's traditional way of life and sustenance?

*Emor* gives us a hint of how we may approach these questions. Our world is at a crossroads, and how we tend to nature will determine the future of our planet. The Torah teaches us: if you must take an animal's life, you can do so—*but you have to understand precisely what it is that you are doing.*

Some animal experiments might be ethically necessary—for example, those that might lead to a cure for a terrible disease. But not all animal experiments are necessary—for example, animal testing for cosmetics. Rampant, uncontrolled whaling is not responsible.

Eating contests or simply gorging ourselves on meat products is not mindful of the value of another living being.

In the midst of a book that focuses on sacrifices serving God, the Torah reminds us that even if it is for a higher purpose, a life is still being taken.

# God Said *What?*

Shulamit Reinharz, PhD, and Ellen Golub, PhD

**The Eternal spoke further to Moses: Speak to Aaron and say: No man of your offspring throughout the ages who has a defect shall be qualified to offer the food of his God ... no man who is blind, or lame, or has a limb too short or too long....** (Leviticus 21:16–18)

Did you ever think it was strange that we are supposed to understand our twenty-five-hundred-year-old Torah when it is written in a language that we struggle to comprehend? And by language, we don't just mean Hebrew. Each week, we turn to the text and try to get it. English translations help, of course. Rabbis and sermons can be useful. Some of us will even turn to Rashi and his commentary to get some insights. But that's not all that's needed.

In general we assume that Bible stories make good points; they show the way we should live. That pretty much works for Genesis and Exodus. But then there's Leviticus. That's where the narrative about

---

**Shulamit Reinharz, PhD,** is Jacob Potofsky Professor of Sociology at Brandeis University, where she created the Hadassah-Brandeis Institute in 1997 and the Women's Studies Research Center in 2001, both of which she directs.

**Ellen Golub, PhD,** is professor of Journalism and writing coach for the college newspaper at Salem State University and a research associate at the Hadassah-Brandeis Institute.

people and families morphs into a long list of strange rules and even stranger ideas.

The name of the Torah portion *Emor* means "say" or "tell," as in "Tell the people what the rules are." The first thing to figure out is who is telling whom to do what? The answer is that God is commanding Moses to tell his brother, Aaron, to instruct his fellow priests (*kohanim*) about the rules of the priesthood.

Specifically, God outlines the privileges and responsibilities for priests who will be carrying out religious rituals.

*Kohanim* act on behalf of the Jewish people as a whole. *Emor* instructs them how to offer animal and grain sacrifices on the altar in the Temple. This ancient practice means slaughtering the animal, burning the carcass on the altar, and sprinkling drops of the animal's blood in specific ways. After the destruction of the Temple in Jerusalem, sacrifices could no longer be performed, and prayer took its place as a way for Jews to draw closer to God.

*Emor* is very specific about who may, and who may not, act as a priest (*kohen*). Women are excluded, as are people who have any physical imperfections. One leg shorter than the other? Unfit. A dwarf or hunchback? Unfit. Blind, bruised, scarred, homosexual— all make a man unfit for priestly service in the Temple.

Some of us might be offended by rules such as animal sacrifice. Today there are many people, for example, who do not use shampoos that are tested on animals.

And yet, in our Torah portion, God demands that the choicest animals be slaughtered on the Temple altar. So too, in modern times, laws protect the rights of people with disabilities. But the God of *Emor* does not allow disabled people to be priests. Nowadays it is difficult to accept the idea of a special caste of Jews—men descended from Aaron. Why should they, alone, have exceptional privileges? To this day, in Orthodox and Conservative congregations, *kohanim* are still "special." They are the first to be honored with an *aliyah* to the Torah, and it is their unique privilege to bless the congregation.

These contradictions between *Emor* and contemporary morality can present a real problem. One way to deal with this is to understand the Torah as continuously giving us paradoxes and dilemmas to unravel. Over the centuries, rabbis and scholars have struggled with the question of how to read the Torah. What do we do if the words of Torah come into conflict with the values of the time? How are modern people who believe in equality and fairness supposed to understand the Torah's often-strange demands?

The Rabbis tell us that there are two starkly different kinds of rules: *chukim* (decrees) and *mishpatim* (laws). *Mishpatim* are laws that make sense—laws that good and wise people might have invented on their own, like not murdering and not stealing. For instance, *Emor* mentions the *mishpat* of *leket*, the commandment that farmers not harvest the produce in the corners of their fields. Rather, they must leave areas for poor people to glean. This law leads to one of the Torah's earliest and most radical ideas: for those in need, charity (*tzedakah*) is a legal right.

But *Emor* also deals in *chukim*, or divine decrees—rules that we find incomprehensible and irrational, like sacrificing animals. That type of commandment may confuse us. For example, if the Torah says (in Genesis) that all humans are created in the image of God, why does it then decree that only unblemished people can be *kohanim*?

Nowadays young Jews are idealistic. For example, teenagers use the celebration of their bar or bat mitzvah as an opportunity to ask guests to give to charity. On this occasion, lots of kids becoming a bar or bat mitzvah participate in social justice projects themselves. We suggest that this idealistic impulse can be applied to analyzing the Torah and seeking its challenging inner wisdom. If you can accept the fact that the Torah deals in ideas that are beyond human understanding, then it becomes interesting to try to puzzle out the meaning of these apparently irrational concepts. As the ancient sage Ben Bag Bag wrote in *Pirkei Avot*, "Turn it and turn it again, for everything is in it. Contemplate it. Grow old over it, and never depart from it, for there is no finer pursuit" (*Mishnah Avot* 5:26).

Our tradition does not require us to accept everything at face value, but it does expect us to study and debate. The Torah invites us to think in complex ways and interpret each chapter. You can read the Torah portion every Shabbat and gain inspiration from the meaning and choices you find there. From your own explorations, you can go on to figure out how you can live a Jewish life.

Like Jacob, who wrestled with God and whose name was changed to Yisrael (the one who struggles with God), each week we engage with the text, trying to discern what it means to us. It is that engagement, like Jacob's, that has made us a nation of thinkers and commentators, of relentless seekers and interpreters. As we turn the Torah over, Shabbat after Shabbat, working to understand each word and mark, we earn the right to be called the children of Yisrael, the Jewish people.

# בהר

# *Behar*

## God's Reset Button

### Rabbi Mike Comins

**When you enter the land that I assign to you, the land shall observe a sabbath of the Eternal. Six years you may sow your field and six years you may prune your vineyard and gather in the yield. But in the seventh year the land shall have a Sabbath of complete rest … you shall not sow your field or prune your vineyard.**
(Leviticus 25:2–4)

In *Behar*, we once again understand what the Torah's greatest priority is: *social justice*. It's not only people that have rights. Nature does, too.

Once every seven years, the land must be left alone, unused and uncultivated. This is how the ancients, who had poor fertilizers, protected the health of the land. But here is what is amazing about the Israelites. Even though you worked your farm during the past six years, everyone (even wild animals) is entitled to whatever grows on its own during the sabbatical year. You aren't allowed to take any more food for your family than anyone else.

Why? Because in a just society, everyone must have access to food, especially when it is scarce. In the end, you're not the ultimate owner of your land; God is.

---

**Rabbi Mike Comins** is a licensed Israeli desert guide and the founder of the TorahTrek Center for Jewish Wilderness Spirituality.

Even more radical, during the fiftieth, jubilee year, all land returns to its original owners, and slaves are set free.

Just think about what the Torah is actually saying here. This is huge.

In ancient Israel, the biggest industry was agriculture. When drought came and crops failed, the rich became richer, because less fortunate people had to sell their land in order to eat. They became sharecroppers, or worse—they might sell themselves into slavery in order to survive. It was Egypt all over again. New Pharaohs arose from within the Jewish people.

But not for long. The Torah says "no" to this kind of injustice, because every fifty years it pushes the "reset" button, and it starts over. The land also lay unused during the jubilee. And because the forty-ninth year was a sabbatical year (seven times seven, right?), farmers didn't farm for two years in a row!

Just as the Israelites released their slaves and celebrated freedom for all, they had to remember their first home: the wilderness. For six years, they fought off the desert by growing their crops. For six years, they brought civilization and order into the wilderness. But in the sabbatical and jubilee years, they didn't do anything with the land. They let it go wild—which really means: they invited the desert back into their homes!

To a person like me, these connections among wilderness, justice, and Judaism are crucial. I grew up hiking and backpacking in the Sierra Nevada mountains of California. To this day, if you ask me, "Where do you feel closest to God?" I would have to say, "Easy—in nature."

When I was in high school, I played football and ran track. Nothing made me happier than working my body. I liked my studies and I loved being Jewish, but I didn't know what they had to do with my most spiritual and happiest moments.

Fortunately, things changed for me in college. I went on solo backpacking trips, because that was the ultimate freedom. Everything I needed was on my back, and I went wherever I wanted to go.

Or, so I thought.

In reality, if I wanted to climb a peak and return safely, I needed to monitor the weather and revise my plans accordingly. I hiked on main trails, so that if I twisted my ankle and couldn't walk, someone would find me. I needed to protect my food from bears and be alert for rattlesnakes. I was experienced and I knew what I was doing, so I felt safe. But if I wanted to reach my goal, I couldn't do whatever I wanted. I had to pay close attention, and whatever the wilderness "told" me to do, I did.

I was *commanded*. To be free, I surrendered to the truth of a reality that was larger than me.

Where did we Jews become a people? While wandering in the desert.

One of the first things that Moses did after the Exodus was to appoint judges to administer justice for all (Exodus 18:13–16). If we were to survive in the harsh wilderness, we had to pull together and treat each other fairly. We could not hoard the food on which our lives depended (Exodus 16:4). To be free, we had to surrender to a larger, moral reality.

We were *commanded*. In the wilderness, justice is not an option.

That's why it always made a lot of sense to me that our ancestors received the Torah in the desert. They literally brought the desert into their homes every seventh year to remember their origins. In the Sinai desert, the people not only received the values and laws for a just society, but they also had to *live* them. What better preparation for life in their permanent, civilized home, where greed and hoarding wealth might threaten their ability to survive as a nation? This message is just as relevant for us today as it was for our ancestors.

And, if you are the kind of person who feels most spiritual in nature and loves to challenge your body as well as your heart and mind, you can remember what God taught the ancient Israelites in the Torah.

When you're in the wilderness—hiking, biking, skiing, or paddling—you don't have to leave your Jewish self behind. On the contrary, you're returning to where our people and our values were born.

# Shabbat and the Power of the "Regular" and "Routine"

Rabbi Michael L. Feshbach

**You shall keep My Sabbaths, and venerate My Sanctuary, Mine, the Eternal's.** (Leviticus 26:2)

It is the middle of a school year, and suddenly, unexpectedly, a teacher must step down. The administration finds a new teacher, and she enters the class. She wants to get to know her new students as quickly as possible. The curriculum tells her it is time for a book report, and she faces a choice.

She can let the students choose any book they want to read, and she can learn about her students from the choices that they make.

Or she can assign the entire class the same book and see how different students with different personalities interpret the book in different ways.

In our culture, it sometimes seems that everything we do has to be new and exciting. After all, what's the most hated word in a teenager's vocabulary? *Boring.*

Maybe it's OK for some things to be, well, if not exactly boring, then at least predictable. Our Torah portion teaches us, "You shall keep My Sabbaths...." Sabbaths—in the plural.

---

**Rabbi Michael L. Feshbach** is senior rabbi of Temple Shalom of Chevy Chase, Maryland.

We don't invent Shabbat every week. That's why it is so powerful, because it comes so frequently and therefore it is so familiar.

If you measure Shabbat by what's cool and trendy, it will fail every time. Movies are usually more exciting; plays are usually better drama; concerts will usually have better music. Shabbat is not about what's new; it's actually about making *yourself* new.

That's how Shabbat can work for you—through repetition, regularity, and routine. It is probably totally unlike anything that you are accustomed to—but it works.

Shabbat is the "control-alt-delete" on our lives. And it's not because we do it sometimes; it's because we are able to do it once every seven days.

Shabbat is the gift that keeps on giving. And it is a gift that you can accept.

# בחקתי
# *Bechukotai*

## "Girls Rule! Boys Drool."

### Rabbi Marshal Klaven

**When anyone makes a vow to support the tabernacle ... if it is a male from age five to twenty, his value is equivalent to twenty shekels; while a female's value [at the same age] is ten shekels.** (Leviticus 27:2, 27:5 [my translation—MK])

"Girls rule! Boys drool."

"Nah uh, boys are cool! Girls are fools."

These supersophisticated schoolyard chants prove something very important: practically from the very moment that we are born, we begin to value males and females differently.

It's not new, of course. Our ancestors did it, as well, in their own way.

Specifically, our portion states, "When anyone makes a vow to support the tabernacle ... if it is a male from age five to twenty, his value is equivalent to twenty shekels; while a female's value [at the same age] is ten shekels" (Leviticus 27:2, 27:5).

Unfortunately, there is no way to get around it: historically, men have been valued higher than women.

Sure, on the whole, we have made progress toward greater gender equality. But there are some Jews who continue to maintain

---

**Rabbi Marshal Klaven** is director of rabbinic services for the Goldring/Woldenberg Institute of Southern Jewish Life (ISJL), serving over one hundred congregations of various movements in thirteen states.

gender inequality. They say that for society to function properly, men and women should have separate roles.

Even God, some say, appreciates such distinctions. According to the midrash:

> When Moses went out to witness the harsh labors of his brethren, he saw women being forced to do men's work, and men being forced to do women's work. Therefore, Moses rearranged their work according to their gender. God said, "Since you have ordered the burdens of My children according to their gender, so should you continue to order them [i.e., lead them] into the future."
>
> (Midrash, *Vayikra Rabbah* 27:2)

As the midrash teaches, we can, and should, appreciate genders as being different. But, that does not mean we should *value* them differently. When we value genders differently, we actually decrease our overall value as a society. As the former prime minister of Great Britain Margaret Thatcher acknowledged, "The greatest resource of all is human beings." This does not mean, as the movie *The Matrix* depicted, that some day machines will harvest people for energy. Thatcher meant that when we weed anyone out of society based upon external factors like gender, we not only do an injustice to them but we also do an injustice to ourselves.

Therefore, let's cut out statements like "Girls rule, boys drool" or "Boys are cool, girls are fools." Because, as this Torah portion also states, before the age of one month we are all equal in value (Leviticus 27:6). It is only as we progress through life that we make the mistake of placing a value on those differences. In the sight of God, we are all created equal, each reflecting an equally valued part of the divine image. If we wish to see the whole of the Divine in this world, then we must begin to realize that everyone has equal worth—whether male or female, young or old, black or white, heterosexual or homosexual. For, in doing so, may we come to build—as was the inspiration of our ancestors—a sanctuary in which a stronger and more caring society may reside.

# A Big "If"

Rabbi Shira Stutman

**If you follow My laws and faithfully observe My commandments ...** (Leviticus 26:3)

Alexis stood on the bimah to give that week's *devar Torah* on *Bechukotai*. When we were preparing her speech, we never got past the first few words: "If you walk in My laws ..." (Leviticus 26:3 [my translation—SS]).

"What does it mean to walk in God's laws?" Alexis asked. Her heart was heavy with conflicts from school. She certainly didn't feel close to God.

We studied the Hasidic commentary Sefat Emet, which says, "'If you walk in My laws' means that wherever we walk, God is there. When we act in godly ways, every place can become like a synagogue."

**Me:** "How wonderful! God is everywhere!"

**Alexis:** *Snort.* "Today, I found out that my so-called 'best friend' was talking about me behind my back. So where's God in that!"

**Me:** *Cue the adult platitudes ...*

**Alexis:** *Dead stare.*

**Me,** trying again: "Perhaps the right question isn't 'Where's God in that situation?' but instead, 'Even when someone else doesn't do so, how

**Rabbi Shira Stutman** is director of Community Engagement at Sixth & I Historic Synagogue in Washington, DC.

can *I* behave in, or walk, in godly ways?' Real life isn't a television show, with easy answers at the end of every half hour. You have relatively little control over whether your best friend chooses to 'walk in God's ways' or not. You only have one choice—*how you decide to react.* When you're sitting with a friend who wants to tell an unfair, untrue, and/or unnecessary story about another person, you can choose to redirect the conversation away from *lashon ha-ra* [gossip]. We can decide how we want to react, and that's what gets us walking in 'godly' ways."

A month later, Alexis began her *devar Torah* with the following story, which she learned from Elie Wiesel:

> One day, a righteous person came to save Sodom from sin and from destruction. He preached to the people, "Please do not be murderers, do not be thieves. Do not be silent and do not be indifferent." He went on preaching day after day. But no one listened. He was not discouraged. He went on preaching for years.
>
> Finally, someone asked him, "Rabbi, why do you do that? Don't you see it is no use?"
>
> He said, "I know that it is of no use, but I must. And I will tell you why: in the beginning I thought I had to protest and to shout in order to change *them.* I have given up this hope. Now I know I must protest and shout so that they will not change *me.*"[6]

Alexis continued, "In Judaism, we believe that people have free choice. Every minute of every day we can make certain choices. We usually know what the right one is, but we can't always choose it, and sometimes we just don't want to. But we can try.

"Unfortunately, I've learned to not always expect kindness and generosity. I've also learned, though, that while we can't control other people, we can control ourselves. If we take the high road— and the long view—our own acts of kindnesses and generosity will ripple outward and create a better world."

Amen to that.

Bemidbar/
Numbers

# במדבר
# *Bemidbar*

## Standing Guard
### Rabbi Jonathan E. Blake

**The Levites, however, shall camp around the Tabernacle of the Pact....** (Numbers 1:53)

What or who represents the greatest threat to you as a Jew today?

There are two possible answers.

On the one hand, you might believe that the greatest threats to the Jewish people today are *external* threats: anti-Semitism, "anti-Israelism," and the threat of a nuclear Iran, whose president, Mahmoud Ahmadinejad, denies that the. Holocaust happened and would like to see Israel disappear from the map.

On the other hand, perhaps *internal* threats to the Jewish people are more dangerous. Jews from different streams of Jewish life, like the ultra-Orthodox and the non-Orthodox, are constantly going at it. Some Jews don't even like it when other Jews express different opinions on Israel and what it means to be Jewish.

And then, there's that old threat—assimilation. There are many Jews who just want to be like everyone else in America. Throw in rising rates of intermarriage and the fact that fewer people are choosing to join synagogues.

Each of these, and all of these together, might lead to the weakening of the Jewish community—not because of external factors, but from the inside out.

---

**Rabbi Jonathan E. Blake** is senior rabbi of Westchester Reform Temple in Scarsdale, New York.

So which type of threat is more dangerous to us as Jews—the external or the internal?

In our Torah portion, we read that the Levites, the biblical priests, took on the responsibility to "stand guard around the tabernacle" (Numbers 1:53), the central shrine in the wilderness. The Levites served as the tabernacle's security force!

When you consider what we know about the Levites, it's an intriguing choice. Although other tribes consisted of warriors, the Levites were religious professionals. They ministered to the ancient sacrificial system, conducted communal rituals and celebrations, taught sacred texts, and even composed and performed religious poetry and music.

Perhaps the Levites' main function in guarding the tabernacle had nothing to do with their skills as security guards and everything to do with promoting a vibrant Jewish life for the entire community. After all, the entire tabernacle was already fortified with a heavily armed military encampment, composed of all the other tribes.

What was the job of the unarmed Levites? Teaching holy words, bringing uplifting music and ritual to worship, and ministering to the needs of the people.

I imagine the Levites made it their top priority to ensure a thriving Jewish congregation, aware that no external threat could ever destroy a community that was strong and united from within.

# "They've Given You a Number, and Taken Away Your Name"

Rabbi Joshua Hammerman

**Take a census of the whole Israelite community by the clans of its ancestral houses, listing the names, every male, head by head.** (Numbers 1:2)

I've never been great at math, but I've always had a fascination with numbers.

"Who knows one? I know one!" we sing at the Passover Seder—the same event that boasts four cups, four children, four questions, three matzot, and ten plagues.

Come to think of it, Jews are *obsessed* with numbers. We even have an entire book of the Torah called Numbers, though in Hebrew it has an entirely different name—*Bemidbar*, "in the wilderness," which is also the name of this Torah portion.

*Bemidbar* contains a count of the Israelites. It is very rare for the Bible to contain a census, or count, and Jews have always been a little nervous about such counts.

But wait: how could a tradition so obsessed with numbers be so afraid of counting people?

Here's the answer.

*We don't want to turn people into numbers.*

---

**Rabbi Joshua Hammerman** is rabbi of Temple Beth El in Stamford, Connecticut.

In the haftarah (the prophetic reading) that goes with this Torah portion, the prophet Hosea seems to be sending that message when he states that the number of the people in Israel cannot be counted, much like grains of sand. Rashi, the great medieval commentator, says something similar in a commentary to Exodus 30, which also contains the story of a census: "The evil eye controls something that has been counted." The Talmud echoes the idea that God only imparts blessing to that which is not quantified. In very traditional Jewish worship services, when people calculate whether there is a minyan (quorum of ten worshippers), they'll count "*Not* one, *not* two, *not* three …" to fool that "evil eye."

Yes, that practice probably seems superstitious, but what is it really saying to us? It is saying something very big and very valuable: *a human being is more than the sum of his or her parts*. We can't be reduced to merely our statistics: our age, our phone number, our Social Security number. We are more than all of that.

We can learn this, terribly, from the Nazis. When the Nazis wanted to totally dehumanize someone, what did they do? They assigned him or her a number, and they tattooed that number on the person's arm. After all, if you can reduce an entire life to a number, then it makes it that much easier to erase that entire life.

As someone who loves sports, I look closely at statistics, but I know that while a player's stats can be impressive, they never tell the whole story. A basketball player's scoring averaging doesn't tell us whether he can block out, set picks, or make a perfect pass. For me, the number "twelve" will always remind me of my favorite quarterback, Tom Brady, and "fifty-six" is Joe DiMaggio's hitting streak, but we cannot measure the accomplishments of these players in numbers alone. When we rate someone's looks numerically ("She's a ten!"), it may be flattering, but we have just turned that person into an object.

In the words of the theme song to the old television show *Secret Agent*, "they've given you a number, and taken away your name."

We live in a digital age. After all, when you really think about it, what are all of those photos on our computers, or the streaming music, or the text messages, or the Skype chats, or the Google searches? They are all based on computer language, and computer language is nothing more or less than infinite combinations of ones and zeros.

There can be something very powerful—even sacred—about the relationships and connections that we forge online in that virtual world.

But the Torah suggests that from time to time, we step back from the virtual to the real, the world of infinitely complex and infinitely beautiful human beings created in God's image.

We are more than our numbers.

# נשא

# *Naso*

## Accessing Your Superpowers

### Rabbi Sarah Mack

**If anyone, man or woman, explicitly utters a Nazirite's vow, to set himself apart for the Eternal, he shall abstain from wine and any other intoxicant; he shall not drink vinegar of wine or any other intoxicant, neither shall he drink anything in which grapes have been steeped, nor eat grapes fresh or dried.** (Numbers 6:2–3)

Let me tell you about a biblical superhero. When a lion attacked this young man, he tore the animal apart with his bare hands. When the Philistines threatened the Israelites, he caught three hundred foxes, lit torches on their tails, and set them loose in the Philistine settlement, destroying their crops. When he was taken prisoner, the ropes that bound him melted off his hands.

This young man is Samson, and you can find his story in the book of Judges. Samson had taken a Nazirite vow, the details of which appear in Numbers in *Naso*. A Nazirite is forbidden from drinking wine or consuming grape products; he may not cut his hair, and he is forbidden from coming into contact with a human corpse. The Torah text says that becoming a Nazirite was voluntary and temporary. The portion even includes a ritual to release the

---

**Rabbi Sarah Mack** is a rabbi at Temple Beth-El in Providence, Rhode Island.

172

Nazirite from his vow once the term is complete. In an egalitarian twist, both men and women could become Nazirites.

While the details of *how* to become a Nazirite are clear, the "why" is not as clear.

My students were skeptical. "How can staying away from grapes really keep a person on track?" they asked.

What really matters here is *self-control*. For Samson (and others in biblical times), avoiding wine and the other elements of the Nazirite vow were powerful deterrents.

For us, it might be something different altogether. Each of us has our own superpower—a skill that sets us apart from everyone else. And, each of us needs a spiritual brake to make sure we use that ability for good.

Ibn Ezra, a commentator in twelfth-century Spain, said this about the Nazirite vow: "The same word that means 'explicitly utters' [*yi'palei*] also means 'to do something wondrous.' For most of the world simply follows its appetites."[1]

The wonderful thing about the Nazirite vow is that while most people follow their desires and lusts, the Nazirite does the opposite. Our passions can empower us to achieve wonderful things, or they can get us into trouble. Learning to harness those passions enables us to access our own superpowers.

# Jealousy Is Like Poison

## Ethan Klaris and Rabbi Burt Visotzky

If a man's wife goes astray and transgresses against
him, and another man sleeps with her; and unknown
to her husband, he has sex with her, and she keeps it a
secret that she is unfit, yet there is no witness, nor was
she forced, and the husband becomes very jealous of
his wife ... that husband brings his wife to the priest....
Then the priest shall stand her before God, and the
priest shall take sacred water in a clay vessel and add
dirt from the floor of the Tabernacle.... And the priest
shall uncover her head ... while in his hands is the
bitter water of the curse.... And the priest shall adjure
the woman and say, "May God cause your thighs to sag
and your belly to burst." ... And the priest shall write
this curse on a scroll and dissolve it in the bitter water.
And he shall make the woman drink the bitter water....
If she has transgressed against her husband, the bitter
water will burst her belly and make her thighs sag, and
she will be accursed among her people. But if she is

**Ethan Klaris** is a student at Horace Mann High School in New York.

**Rabbi Burt Visotzky** teaches at the Jewish Theological Seminary in New
York.

**not unfit, but rather the woman is pure, then she shall become pregnant. This is the Torah of jealousy, when a woman goes astray while married, or if her husband has a fit of jealousy.** (Numbers 5:12–30 [my translation—BV])

Nowadays, most American Jewish teenagers are not married. So this passage from Numbers about the "suspected wife" (*sotah*) may not seem immediately relevant to you.

But imagine if a guy came to a party with a girl, and then she went off with a different guy, and they locked themselves in a room for half an hour. The first guy might be really jealous; he might even say to his buddies that the girl is a slut. That name, "slut," might stay with her all through high school—whether she did anything wrong or not, or whether the guy intended it to or not.

But if a guy did the same thing as that girl, he might just be considered a "player." This might not be fair, but it is real. Jealousy is a dog. And sometimes we learn the hard way that gossip isn't fun. It's like killing someone, because it can be as hard to get your reputation back as it might be to get your life back.

Maybe that's a good reason why personal relationships should stay personal and not play themselves out in public. Public displays of jealousy and gossip lead people to believe the worst. By making your jealousy public, you surrender your relationship to whatever anyone else makes of it.

But what about this "trial by ordeal" that the Torah is commanding? Where is the court system that the Torah earlier (in the book of Exodus) worked so hard to establish?

And does this trial by ordeal really work? Since it seems to depend on God, or God's name, to activate the poison in the bitter waters, what does this teach us about God?

And if it ever, even once, does not work, the *sotah* ritual completely undermines our belief in God and the Torah.

What does this mean for us today? Should we understand the Torah to simply be a set of rules for a small tribe in ancient times?

Or should we, perhaps, read the Torah text as an allegory for our own time? If that's the case, why do people still read it so literally? If you think about the guy and the girl at a party, you can see how the Torah text might help us think our way to what is right and what is wrong for us, now.

# בהעלתך

## _Behaalotecha_

### Facing the Wilderness

Rabbi Elliot J. Cosgrove, PhD

**They marched from the mountain of the Eternal a distance of three days. The Ark of the Covenant of the Eternal traveled in front of them on that three days' journey to seek out a resting place for them; and the Eternal's cloud kept above them by day, as they moved on from camp.** (Numbers 10:33–34)

There is a parable about the owner of an antique store and his apprentice. The owner would manage his shop from the back of the store, while the young apprentice would meet with customers who came into the store. To the dismay of the owner's family, the owner never went on vacation, for fear of losing his grip on the affairs of his business. A customer would come in, and from the back of the shop the owner would overhear the exchange between the young apprentice and the potential antique buyer. "The price you offer for this antique is very low," the apprentice would say. "I will have to check with the owner." The owner would shake his head in the back, knowing it was not time for him to go away.

Over time, the owner heard how his apprentice was beginning to shift his tone—just slightly: "The price you offer for this piece is far

---

**Rabbi Elliot J. Cosgrove, PhD** is rabbi of Park Avenue Synagogue, New York City.

too low; the owner would never agree to it." Again, the owner would shake his head, knowing it was not yet time to go away.

Finally, one day, from the back of his shop, the owner overheard the apprentice speaking to a customer: "The price you offer is far too low. I could never sell you this antique for that price."

At that precise moment, the owner smiled inwardly. He knew that he could now go away for that badly needed vacation. He knew that the apprentice was ready to be on his own.

And why? Because the apprentice had begun to think and speak *for himself.*

That story is all about growing up and letting go. Independence can only come when an individual shows that he or she can be *accountable.* Growth—personal, educational, or in the context of a family—actually depends on two parties acting together. One individual must let go, and the other must exhibit the quality of self-reliance.

Our Torah portion describes the children of Israel as they face the open expanse of their future. In both a physical and a spiritual way, they are facing the wilderness (*midbar*). Having left Mount Sinai behind them, they set out on their wilderness trek toward the Promised Land. Over the coming weeks, we will read of the Israelites' long and troubling forty-year journey toward the steppes of Moab—to the very banks of the Jordan River.

In a very real way, these stories describe how the *children* of Israel become the *adults* of Israel. These are also stories of a God who is refining a relationship with a people, engaging in the sacred and difficult task of knowing how to hold on and how to let go.

If, as philosopher Ralph Waldo Emerson noted, "discontent is the want of self-reliance," then it follows that we can achieve happiness only through self-reliance. The desert is a frightening expanse, filled with pitfalls and the possibility of failure. But it is the wise and courageous person who recognizes that it is actually only in the *midbar* that we can truly find ourselves.

There is no task more essential to the human soul than coming into your own and letting those around you be given the chance to do the same.

Is it difficult? Without a doubt.
Is it necessary? Absolutely.
It is what the *midbar* of life is all about.

# What Makes a Leader Powerful?

## Deborah Meyer

**Did I conceive all this people, did I bear them, that
You should say to me, "Carry them in your bosom as
a nurse carries an infant," to the land that You have
promised...?** (Numbers 11:12)

When you think of a powerful leader, what image comes to mind?

Hold onto that thought for a second, and consider this gender-bending story from the Torah.

Everybody who has had more than a day of Jewish education knows about Moses. Moses hears God speaking to him out of a burning bush, he carries the tablets that contain the Ten Commandments, and he leads the people out of Egyptian slavery through the desert to the border of the Promised Land. Moses is clearly a very powerful guy.

On the way from slavery to freedom, however, Moses has a moment. The people are complaining about food and water, and they even moan that life was better when they were in Egypt. In one of the most emotional pleas to God in the entire Torah, Moses asks, "Did I conceive all this people, did I bear them, that You should say to me, 'Carry them in your bosom as a nurse carries an infant,' to the land that You have promised...?" (Numbers 11:12).

---

**Deborah Meyer** is founder and executive director of Moving Traditions, an organization that enhances Jewish life so that women and men and girls and boys are able to reach their full human potential.

You might now be thinking, "What is going on here?" Does Moses really think that his role was to be the Jewish people's *mother*?

This Torah portion speaks about leadership—in two ways.

First, Moses sees being a mother as being synonymous with the most important, and perhaps most difficult, aspects of leadership. What images of leadership does Moses use? The images are of *birth* and *nursing*. This can help women recognize that they, too, have critical skills to help create a nation. When boys and men read this, they can realize that in order to lead people, you must understand the power of birth/creation and nurturing.

Look what happens next. In Numbers 11:14, Moses says, "I cannot carry all this people by myself, for it is too much for me." And what does God do? God says, in essence: You are right, you can't do it all by yourself! Get other people involved. "Gather for Me seventy of Israel's elders.... They shall share the burden of the people with you, and you shall not bear it alone" (Numbers 11:16–17).

Moses has been trying to be both father and mother to the people, and he is in danger of burning out. As leaders, we have to know when to bring in others to help share the burden.

To be a truly powerful leader, we need to bring together all of those with wisdom to contribute—both women and men. And, like Moses, we must draw on all of our gifts as leaders, no matter whether these gifts are defined as masculine or feminine.

Now when you imagine a powerful leader, what comes to your mind?

# שלח לך
## *Shelach-Lecha*

## They Could Be Giants—So Could You!

Dr. Erica Brown

**But the men who had gone up with him said, "We cannot attack that people, for it is stronger than we."**
(Numbers 13:31)

Perception is reality—or so they say. Who we are is often, in our eyes, not a matter of what we do but how we think about ourselves, usually refracting our self-image through what we think others think about us.

A fifteen-year-old boy buys a pair of jeans and he thinks he looks great in them, until one popular girl says that she hates them. He goes home, puts them in the closet, and never wears them again.

A beautiful thirteen-year-old girl looks in the mirror. When her friends look at her, they see a thin, attractive, special person. But all she can see is every imperfection. "I'm fat," she says—even when the scale says otherwise. For her, it is fact, not fiction.

People act based on their own perceptions. Sometimes, they *fail* to act because of *self-perception*.

When we turn to Numbers 13, we find that perception becomes such a strong reality that we almost give up on our national dream.

A group of leaders are ready to go into the Land of Israel to scout out the Land. Their mission is to bring back their impressions and report them to their fellow Israelites.

---

**Dr. Erica Brown** is scholar-in-residence for the Jewish Federation of Greater Washington, DC.

They return with a mixed report. On the one hand, they say, the soil is extraordinary. The fruits are beyond belief. They say that there is milk and honey there; at a time of intense thirst and hunger, the vision of a land of plenty brings comfort and hope.

But the report does not end there. The cities are fortified and daunting, the spies say. It will be impossible to conquer the native people. The Land actually eats its inhabitants. The Land destroys anyone who lives there. So it hardly matters that the fruits of the Land happen to be good.

And then, in a final blow, they describe the military might of the people in Canaan—and they can only compare how strong the Canaanites are to how weak they imagine themselves to be. They describe mythological races of giants: "We saw the Nephilim there—the Anakites are part of the Nephilim—and we looked like grasshoppers to ourselves, and so we must have looked to them" (Numbers 13:33).

Feeling small and timid, they not only say that the inhabitants have the DNA of giants, but they also compare themselves to those giants. We are grasshoppers, they say—as insignificant as insects. The "giants" might step on us and trample us.

The people hear the report and weep. Joshua and Caleb, the only two leaders to go into the Land and return with a positive report, tell the people that they should go up to the Land and conquer it. The dream is still within reach.

When you have two opposing views, which one is real? Who is right?

To answer this question, one of my students once directed me to a later chapter in Numbers—chapter 22. There, we find an outside observer, Balak, king of Moab. He wants to curse the Israelites, precisely because he sees them as a serious military threat. And how does Balak describe the Israelites? Not as grasshoppers. Hardly. He describes them as *oxen*. An ox is large, bulky, stubborn, and strong. The ox is a far cry from the grasshopper.

It takes convincing, but we make it to the Promised Land. Imagine if we convinced ourselves that we really were grasshoppers, and instead of making it to Israel, we all died in the desert, crushed like insects.

Sometimes we think of ourselves as weaker than we are. Others see us as stronger. Perception and reality tell a mixed truth. In the universe of perceptions, why not go with the perception of our strengths rather than our weaknesses?

I invite you to go with the more encouraging perception.

Maybe when others say that we are strong and beautiful and talented, we will train ourselves to hear them. And maybe, just maybe, when someone else feels small and powerless, we can help him or her find his or her inner giant.

# Don't Be a Grasshopper!

### Rabbi Sheldon Zimmerman

**All the people that we saw [in the Land] are men of great size ... and we looked like grasshoppers to ourselves, and so we must have looked to them.** (Numbers 13:32–33)

Come with me on a journey back through time.

You and I are part of the Israelite people. We have gotten out of Egyptian slavery. We are free. Slowly but surely, we are making our way to the Promised Land of Israel, the land God promised to our ancestors. Through all those years of slavery, we have waited, and now we are about to enter the Land.

But, we can't just walk into the Land. Yes, God will lead us, but we will have to fight for it. Moses tells us that we need to know more about the Land before we enter. God tells Moses to send people to spy out the Land, to sense its strength, how fortified the cities are, the nature of the people and armies we would encounter, and to figure out how difficult the battle will be. We all have so many questions.

But, God says not just *shelach*, "send," but *shelach-lecha*, "send *for yourself*." Send the spies—for your own benefit, not Mine. It's as if God is saying, "Moses, your people have doubts. So, to be more confident, send people to take a look, to investigate, to learn and prepare. I'm not asking for blind faith here; go and look for *yourselves*."

**Rabbi Sheldon Zimmerman** is rabbi of the Jewish Center of the Hamptons in East Hampton, New York.

So, Moses sends out spies—not just anyone, but tribal leaders. They complete their task, and then they return and give their report.

"It is a good land," they say. "It flows with milk and honey, but the cities are large and fortified, the people are extraordinary fighters and gigantic. They are too powerful for us."

We become very nervous. "How can we do this? We are still slaves. We haven't trained to be fighters. What weapons do we have?"

One of the spies, Caleb, tells us that we can do it. But that's not enough. How can we accomplish this?

The other spies say, "The people of the Land are giants. We looked like grasshoppers to ourselves, and so we must have looked to them."

The people rebel against their leaders, Moses, Aaron, and Miriam: "We are not going. The inhabitants of the Land are far too strong. Let's go back to Egypt." God then tells us that not one of us would enter the Land at all. We lose our opportunity. How tragic!

*But the spies weren't lying.* They gave a true description of the Land. Archeologists have dug in the Land of Israel, and they have discovered that yes, the cities were heavily fortified; the people were well armed, and they had mighty armies.

But we saw ourselves as too small, too weak, too fragile. We saw ourselves as grasshoppers. So, that's the way they must see us, we said to ourselves. We'll never be able to do it.

How often in our own lives do we shy away from challenges? The challenges may be difficult. Perhaps it is an athletic or artistic challenge, or schoolwork, or helping the poor, or confronting those who are unjust.

True, the challenges are difficult. But if we believe that we are just too small, fragile, and weak, that we do not have the capacity, the ability, and the courage to do something, to make it happen, then we will never attain the dreams and hopes we have for ourselves.

If we are only grasshoppers frightened that others will step on us and destroy us, then what do we expect them to believe? What will they see? There is nothing wrong with being frightened of difficult tasks. But if we see ourselves only as grasshoppers, then we will never overcome fear to become the people we can become. What would have been had Martin Luther King Jr. seen himself as a grasshopper—or the founders of Israel, the pioneers of America, those who traveled in space, or Steve Jobs?

That generation of slaves lost the gift that God had promised them. They defeated themselves. They lacked faith in God and themselves.

Remember, you can do great things.

Dream great dreams. Aim higher. Be the person you can truly become.

# קרח
# *Korach*

## Rebels for What?

### Rabbi Jessica Brockman

**You have gone too far! For all the community are holy, all of them, and the Eternal is in their midst. Why then do you raise yourselves up above the Eternal's congregation?** (Numbers 16:3)

My sister was wild in high school. She drank and smoked and snuck out of her room to meet boyfriends at night so many times that my parents had to put a lock on her window as a deterrent. I was not this way. I was good and sailed under the radar in high school. My parents always noted that at my high school graduation the assistant principal could barely pronounce our last name, because he had never met me, while at my sister's graduation four years later, the name rolled off his tongue easily, because he had spent so much time with my sister and our parents in his office.

Our Torah portion tells the story of the rebellion of Korach, a respected and wealthy leader who challenges Moses's authority. He convinces 250 other respected men to follow him. Like my sister, Korach is wild, rebellious, and a troublemaker.

What or *who* are they rebelling against? Korach and his followers think that Moses and Aaron are acting as if they are holier than everyone else—"All the community are holy, all of them, and the

---

**Rabbi Jessica Brockman** is associate rabbi at Temple Beth El of Boca Raton, Florida.

Eternal is in their midst. Why then do you raise yourselves up above the Eternal's congregation?" (Numbers 16:3)—and that is the cause of the rebellion.

Sometimes, rebellions can be good. Throughout your life, when you confront all sorts of authority figures, it can be important to speak truth to power.

So, when does rebellion become a problem? When it is not for a noble, true, or good reason.

That is the way it is with Korach and his followers. It's not as if Moses and Aaron are arrogant. They are humbled by their position and relationship with God. As soon as Moses hears Korach's criticism of him, Moses falls to the ground, perhaps embarrassed that anyone would accuse a man who strived toward modesty of being self-important. God is on Moses's side, and as the story continues, the earth ultimately swallows up Korach and his followers.

There can be little doubt about it: Korach was probably charismatic. He convinced more than two hundred people to rebel against Moses, who, according to the Jewish tradition, was the greatest prophet, ever. So, even though Korach could influence others and bring them along, it wasn't for good. And the fact that not one person in his group stood up and challenged Korach's unfounded criticism meant that perhaps Korach simply surrounded himself with "yes-men" and "yes-women" who wouldn't challenge him or question his motives.

There are many Korach types in your midst—those who want to bring you along in one way or another to a path or a place that may not be the smartest or best place to go. And if these people are charismatic enough, often they will succeed.

The challenge comes in figuring out who is a Korach and who is a Moses. Our task in life is to avoid following the Korach types and instead work to emulate the Moses types.

Because, really, at the end of the day, isn't Moses what we all strive to be?

A rebel with a cause.

# Teaching Lasts Longer Than Politics

Rabbi Michael Paley

**You have gone too far! For all the community are
holy, all of them, and the Eternal is in their midst.
Why then do you raise yourselves above the Eternal's
congregation?** (Numbers 16:3)

Who's in charge? That is the basic question of this provocative Torah portion.

To set the scene, Moses has just sent spies to scout out the Land, who returned with a bad report, and now the entire people have learned that they will wander in the desert for forty years and will ultimately die before reaching the Promised Land.

Wasn't this a massive failure of leadership? Moses may have led us out of Egypt, but he has clearly failed at getting us into the Land. The time is ripe for a rebellion by the people.

And so, the rebellion begins. Korach, a member of Moses's tribe and family, gathers some friends and confronts Moses and Aaron: "You have gone too far! For all the community are holy, all of them, and the Eternal is in their midst. Why then do you raise yourselves above the Eternal's congregation?" (Numbers 16:3).

I am a person who has spent a lifetime questioning authority, and so I find this to be a pretty good question. Who appointed Moses, and

**Rabbi Michael Paley** is Pearl and Ira Meyer Scholar in Residence and the director of the Jewish Resource Center of the UJA-Federation of New York.

how long was his tenure supposed to be? In a democracy, we believe that everyone is equal and holy, and *we* appoint the leader—not a burning bush or a magic staff. Had there been a general election, I might have voted for Korach.

The Rabbis of the Talmud say that this argument between Moses and Korach was not for the good of the people. Rather, it was only about Korach's ego. Korach was jealous of Moses, and he only wanted power. Who doesn't know someone like that? But the people are stuck in the desert, and most of them are not getting out, so maybe Korach had something to offer.

The great Orthodox sage Rabbi Joseph Soloveitchik uses this conflict to analyze the nature of Jewish power. In Jewish tradition, at least until the State of Israel, in general, every Jew had the right to act as he or she desired. There was no centralized authority; there was neither a "pope" nor president.[2]

Soloveitchik says that Korach's mistake might have been that he aspired to be the *king*, whereas Moses merely wanted to be the *teacher*. That is why we call Moses *Moshe rabbeinu* (Moses our teacher), and not *Moshe malcheinu* (Moses our king).

The distinction is subtle. Kings often base their leadership on what would make them happy or by finding out what the people think—the "common sense" of the people. But Moses based his leadership on the hope that he could elevate not just *himself*, but the entire *people*. In Jewish tradition, our leaders are teachers, and teachers have influence that lasts long after the political battles are over.

Moses understood that the commandments would not be fashioned by the people, but that they would stand the test of time and shape the people around them. Korach's rebellion was for the moment, but Moses's vision was for the future—and the length of one's vision is the key to leadership.

The story ends dramatically: Moses and Korach square off, face to face. An earthquake opens up the ground, and Korach falls in. This is an effective, and even impressive, way to end an argument, even though it's not the sort of thing that we can pull off on a regular basis.

In the long run, I find Moses's vision much more convincing than a convenient natural disaster. I suspect that you might feel the same way.

# חקת
## *Chukat*

### Speak Up and Speak Out!

Emilia Diamant

**The community was without water, and they joined against Moses and Aaron.** (Numbers 20:2)

In *Chukat*, the Israelites find themselves in the middle of quite a bit of drama. Miriam dies, they get *real* thirsty, Moses disobeys God's commandment to speak to the rock instead of striking it, God gets mad and tells Moses and Aaron they won't enter the Land of Israel, Aaron dies, and then they all battle against some Amorite kings and their armies.

Whew.

For just two chapters of Torah, that's a lot of action. And, in fact, this is one of the most action-filled portions in the book of Numbers. The Israelites are faced with some tough questions: "Who do we listen to?" "Who is our leader now?" "Whom can we reach out to for help?"

But the problem is that we don't actually hear the voice of the Israelites. We are only imagining what they would have been saying. They experience the death of major leaders, war, and shocking news about Moses—and there's not a peep out of them.

Are they scared? Do they want to break off on their own? The Torah does not offer us the voice of the people, except for the occasional complaint or exclamation.

---

**Emilia Diamant** is school principal and youth director at Temple Beth Or in Raleigh, North Carolina.

The easy explanation might be that Moses, or Aaron, or Miriam, or even God speaks for the Israelites, expressing their concerns or their needs; that these voices are symbolic and therefore easier to understand.

That doesn't quite sit right. There were (according to the Torah) hundreds of thousands of Israelites, and as we know, Jews tend to have opinions. Beyond the kvetching about water, how did they feel when Miriam died? Did they mourn Aaron? Do they trust Moses? There's no way they didn't have something to say.

It's easy to see where the voice of the people can get lost in the shuffle. The newspapers report on what politicians, academics, and leaders say. But we rarely hear from the people—the ones experiencing the events in the headlines, the ones who most intensely feel the impact of the economy or the passing of legislation. Sure, local cable channels interview random citizens for the eleven o'clock news, but beyond that, there's no real discussion.

So, what do the Israelites do? What do we do to make our voices heard?

We ask questions—of our parents, our friends, our legislators, our rabbis, our sages. We seek to understand so that we can then make ourselves heard. Whether it's in a public protest, a letter to the editor, or a *devar Torah* to our congregation, our voices are valuable and important. Even if we didn't hear the Israelites then, we can make sure our voices are heard now. It is up to us to speak and make sure someone listens.

# No Leading While Angry!

Rabbi Edward Feld

**Listen, you rebels, shall we get water for you out of this rock?** (Numbers 20:10)

If you're looking for puzzling stories in the Torah, this portion contains one of the best.

Miriam, Moses's sister—the one who protected him as his basket flowed down the Nile—dies, and suddenly the Israelites have no water as they travel through the desert; the well at the oasis at which they are camped has dried up.

They complain to Moses that the liberation from Egypt was useless—it would have been better to have died in the recent revolt.

God then tells Moses to speak to the rock, so that water will miraculously pour forth from it. This is actually not as strange as it sounds, because in the desert, there are often hidden underground sources of water that can gush a waterfall, and often without much warning.

But Moses disobeys God. He hits the rock, yelling at the Israelites, "Listen, you rebels, shall we get water for you out of this rock?" (Numbers 20:10). Immediately, God responds to Moses and Aaron, "Because you did not trust Me enough to affirm My sanctity in the sight

---

**Rabbi Edward Feld** directs the Rabbinic Companionship Program, counseling and coaching rabbis in the field, and is the senior editor of Mahzor Lev Shalem, the new Conservative machzor (High Holy Day prayer book).

of the Israelite people, therefore you shall not lead this congregation into the Land that I have given them" (Numbers 20:12).

And, indeed, both Moses and Aaron die before entering the Land—with this Torah portion actually containing the report of Aaron's death.

But the punishment doesn't seem to fit the crime. What did Moses do that was so terrible? God may have said that Moses should speak rather than hit the rock, but the difference between the two acts doesn't seem so significant. If someone changes a command ever so slightly, does it deserve a death penalty?

Perhaps, then, it is a lesson in the inexplicable nature of our fate. Things happen to us that are undeserved—we make a mistake and the consequences are so much more than anyone could have imagined.

It is interesting: this story occurs in the Torah portion called *Chukat*, which is related to the term *chukim* (laws). The ancient Rabbis said that *chukim* were biblical laws that are simply beyond our understanding—like the laws of kashrut, or *shatnez*, the prohibition of mixing wool and linen in the same garment. We do them simply because God commands us to do them.

And so, Moses deviates just a little bit from God's command, and the consequences are beyond anything he might have reasonably expected. Maybe consequences are never what we expect.

The ancient Sages could not accept that God would act irrationally, so they searched for other explanations for the harshness of Moses's punishment.

One sage suggests that when Moses and Aaron speak to the people, they never mention God. Rather, they say, "Shall *we* get water for you out of this rock?" (Numbers 20:10). It is as if Moses and Aaron no longer credit the Divine with the power that they exercise. They turn the people's complaints into a test of their own leadership and a challenge to their own self-worth. They can only see the people's revolt in personal terms. God's response is to assert that God needs to be sanctified above all.

Other interpretations suggest that Moses and Aaron are punished because of the anger they display. They call the people "rebels" and taunt them with what is about to happen, rather than proclaiming to the people that God is about to show them kindness. Perhaps we can understand their bitterness and their frustration. Several verses before this (Numbers 20:1), Miriam has died, the brothers are grieving, and suddenly leadership has become too burdensome for them. They no longer behave in loving ways. Rather, they respond with anger, and God's judgment is that therefore they no longer can exercise leadership. Angry leaders are not true leaders. The leaders who deserve respect are those who truly love their people, understand them, and respond to their troubles with compassion.

Ultimately, leadership is not about an ego trip or about seeking personal honor. It is about having a vision that is worth putting into action. If the people who are supposed to follow do not believe that their leaders respect and love them, then the vision of the leaders is ultimately worthless.

# בלק
## *Balak*

---

## Because That's What Jews Do
### Robert Bildner

**There is a people that dwells apart, not reckoned among the nations....** (Numbers 23:9)

This might be the funniest Torah portion of them all. But it also raises a serious question for Jewish teens.

A Moabite king, Balak, hires a sorcerer, Balaam, to curse the Israelites. It doesn't work out that well. God throws a sword-carrying angel in Balaam's path. And then, two thousand years before *Shrek*, God gives Balaam's donkey the power to talk and to complain to Balaam, and then God changes Balaam's curses against the Israelites into blessings.

Like this one: "There is a people that dwells apart, not reckoned among the nations ..." (Numbers 23:9).

Really? Is it such a blessing for Jews to be different?

To quote one of the other great talking animals of world literature, Kermit the Frog, "It's not that easy being green."

It's not always a blessing to be different.

Here's a short list of things that make Jews different:

• Preparing for bar or bat mitzvah—no one else has to do that.

---

**Robert Bildner** is an attorney, entrepreneur, and activist in the Jewish and secular worlds. He is one of the founding directors and current treasurer of Repair the World and, together with his wife, Elisa Spungen Bildner, founded the Foundation for Jewish Camping.

- Attending High Holy Day services—ditto.
- Keeping kosher when it's hard to find things to eat—double ditto.

Let's face it: the Jews are a tiny minority, surrounded by people of different faiths and religious practices. It's not easy.

But here's another major difference—and this one really counts. God commands the Jews to repair the world—to perform *tikkun olam*. Yes, gentiles do it as well (think Bono). But for Jews, this is our *job*: to bring *tzedek* and *mishpat*, righteousness and justice, to everybody. Just think of all the laws and sacred texts in Judaism that obligate Jews to serve our communities and the world, feeding the poor, providing housing and medical care, protecting the environment, and advocating for civil rights and social justice. (To learn some good texts on these subjects, check out http://on1foot.org.) *That's Jewish.*

Sure, many young American Jews teach in Teach for America; they work in food pantries; they build low-income housing. But they're just not connecting the dots. In a recent study, only 27 percent of young Jews surveyed believed that their community service activities were based on Jewish values.

Don't they get it? This is what Jews do!

That's why, a few years ago, I joined with other philanthropists and activists in founding Repair the World. "Repair" advocates for Jews to be a force for social change, while understanding the Jewish basis for doing so.

Here's just a short list of items on Repair's service menu: mentoring and tutoring disadvantaged children; providing companionship for elderly Jews; helping immigrants; volunteering in response to natural disasters; engaging in sustainable agriculture while providing food to the hungry; teaching English to low-income students in Israel. Check out our website, http://weRepair.org. I'm proud of what Repair the World has done, the alliances that it has created, and the energy that it has generated.

And why is Repair the World doing all this?

*Because that's what Jews do.* Balaam might have been right. We are "a people that dwells apart." It's tough to be a Jew, but it is a joy to be a Jew when we Jews have so much to do to make the world better.

We don't need a talking donkey, or a singing frog, to help us figure out that this is what we do—because we are Jews.

# How Good Are Your Tents!

Cantor Ellen Dreskin

**How fair are your tents, O Jacob, your dwellings, O Israel!** (Numbers 24:5)

*Mah tovu ohalecha Yaakov, mishk'notecha Yisrael,* "How good are your tents, O Jacob, your dwellings, O Israel!" (Numbers 24:5 [my translation—ED]). We sing these words at the beginning of every morning service—the words of Balaam, a wicked sorcerer hired by Balak, the king of Moab, to curse the Israelites as they pass through his kingdom on their way to Canaan.

But it just isn't happening. Balaam opens his mouth and what comes out? A blessing. One line from the mouth of a non-Israelite magic maker, and several thousand years later, we're still singing it every morning.

Why? Perhaps because these simple words emphasize the blessing of each individual's unique role in our community, the blessing that is contained in every aspect of our own personalities, and our obligation to attempt to speak blessings and *be* blessings at every moment of our lives.

Let's take a closer look.

The verse appears repetitive. Aren't "tents" and "dwellings" pretty much the same thing? And aren't "Jacob" and "Israel" the same guy?

Maybe. Maybe not.

---

**Cantor Ellen Dreskin** serves as coordinator of the Cantorial Certification Program at the Debbie Friedman School of Sacred Music at Hebrew Union College–Jewish Institute of Religion in New York.

Tents are temporary shelters—here today, gone tomorrow. Jacob, a name that comes from the Hebrew word for "follower" or "heel," arrived in this world literally hanging onto the heel of his twin brother, Esau. While his brother hunted game, domesticated Jacob was content to stay home and cook the stew. He was definitely quite comfortable in a tent.

But that's Jacob. Israel is something—or *someone*—else.

Israel, the name that Jacob receives following an all-night wrestling match with some sort of angel, literally means "he will struggle with God."

Israel is not a follower, but a *leader*—and leadership most often involves challenge and struggle. Leadership happens in those places and times where we really dwell, where there is really something at stake. Israel dwells in and thrives through challenging the big questions and injustices of the world.

Some of us spend our days or lives as tenders of the home or workers behind the scenes. Some of us, however, are more inclined to be wrestlers with forces stronger than our own, dwelling in those places that require great courage and strength.

Every family, every community, and the entire *world* benefit from both Jacobs and Israels. And the capacity for both is within each of us. And both are good. That realization is the blessing that Balaam bestowed upon us.

It's all good: each day, whether I join my community as a follower or a leader; whether I am close to home or at camp or in college or visiting foreign lands; whether my mind is tranquil or I am dwelling in divine wrestling rings and ready to wage war with the world, it's all good.

Each of us has days of "Jacob-ness," as well as days of "Israel-ness." Some people spend their lives entirely in one world or the other. I acknowledge the unique contributions of the day, gifts brought by each and every member of my community in whatever space we may come to worship. No matter who or where you are, blessings can emerge from your life as well as your lips.

If the wicked sorcerer Balaam could do it, then so can I.

# פינחס
## *Pinchas*

## It's Not Fair!
### Rabbi B. Elka Abrahamson

**The daughters of Zelophehad ... came forward.... They stood before Moses, Eleazar the priest, the chieftains, and the whole assembly, at the entrance of the Tent of Meeting, and they said, "Our father died in the wilderness.... Let not our father's name be lost to his clan just because he had no son! Give us a holding among our father's kinsmen!"** (Numbers 27:1–4)

How many times in the last week (the last hours?) have you said these words: "It's not fair!"

And if you have not said them out loud, how many times have you thought them to yourself—the unfair grading practices of a teacher, or what a friend did, or a sibling, the coach or ref, and of course, a parent? It would be "fair" to assume you wanted to shout it from the rooftops, convinced that if you yelled it loud enough and with enough feeling, you might alter a decision, a grade, the score, or outcome—all based on your clear perception of the situation.

"It's not fair!" we scream—and the predictable (and dreaded) response to your forceful appeal is the all-too-common phrase "Life's not fair."

**Rabbi B. Elka Abrahamson** is president of the Wexner Foundation, based in Columbus, Ohio, which strengthens Jewish leadership in North America and Israel.

But sometimes, when your plea is just, when the motives are not just about your own needs and the situation truly calls for a new look, the response could be, "You are absolutely correct. Let's make it right."

When that happens, you are not alone. You are in historic company. You echo an ancient voice.

In our Torah portion, five young women—the daughters of Zelophehad—stand up and say, in essence, "It's not fair!" These sisters—Mahlah, Noah, Hoglah, Milcah, and Tirzah—appear three times in the Torah, but this is the first time that we learn their names.

The scene unfolds as the Israelites are preparing to inhabit the Promised Land. A tribe of connected wanderers that has been pitching tents for forty nomadic desert years is about to transform itself into a permanent community. The children of Israel will, at last, get to enter the Land of Israel.

Yes! A home of our own, a roof over our heads, a place to plant, a home field.

Yes, except for that fairness thing. Mahlah, Noah, Hoglah, Milcah, and Tirzah get to talking and they realize that given the laws of inheritance as applied to women, they will be denied their own lot.

And this is totally not fair.

They approach Moses and the community's elders to plead their case. They explain that their father died in the desert, leaving five daughters, but no sons, behind. "Let not our father's name be lost to his clan just because he had no son! Give us a holding among our father's kinsmen!" (Numbers 27:4).

Moses takes the case of the daughters before the Holy One. OMG!

And it gets better. God says, "The plea of Zelophehad's daughters is just: you should give them a hereditary holding among their father's kinsmen; transfer their father's share to them" (Numbers 27:7). As if this is not enough, God adds a new law to the Torah, saying that if there are no sons, daughters are permitted to inherit land.

When one person, or five sisters or brothers speaking as one, press against what is "unfair" with selfless motives and a reasonable alternative, that's how change can happen. The daughters of Zelophehad did not *start* with their own needs. Their claim started with a respect for the past, preserving their father's legacy. Nor did it *end* with their own needs. They hoped for a future home among their community in the Promised Land.

Moses heard them, God heard them, and thanks to our Torah portion, in every generation we can hear the echoes of these ancient voices. They tweet a succinct message from the rooftops: "Let's make it right."

You are not alone.

# A Fanatic Named Pinchas

Jerry Kaye

**The Eternal spoke to Moses, saying, "Pinchas, son of Eleazar son of Aaron the priest, has turned back My wrath from the Israelites by displaying among them his passion for Me...."** (Numbers 25:10–11)

Wait until you hear this story! If it wasn't already in the Torah, it could have been written by Stephen King.

So this guy and this girl are seriously fooling around in front of everybody, and then they step into a room. Another guy walks in, finds the two of them in a world-class clinch, and runs them through with a spear—both of them with one stab of the spear!

You know people who are fanatic about some idea, politics, right and wrong, or even a baseball team. They will go as far out as they can to show how much they absolutely love their favorite ... (fill in the blank). You can give money, wear the button or the T-shirt, and everybody will know what you care about.

There are people who are *really* committed to an idea and who are willing to do just about anything for it. I bet you know people like that in school, or in sports, or even in your synagogue. They are ready to let everyone know that their idea is the best and the most right.

---

**Jerry Kaye** is director of the URJ Olin-Sang-Ruby Union Institute in Oconomowoc, Wisconsin.

So, this is the story of a guy named Pinchas. His story actually started out in last week's Torah portion, when the pagan king Balak hired the prophet Balaam to curse the Israelites. But he could only bless them with the words "How fair are your tents, O Jacob, your dwellings, O Israel!" (Numbers 24:5). You can imagine how ticked that king was when he paid good shekels for a curse and got only a blessing.

So, the cursing stuff didn't work.

The king's next great idea: persuade the Moabite women to go after the Israelite guys, get them all hot, and then bring them around to idol worship. God was incredibly ticked and started a plague that knocked off twenty-four thousand Israelites.

Then comes the spear story. Pinchas is furious about what Zimri and his "gf" Cozbi are doing. He runs them through with a spear. This, believe it or not, made God pretty happy. God stopped the plague, made Pinchas a hero, awarded him a "covenant of peace" (sort of like a medal, but better), and let him be a priest. Not bad, huh?

Sure—unless you think about how Pinchas should have known the commandment not to murder. The Talmud says that if Pinchas had gone to a rabbinical court using Jewish law to justify his behavior, this is what the court would have told him: "The law may permit it, *but we don't follow that law*" (*Sanhedrin* 82a).

So, here's the question: just because you *can* do something, does that mean you *should* do it?

Think about the people you know who are really fanatics about what they think is wrong. Think about the people who kill doctors who perform abortions, the man who assassinated Israel's Prime Minister Rabin, and suicide bombers who kill innocent people.

So, yes—you might be absolutely positive that you are right. But do you *really* have to hurt the other person—either with fists or words?

Can you put some limits on your own fanaticism and certainty?

# מטות

# *Mattot*

## Silence Is Consent

### Rabbi Laura Geller

**If a woman makes a vow to the Eternal or assumes an obligation while still in her father's household by reason of her youth, and her father learns of her vow or her self-imposed obligation and offers no objections, all her vows shall stand and every self-imposed obligation shall stand. But if her father restrains her on the day he finds out, none of her vows or self-imposed obligations shall stand; and the Eternal will forgive her, since her father restrained her.** (Numbers 30:4–6)

Some time ago, I received an e-mail with the subject line "The Arab Mentality." It described a Palestinian woman who had been badly burned and successfully treated in Israel, only to be later arrested for attempting to infiltrate Israel's borders as a suicide bomber. The sender included the names of all those who had received the posting. My name was in the middle of the list.

As I often do when I receive e-mails like this, I consulted with the Anti-Defamation League (the principal American Jewish organization that fights anti-Semitism and bigotry) to see whether the story was true, and indeed, it was.

**Rabbi Laura Geller** is senior rabbi of Temple Emanuel in Beverly Hills, California.

But I was still uncomfortable with the e-mail. I believed that labeling this posting "The Arab Mentality" was like an anti-Semite titling a posting about Bernie Madoff "The Jewish Mentality." No question that this particular woman was a terrorist, but to suggest that her actions described the mentality of an entire group of people—"the Arabs"—struck me as clearly wrong.

I get a lot of e-mails like this—e-mails describing situations, sometimes true and often not true, that slander Arabs and Muslims as a group. I'm never sure how to respond. The easiest thing to do is to simply delete them.

But if I just deleted the message, what was I saying by my silence? Other congregants were on the same response list; they knew I had seen it too.

This Torah portion is part of why I felt I had to respond. *Mattot* begins with a description of the importance of vows. The primary focus is the vows that women make. As *The Torah: A Women's Commentary* suggests, "The chief concern seems to be to regulate the impact that a woman's vow might have upon the household ... her father or her husband."[3] In a patriarchal culture, this would not be surprising; her father or husband can veto her vows. What *is* surprising is that the veto has to happen on the day that he finds out about it.

The *Shulchan Aruch* (the classic code of Jewish law, written in the sixteenth century) makes it very clear: "They can only cancel the vow within the day they heard it. That is, if they heard the vow at the beginning of the evening, they may cancel it all night and the entire following day. If they heard [the vow] close to the time that the stars appear, they can cancel it only until the stars appear. Beyond that time, they cannot cancel it...."

As Rabbi Brad Artson (see p. 136) has pointed out, this is strange, because if these fathers and husbands have the power to veto the woman's vow, why does it have to be immediate? Here's the Talmud's answer: "Silence is like consent" (*Yevamot* 88a). Once you know what the promise is, if you don't speak up, it is as though you are also responsible for it. Once you know what is going on, if you don't speak up, you are also responsible.

Someone forwards a derogatory e-mail that tarnishes all Arabs and I say nothing? *Silence is like consent.*

The Maharal of Prague (a sixteenth-century scholar) made this very clear when he wrote that individual piety is not enough; no matter how pious we are, we will be held accountable for the sin of not protesting against something that is wrong. His position has echoes in the Talmud: "Whoever has the ability to prevent his household from sin and does not is accountable for the sins of his household; if he could do so with his fellow citizens and does not, he is accountable for his fellow citizens; if the whole world, he is accountable for the whole world" (*Shabbat* 54b).

So, maybe I can't prevent the whole world from sin, or my community or even my family. But if I do nothing, then I am still accountable.

So, back to the e-mail dilemma.

This is how I responded: "I am not sure that sharing e-mails like this is necessarily helpful in the ongoing discussion of what is best for Israel. This is a not a story about the 'Arab mentality' in general. It is rather the story of a particular Arab woman."

This issue comes up in so many different ways. How often does a picture appear on your Facebook page that makes fun of someone you know? How often are you in a chain of cyberbullying? How often does someone share gossip that humiliates someone you know?

This week's Torah portion asks us to be careful about what we say—the vows and promises we make. And it also demands of us to be careful about what we don't say, because "silence is consent."

# *Dugma* Is Dogma

Ira J. Wise, RJE

**Moses became angry with the commanders of the army,
the officers of thousands and the officers of hundreds,
who had come back from the military campaign.**
(Numbers 31:14)

You've heard of the Holocaust and the six million? Of course you have. Twenty-two years later, much of the world feared that another two or three million Jews might be killed.

It was late May 1967, and the combined forces of five Arab nations were massing on Israel's borders. It seemed to many that the tiny Jewish state would not survive. This led to the famous Six Day War. You know how it turned out, because Israel is still very much alive.

There are many amazing stories that emerged out of that war, but one of the most impressive tales concerns Israeli army officers.

If you listen to the stories of those who have served in the armed forces of other nations, it often sounds like the higher an officer's rank, the further from the battle he or she seems to be.

That's not how it was, or still is, in the Israel Defense Forces. During the Six Day War, as soldiers ran into battle, their officers shouted a very important and usual word to their soldiers: "*Acharai!*" ("Follow me!")—and that has become the motto of the officer corps of Tzahal (the Israel Defense Forces).

**Ira J. Wise, RJE,** is director of education at Congregation B'nai Israel in Bridgeport, Connecticut.

In our Torah portion, we read about the Israelites fighting a war with Midian. True, the Israelites won the war, but the army had not acted in the way Moses expected. "Moses became angry with the commanders of the army, the officers of thousands and the officers of hundreds, who had come back from the military campaign" (Numbers 31:14).

Why did Moses yell at the officers, and not the soldiers?

There are many kinds of leaders, and there are thousands of books about leadership. There are hundreds of theories about what makes someone a good leader. When all is said and done, a leader is someone who others believe is worth following. The midrash suggests that Moses was angry with the officers—and not the foot soldiers—because the officers are responsible for the actions of those they command (Midrash, *Sifrei Bemidbar* 157). Officers need to be examples. They need to shout, "*Acharai!*"

In Hebrew, we say that a leader must be a *dugma ishit*—a personal example. The power of personal example is enormous. As the saying goes, anybody can talk the talk. A true leader is someone who walks the walk—who puts words into actions. This is someone who shouts, "*Acharai!*" and leads through example. This is someone people will follow. This is a leader.

So ask yourself, "When will I shout, '*Acharai*'? How am I an example? Would I follow someone who does what I do the way I do it?"

If you like your answer, then keep doing what you do, and others will follow. If you don't like your answer, change what you are doing.

# מסעי

# *Maasei*

## Second Chances

### Rabbi William Cutter, PhD, and Georgianne Cutter, MSW/LCSW

**Speak to the Israelite people and say to them: When you cross the Jordan into the land of Canaan, you shall provide yourselves with places to serve you as cities of refuge to which a manslayer who has killed a person unintentionally may flee.** (Numbers 35:10–11)

Everyone needs a second chance! And no one likes to be accused of having done something wrong (a crime or even a social misstep) without evidence and a fair hearing.

Our Torah portion has two big themes: the importance of fairness and having evidence. As our ancestors journeyed across the desert, they probably didn't have much time to think about forming a society. But, when they finally settled in the Land, it was time for them to develop the laws and rules that would help them all get along as part of a sacred community.

One of those first laws was about "the city of refuge."

**Rabbi William Cutter, PhD,** is professor emeritus at Hebrew Union College–Jewish Institute of Religion and teaches literature and human relations.

**Georgianne Cutter, MSW/LCSW,** teaches in the Hebrew Union College–Jewish Institute of Religion School of Education.

Imagine: You killed someone, but it was an accident. You would probably be afraid that a mob would come after you seeking revenge. There should be places to which accidental murderers could flee and where no one could harm them. To accomplish this, the Bible lays out a plan for cities of refuge.

Think about the times in your life when a second chance would have made a difference. Think about the times when you might have been too quick to judge a friend or classmate before having full evidence.

The city of refuge, therefore, is not merely an ancient and obscure concept. We do not have cities of refuge anymore, which is actually too bad, because the idea remains a noble lesson for our time. Even and especially today, many of us need "cities of refuge"—places (physical or emotional) that will provide refuge from overly harsh judgment.

Consider, as well, another important part of this Torah portion: the story of the daughters of Zelophehad (Numbers 36). Their father died without having sons, and therefore, they have a very simple and logical request—that they be allowed to inherit from their father.

Yes, the story is about inheritance, but it is actually about something much bigger than that. It is about the Jewish commitment to equal treatment of men and women even when inheritance isn't involved. The original idea—that only sons could inherit—turned out to be wrong. The daughters of Zelophehad appealed, and they—and all Jewish women—got a second chance.

And, yet another piece. Our Torah portion describes how the Israelites were to conquer the original inhabitants of the Land (Numbers 33:50–56), and then it goes into great detail, drawing the borders of the ancient Land of Israel (Numbers 34). These sections are, perhaps, too aggressive for our modern sensibilities. But they *do* express the Jewish love for the Land, our sense of historical commitment to the Land, and our love of the idea of building the Land into a home for the Jewish people.

But here again, we have to believe in second chances. *History has given us a second chance to interpret these verses.* We have maintained our attachment to the place where Jews have settled and that Jews visit—a Land that invites us to participate in and to experience the great modern revival of Jewish life.

But as for the violent aspects of the Torah portion, we reject them, and so we have a second chance to encounter these verses for our time.

And here's the bottom line: we always have a second chance—and a third, and a fourth, and a fifth chance—to read Torah and to interpret it, and to reinterpret it. It's never too late to find meaning in Judaism.

# Are We There Yet?

### Rabbi Baruch Frydman-Kohl

**These were the marches of the Israelites who started out from the land of Egypt....** (Numbers 33:1)

"Are we there yet?"

Almost.

Forty years have passed since leaving Egypt. The children of Israel are at the edge of the Promised Land. Refugees and slaves have matured into a confident nation, battle tested and prepared for its new challenge.

Initially, our Torah portion offers us a looking back, a review of the forty-two locations where the children of Israel stayed during their years in the wilderness. Rashi, the medieval commentator, cites a classic midrash that compares the review of the journey to a parent who is bringing a child home after an extended trip, reminding the child of the places in which they found shelter and faced challenges. Many parents do this with their children: "Do you remember when we went canoeing here?" or "Do you recall when we had to stop for your sister here?"

Then Moses turns to the future. The Israelites must enter and take over possession of the Land from its current residents. The Torah has a very high standard of moral integrity for the residents of the Land. In Genesis 15:16, the mention of "the sins of the Amorites"

---

**Rabbi Baruch Frydman-Kohl** is Anne and Max Tanenbaum Senior Rabbi of Beth Tzedec Congregation, Toronto, Canada.

(the original Canaanite peoples) means the ultimate removal of the existing inhabitants of the Land. In Leviticus 26:33, the Israelites are warned that their evil behavior can also lead to exile. To live in the Land that was promised to Abraham, the people of Israel will have to follow the path of the first Hebrew, living up to the ideals of *tzedak* and *mishpat*, righteousness and justice.

But what will happen after the Israelites conquer and settle the Land? Here, the Torah engages in urban planning.

There are two types of urban centers: cities of refuge (for people who have accidentally killed others) and cities for the Levites (those who assisted in the ancient desert sanctuary, who did not receive any tribal land). The Torah teaches that there should be green space in and around the cities, creating a model of ecological balance and awareness. Finally, Moses reviews issues of inheritance as they apply to the daughters of Zelophehad and for all Israelite families.

Earlier, Moses had clarified the issues of leadership succession. A successor for Aaron the High Priest was anointed, and Joshua prepares to lead the people after Moses. The sacred calendar and basic laws have been set. In *Maasei*, Moses momentarily looks backward at the journey and then directs the people to imagine a change from wilderness wanderers, with no place of their own, to living in the Land of Promise.

We are finally "in the steppes of Moab, at the Jordan near Jericho" (Numbers 33:50).

The journey is complete. The plans are finished. Everything is in place. It's time to go in.

What are your plans? How will you figure out your own journey?

*Devarim/*
Deuteronomy

# דברים

## *Devarim*

### Trust the Rebellion

Rabbi Ken Chasen

**Yet you refused to go up, and flouted the command of
the Eternal your God. You sulked in your tents and said,
"It is because the Eternal hates us that God brought us
out of the land of Egypt...."** (Deuteronomy 1:26–27)

I spent most of my childhood wanting to grow up as quickly as
possible. In the race to independence, my older brother was always
three years ahead of me. When we were little, I resented his later
bedtime. As we grew, it was his later curfew that seemed especially
unjust. It felt like I would be a child forever.

My frustration frequently tumbled out of me in anger that was
directed at my parents. I railed against their hypocrisies, picked at
their emotional vulnerabilities, and demanded respect and freedom.
For a while, it seemed that the most prominent sound in our house
was the noise of doors slamming.

My rage bewildered my parents. Usually, they couldn't even
see it coming. And what intensified my rebellion? The very actions
they took with hopes of granting me a better future. The more they
"loved" me by establishing expectations, the more deliberately I
rejected those expectations, determined to prove myself a worthy
adversary.

---

**Rabbi Ken Chasen** is senior rabbi of Leo Baeck Temple in Los Angeles,
California.

221

Back then, I felt that my oppression was somehow unique to my family. However, now that I have a teenaged son of my own, I have come to regard the sometimes-violent push-and-pull of adolescence as something necessary, common, painful, and yet strangely holy.

Perhaps that is why the Torah actually sanctifies this kind of rebellion—through the relationship between God the Parent and the adolescent Israelites.

In *Devarim*, Moses addresses the Israelites as they prepare, at last, to enter the Promised Land. He opens with a reminder of how things once were between God and the Israelites, back when the relationship was young. The people embraced God the Parent. Promises were made and kept. The people grew in number. They consented to the plans that were laid out for them.

But then, Moses recalls, as the Israelites grew in their bond with God, the story became more complicated. God's endless rules became irritating to them, and the final straw came when God told them that it was time to enter the Promised Land. They simply weren't interested in doing as they were told. They had plans of their own.

Moses's description of what comes next reminds me of my childhood home: "Yet you refused to go up, and flouted the command of the Eternal your God. You sulked in your tents and said, 'It is because the Eternal hates us that He brought us out of the land of Egypt ...'" (Deuteronomy 1:26–27). If those tents had been fitted with doors, they would surely have been slamming.

God the Parent *hates* our ancestors—the children of Israel?

The defense that follows sounds familiar to anyone who has ever accused his or her parent of hatred: "You saw how the Eternal your God carried you, as a man carries his son.... Yet for all that, you have no faith" (Deuteronomy 1:31–32).

Nowadays, when tensions in my house rise, I sometimes find myself lingering in sweet memories of how it used to be—back when my teenaged son was a small boy that I carried in my arms.

But I know that it can't stay that way. I don't even want it to stay that way. The rebellion must happen. Ultimately, it enabled the

Israelites to grow up, to discover a new trust in their Parent, and to follow their own path into the Promised Land. It will enable my son to do the same.

The medieval Jewish sage Hasdai ibn Crescas taught, "At five, your child is your master; at ten, your servant; at fifteen, your double; and after that, your friend or foe, depending upon his or her upbringing." Growing up is a wild ride. We don't get to stay for very long at any stop along the way.

So, because we can be sure that we won't, in fact, be children forever, our best bet may be simply to trust that the necessary, common, painful, and yet strangely holy journey leads to the Promised Land.

# Angry at God

## Rabbi Harold S. Kushner

**Thereupon I said to you, "I cannot bear the burden of you by myself."** (Deuteronomy 1:9)

When the curtain goes up on the book of Deuteronomy (*Devarim*), Moses is an old man. By the Torah's reckoning, he has reached the age of 120. In this portion and in those that follow, he seems to show the cumulative effect of having worn himself out in the course of his long and productive life. He says things like "I cannot bear the burden of you by myself" (Deuteronomy 1:9) and "Because of you, the Eternal was angry with me" (Deuteronomy 1:37). At times, he even seems to be angry at God, accusing God of treating him unfairly after all his years of loyal service by not letting him set foot in the Promised Land.

Is it permissible for a religious person to be angry with God? Shall we attribute Moses's outburst to frustration at all the things that didn't work out in his life?

Professor Aviva Zornberg of Jerusalem has a different understanding of it. She suggests that Moses complains about God and expresses anger at God to give the Israelites permission, through his example, to express *their* anger at God. And they do, immediately—complaining about conditions in the wilderness, accusing God of hating them for subjecting them to forty years of wandering.

---

**Rabbi Harold S. Kushner** is rabbi laureate of Temple Israel in Natick, Massachusetts.

And then, Zornberg points out, we find something in the Torah we have never seen before: "You shall love the Eternal our God with all your heart ..." (Deuteronomy 6:5). Before this, we have been commanded to obey God, to honor God, to follow God's ways, but never before have we been told to love God, because you can't love someone wholeheartedly, "with all your heart," if you are afraid to be angry with him or her. You will be censoring your emotions. There will be a measure of pretense, of concealment verging on dishonesty in the relationship. Being angry with someone is an inevitable dimension of caring about that person, caring about what he or she does and how he or she feels about you.

I can imagine people being angry with God because of all the tragedies that inflict humanity—famine, flood, and incurable illnesses. The wrong people seem to be blessed with more talent and better looks. Life is not fair, and we wonder why God doesn't do something about it.

Moses's example can teach us the valuable lesson that being angry with someone does not need to fracture a relationship. Anger is a normal part of an honest relationship. We can be angry at our parents or at our friends and still love them, and we can be angry with God and still turn to God for guidance and comfort and to express our gratitude for all the blessings in our lives.

# וָאֶתְחַנַּן
## *Va'etchanan*

## Skydiving and Torah
### Rabbi Marc Gellman, PhD

**But take utmost care and watch yourselves scrupulously....** (Deuteronomy 4:9)

Having fun is not the most important thing in life.

I don't mean to be a killjoy, but this verse from this Torah portion is a commandment from God to protect your life. This is its simple and obvious meaning, and it was how the great sage Maimonides interpreted it in his code of Jewish law (*Mishneh Torah, Hilchot Rotzeiach* 11:4). One of his examples was drinking out of a pitcher of water without first checking to see whether there was a snake in the pitcher.

Of course, some things we do are dangerous to a degree, but they are necessary dangers that we must accept in order to live a normal life. We have to drive cars, fly in airplanes, cross busy streets, and visit sick people in hospitals filled with germs. But those risks are an essential part of life, and unless we lock ourselves in our rooms, hide under the blankets, and wear a surgical mask, we cannot avoid them.

The hard part of these uncomfortable commandments—the truly challenging part—is deciding to do dangerous things just because they are fun.

---

**Rabbi Marc Gellman, PhD,** is the senior rabbi of Temple Beth Torah in Melville, New York.

This is where we go from snakes in a pitcher to skydiving. You jump out of a plane and fall like a stone until the last possible moment, before you pull your rip cord and (hopefully) float down to earth like a fallen leaf. People who skydive do it, so they tell me, because it gives them an adrenaline high. The high comes from cheating death. You could die, but you don't die. What a rush!

But that rush is a violation of these two commandments, because it puts your life in danger for no good reason—other than having fun.

God, through these words in the Torah, is telling us that *fun is not enough of a reason to do something!*

Does this make sense to you? It makes sense to me, but I know it is not an easy idea to wrap your head around. We all do so many things we love that are way too dangerous for our own good, and at some point we should just stop and think, "Is this worth it?" Is having fun enough of a reason to do something that could hurt you?

Look, it's your choice, but the point of religion in general, and Judaism in particular, is to help you make good choices.

So here is my list of fun things in addition to skydiving that violate this commandment: bungee jumping, surfing, skiing, snowboarding, tackle football, smoking pot, drinking, off-road biking, motorcycle riding, diving into too-shallow water, horseback jumping, and going out into the snow without your mittens.

Now, you might say, "Hey, it's my life and my body, and I can do with it what I want." That is a common belief and you might be right, but Judaism takes a very different view.

Judaism teaches that God owns your body (and everything else in the world), and therefore, you have no right to endanger a life that you do not really own. It is like bending the frame of a bicycle that you are borrowing from a friend.

I know that this is a tough idea to accept, but if you *really* own your body, then there is really no reason why you can't do whatever you want with it—including putting drugs into it or even killing it if you give up on life. Judaism firmly and lovingly reminds you that God cares what you do with your body. If life is holy, that includes your life, too. Endangering a sacred life for a brief adrenaline rush is shortsighted, selfish, and basically foolish—no matter who owns your body.

I am thinking of the late Christopher Reeve, the actor who played Superman and who fell off a horse during an equestrian jumping competition in Virginia in 1995. He broke his spine, and he was a quadriplegic for the rest of his life. It was a terrible accident, and I greatly admired his courage after the accident.

But, getting back to the Torah, it was also a terrible and unnecessary waste, and it happened because he was just trying to have fun doing something that was way too dangerous.

So, I would urge you—no, I *beg* you—to consider fun things that are relatively safe: golf, chess, softball (arc pitch), swimming (no diving) in pools with a lifeguard, cross-country skiing in shallow terrain, basketball, baseball (with chest pads to prevent heart injury if you get hit by a line drive), hiking on marked trails, photography, and reading!

I know that I might sound like a meddling, overprotective, and worried parent, but in this case, God is on my side. God is on your side, too, so try to stay safe, and for God's sake—protect your life!

# Curb Your Appetites

Rabbi Elaine Zecher

**You shall not covet your neighbor's wife. You shall not crave [*lo titaveh*] your neighbor's house, or his field, or his male or female slave, or his ox, or his ass, or anything that is your neighbor's.** (Deuteronomy 5:18)

What if you could have everything you ever wanted? Even people who have tons of money don't get everything. There has to be a limit somewhere.

Now, what about just *thinking* that you want something? You may or may not actually end up possessing it. Is it all right to yearn for something (or someone) you won't end up with?

The Torah portion *Va'etchanan* provides an answer to these difficult questions. Back in the book of Exodus, the Jewish people stood at Mount Sinai and received the Torah. That section of the Torah details the Ten Commandments. In this portion, as Moses summarizes the desert experience of the Israelites, we hear those words again. In the past, you may not have paid close attention to the tenth commandment, since it prohibits coveting (desiring) your neighbor's wife. If you are a teenager and you are reading this, it is pretty safe to say that you are not married and that your neighbor's spouse isn't particularly attractive to you.

---

**Rabbi Elaine Zecher** serves as a rabbi at Temple Israel in Boston and chairs the Worship and Practice Committee of the national organization for Reform rabbis (CCAR).

So, what is happening here?

The answer is in one small word: "crave." The Hebrew term is *lo titaveh*. It means *don't have uncontrollable yearnings for that which does not belong to you.*

In other words, wanting stuff is a natural desire. That's OK. But, it doesn't necessarily mean that the *want* will become a *have*.

Is the Torah telling us what we are allowed and not allowed to think? Is the tenth commandment preventing us from even pondering our desires to want?

Yes, and no. When the Israelites had finally reached the other side of the Sea, with their days of slavery behind them, they leaped for joy, singing and dancing over their newfound freedom.

Then they started their desert journey. You can imagine how uncomfortable it might have been. No showers, no real beds ...

But wait! They didn't have that in Egypt, either. Nevertheless, their minds went wild. They couldn't stop thinking about the delicious food they had in Egypt. Leeks! Cucumbers! Yum! They longed for the security of at least knowing they were slaves. Life was much more predictable back in Egypt. With the vast, unchartered wilderness in front of them, they panicked.

The Torah tells us that they were overcome with gluttonous cravings—*hitavu*—from the same Hebrew word for craving in the tenth commandment. They wanted what they wanted, and they wanted it immediately.

Know any toddlers who act like that?

You probably do. Maybe you were a toddler like that. Every little kid hasn't yet learned to control those cravings.

But here's the difference: At this point in your life, you can be more aware of what you crave, yearn for, and want. You can also figure out what is realistically possible to have and what is out of reach.

Why? Because you are growing in your ability to think through and not necessarily to act immediately for that which you desire. It is part of growing up and getting older.

This tenth commandment isn't only about wanting what you can't have. It is also about wanting what you *can* have even though it might be a good idea *not* to have it.

Judaism trusts you to discover the right thing to do. You don't have to make these decisions alone. The Torah is a wonderful gift, because it can help you face the difficult questions of life with your own ability to think and to be guided by Jewish teachings.

# עקב

## *Ekev*

---

# Everything We Do Matters

### Dr. Arnold M. Eisen

**Remember the long way that the Eternal your God has made you travel in the wilderness these past forty years.**
(Deuteronomy 8:2)

Ever since I was a teenager, I have loved Deuteronomy—attracted, I think, by the power of its message. Moses gets one last chance to speak to the Children of Israel before he dies and they must cross over to the Promised Land without him. His need for the Israelites to listen could not be more imperative. "Hear, O Israel," Moses says again and again, "*Shema, Yisrael!*" Moses has to make his words adequate to a reality that he will never know: facts to be built on the ground, things to be done on the far side of the Jordan. The Israelites, once they cross the river to new possibilities, have the task of making all they say and do adequate to the teaching that God and Moses gave them in the wilderness.

Jews still face that task every day. The covenant depends on our fulfillment along with that of other human beings. Justice and compassion will increase in the world only if you and I put them there. Goodness awaits *our* doing. Society awaits *our* word. God needs human partners now as much as ever.

*Ekev* expresses that message in the simple metaphor of a way through the wilderness. "Remember the long way that the Eternal

---

**Dr. Arnold M. Eisen** is the seventh chancellor of The Jewish Theological Seminary, the major educational institution of Conservative Judaism.

your God has made you travel in the wilderness these past forty years" (Deuteronomy 8:2). A paved road exists whether it is traveled or not. By contrast, a path through the wilderness exists only if people walk it regularly. Abandon the path even for a short time and it becomes overgrown. The repeated trampling of feet clears wilderness paths. Each person's journey is made easier by the passage of those who have gone before.

This message remains utterly stirring to me: *what you and I do matters*. Indeed, *everything* we do matters: "When we lie down and when we rise up," when we are sitting in our homes and when we "walk upon the way" (Deuteronomy 6:7 [my translation—AME]). The weights and measures used in the marketplace, the treatment of enemies and strangers, relationships with family and friends, what we eat, how we argue, how we imagine God and worship God, the way we live as a community and steward the planet, and most certainly, how we love.

I used to find the sheer *detail* of this and other law codes in the Torah to be really irritating. I used to be put off by aspects of Deuteronomy's legislation and vision that do not seem right for the present day. No longer. Even when what I read troubles me, or when I cannot live up to its high standards, I am grateful that the Torah's determination to help us pursue justice matches the determination of the forces of injustice in the world. I welcome Deuteronomy's repetitions as a spur to work constantly on doing good, for suffering, ignorance, and evil are the most repetitious things imaginable.

The path of good deeds needs us to walk it and re-walk it, alone and together, every day.

# The Two-Chambered Heart

### Rabbi Micah D. Greenstein

**And now, O Israel, what does the Eternal your God demand of you? Only this: to revere the Eternal your God, to walk only in His paths, to love Him and to serve the Eternal your God with all your heart and soul.**
(Deuteronomy 10:12)

When someone asks, "How are you doing?" what is your response?

This week's Torah portion suggests an eight-letter response.

G-R-A-T-E-F-U-L.

*Ekev* focuses on *the attitude of gratitude*—so much so, that we must thank God not only when we are hungry and about to eat, but also when we are satisfied and full!

A sixteen-year-old girl once offered me a good summary of Judaism. She said, "Do the right thing and give thanks for everything." The author of this Torah portion would have agreed.

But, let's face it. Knowing the right thing to do isn't always easy, and in one of this Torah portion's most wholesome and honest insights, the Torah acknowledges this.

Every Jew is commanded "to love God and to serve the Eternal your God with all your heart [*l'vavcha*] and soul" (Deuteronomy 10:12).

---

**Rabbi Micah D. Greenstein** is senior rabbi of Temple Israel in Memphis, Tennessee.

So, what's the problem? The word for "heart" (which can also be translated as "moral impulse") is not in the singular form, but in the plural.

If this commandment is addressed to each Jew, as a single person, why does the word "heart" appear in the plural rather than the singular?

Because our heart contains two impulses: one for doing good (*yetzer ha-tov*), and one for doing wrong (*yetzer ha-ra*). In fact, the Jewish tradition says that prior to the age of thirteen (bar/bat mitzvah), kids only have a *yetzer ha-tov*. When a child becomes thirteen, that's when the *yetzer ha-ra* kicks in.

There's a famous story about the son of the Chortkov Rebbe, who lived in eastern Europe. The kid was smart, but right before he became bar mitzvah, he became very sad. "My dear son, why are you sad?" the father asked him. "Now that you are thirteen, an important guest is coming into your life—the *yetzer ha-ra*."

"Ah, yes, Papa, but before I became bar mitzvah, I only had the *yetzer ha-tov*. Without the *yetzer ha-ra*, I didn't even know that there *was* evil. But now that I am old enough to be bar mitzvah, I know that both are there."

The Chortkov Rebbe explained, "Very often, we are tempted to do wrong. That's the evil impulse. Now that you are thirteen, you must cultivate the willpower to overcome the evil impulse, so that the good impulse will prevail. That is why the Torah states *l'vavcha* (plural) and not *lib'cha* (singular)—to remind us to love God with *both* impulses. For our impulses," he concluded, "are not evil by definition. It depends on how we use them."

Over a thousand years before that story, a Rabbinic midrash spoke of a horseman who was trying to figure out how to deal with his wild horses. He had three alternatives. He could let them loose, allowing them to cause unlimited havoc and destruction. He could lock them up in the stable and constantly worry that they might escape. Or he could train them and harness them, which would help him and facilitate his labor.

That's the way it is with our instincts. We can let them loose, which is the height of recklessness and irresponsibility; we can lock them up and let them become repressed; or we can channel our impulses into meaningful and constructive activities and deeds.

The midrash concludes with the observation that those who seek a life of purpose and fulfillment (and who doesn't?) will find the training and channeling of human impulses the most promising alternative of the three.

And so, as you go forward in your life journey, learn to put both impulses, good and evil, to work for you.

You really have no choice; you're stuck with them, anyway.

# ראה
## *Re'eh*

# The Vision Thing
Wayne L. Firestone

**See, this day I set before you blessing and curse....**
(Deuteronomy 11:26)

One of the great pleasures of text study is the ability to revisit texts at different times in your life and find new meaning. Although written thousands of years ago, *Re'eh* addresses several issues that remain concerns for all of us today, such as social justice, personal debt, slavery, philanthropy, free will, law, and authority. Interestingly, the part of this portion that has the most profound impact on me at this point in my life is simply the title—*Re'eh*.

*Re'eh* is translated literally as "vision" or "seeing." This relates to how I see both myself and the world.

Over the course of my professional career, I have come to realize that I am a visual learner. This means that I have a better shot at understanding a concept or explaining an idea by using a graphic, chart, or other visual representation. This discovery gave me a profound appreciation for my own sight and its impact on the way I understand the world around me.

Today we are all constantly surrounded by a wide variety of images. Teens are targeted even more rigorously by advertisers because they make up a central segment of shoppers. In commercials

**Wayne L. Firestone** is president and CEO of Hillel: The Foundation for Jewish Campus Life, a global network of Jewish student organizations on college campuses.

during *Glee*, background ads on Facebook chat, and YouTube videos like "Charlie Bit My Finger," we are inundated with icons, logos, and pictures.

Given this constant interaction with visual stimulation, I strive to make it a priority to acknowledge how lucky I am to have the sense of sight, as well as how "seeing" and "visioning" can occur through more than just eyesight.

On a trip to Israel a few years ago, I attended a play produced by a group of blind and deaf actors who formed a theater company called Na-laga'at ("Please, touch!") to creatively use other senses to convey their powerful and moving stories. I greatly enjoyed watching their signature production "Not by Bread Alone," which features onstage ovens in which the actors knead flour and bake loaves of sweet bread between moments of dialogue. Over the course of the performance, the aroma of the bread fills the entire auditorium, and at its conclusion audience members are invited onto the stage to eat the bread.

Seeing is something that many of us may take for granted, so when I hear the word *Re'eh*, I appreciate how each of us is blessed with vision.

# To See Even (and Especially) Those Who Cannot

Rabbi Loren Sykes

**You are children of the Eternal your God.**

(Deuteronomy 14:1)

Meet Tom (not his real name). He is exceptionally gifted. He speaks Hebrew almost fluently. He is a Torah reader. He is gifted with computers. He can program in multiple languages, and he can diagnose and fix problems in an amazingly short amount of time. Tom gets around really well, and he can navigate almost any situation or terrain. He is very successful socially and is a great conversationalist.

Here is the most amazing thing about Tom: he is blind and deaf. Tom was born without eyes and without the ability to hear. Cochlear implants make it possible for him to hear and give him the ability to engage in conversation. A specially programmed GPS device, which works in most situations, helps him move around independently. He is able to diagnose and fix computer problems, as well as do computer programming, because of plug-in devices that talk to Tom about what is going on with the network. He can then diagnose the problem and direct the network to fix that problem. Yet, despite technological advances in hearing, the ability to restore sight to the blind is still elusive.

---

**Rabbi Loren Sykes** is director of Camp Ramah in Wisconsin.

*Re'eh* starts with one simple word that most of us take for granted: "See!" Most of us wake up in the morning, open our eyes, and see what is around us. We don't think twice about it. Judaism even has a morning blessing that praises God for "giving sight to the blind." Unfortunately, too many of us say that prayer without thinking about what it is saying to us—that sight is an incredible gift.

The Jewish world, however, is filled with people who, literally, cannot see. People who are blind are members of synagogues. They work in almost every imaginable field. They are brilliant academics, leaders of social change, and professionals. They are like everyone else, except for one thing: they do not have eyesight. They rely on various tools and technology to help them "see."

Like so many others with physical disabilities or limitations, however, the blind are often excluded from the most basic elements of Jewish community—synagogues, day schools, religious schools, youth groups, summer camps, community centers—and the list, sadly, goes on and on.

How can we change the current reality? How can we change the Jewish world?

Before we take on changing the Jewish world, however, maybe we need to start small. We need to focus on ourselves and on how we behave toward the blind.

Our Torah portion reminds us, "You are children of the Eternal your God" (Deuteronomy 14:1). It doesn't say that only some of us are the children of God. It says "you"—and that means *everyone*.

We Jews have a blessing to say when we see people who are "different": "Blessed are You, Eternal our God, who makes all living things different." It reminds us that all of us are different—not just those who have physical or intellectual differences. We credit God with creating different kinds of people. We bless God for creating difference in the world.

If we are all "children of God," and if we praise God for variety, maybe we can start making change by seeing the whole person, and not just the limitation. Rather than focusing on the blindness of the person we meet, we need to encounter the actual person, to value that person for who that person is and for the gifts that he or she brings to the world.

Once we change our own perceptions, then we can go out and work to make our institutions more open for the blind, the deaf, those with autism, and all kinds of other differences. We all know people in our Jewish communities who want to be included, and who need to be included, and yet are excluded. Our job is simple: to help the Jewish world "see" these exceptional people and welcome them with open arms, to value them as "children of God," and to appreciate the gift of difference.

To learn more about this community, go to www.jdcc.org/ feature-article/jewish-deaf-blind-community and www.jbilibrary.org.

# שפטים
## *Shoftim*

### Judging Ourselves, Judging Others
#### Rabbi Felipe Goodman

**You shall appoint magistrates and officials for your tribes, in all the settlements [*b'chol sh'arecha*, literally, "in all your gates"] that the Eternal your God is giving you, and they shall govern the people with due justice."**
(Deuteronomy 16:18)

Why would the Torah have a whole section dealing with the appointment of judges? After all, if the Torah is all about nice stories and interesting characters, why do we need to learn how the Israelites administered justice in their community? Isn't it obvious that we need judges to administer justice and make sure that accused people receive fair treatment?

If you live in twenty-first-century America, the answer is obvious, but try to place yourself in the shoes of someone who lived three thousand years ago. In those days, justice was not so clear-cut—and it is not so simple now, either.

According to our Torah portion, the Israelites had to appoint judges to sit at the entrances of their cities. It may have served not only as a practical way of speedily delivering justice, but in a very important way, it was also a clear definition of what it means to be a judge.

---

**Rabbi Felipe Goodman** is senior rabbi of Temple Beth Sholom in Las Vegas, Nevada.

Have you ever found yourself in a situation where you judge other people? Have you ever found yourself commenting on the behavior of others by quickly sending a text message or updating your status on Facebook? Often, we press the "send" button too quickly, and we wind up regretting what we have written. How many times have you said something about someone, afterward wishing that you could simply make what you said go away?

Some of us believe that we are experts on everything. After all, our world requires that we be ever vigilant and inform other people as quickly as possible about what happens around us. When we upload a video, when we post a review—aren't we doing the right thing? It all depends whether we know at all what we are talking about. How many of us have reviewed products online and have no idea what we are doing?

Imagine: what would happen if every time you were about to judge others, there would be someone standing there to remind you that you are not really a judge?

Judging and being judged is one of the most difficult things that people deal with during their life. When our text tells us, "Justice, justice shall you pursue" (Deuteronomy 16:20), it is not only referring to the type of justice that comes when someone gets a fair trial or when a criminal is apprehended. It's also about not rushing to judge other people! Our tradition firmly establishes that we shouldn't judge others until we have placed ourselves in their situation. The mere fact that the Torah states that pursuing justice is a gateway to prosperity should serve as a warning of the chaotic fallout of improperly or falsely rendered judgments of other people.

The next time you are about to judge someone else, whether you are doing it on your own or together with a group of people, think of how important it is to refrain from judging unjustly or falsely. God devoted an entire section of the Torah to remind us that there is an important difference between acting with justice and judging others in the process.

# War Isn't All It's Cracked Up to Be

### Rabbi Laurence E. Milder

## When you take the field against your enemies ...
(Deuteronomy 20:1)

There was a popular song in the 1960s that went, "WAR: HUH! What is it good for? Absolutely nothing!"

Now, a lot of people might take exception to that idea. After all, aren't there times when it really is necessary to go to war? What if your country were attacked? What if another people were being oppressed and every other avenue of negotiation had been exhausted?

Other people might argue the opposite: that there is never a just cause for war; that there is always an alternative; that peaceful resistance may appear to be defeat in the short term but will ultimately triumph over any injustice.

There is a lot of war in the Bible, but only a few laws *about* war. In fact, almost all of the laws regarding the conduct of war can be found in *Shoftim*, Deuteronomy 20. But one thing you won't find there, or anywhere else in the Torah, is an explanation of what constitutes a "just war."

The passage begins, "When you take the field against your enemies ..." (Deuteronomy 20:1). If the Torah meant to establish legitimate reasons for going to war, then we might have expected the

---

**Rabbi Laurence E. Milder** teaches Jewish studies and leads the Reform Minyan at the American Hebrew Academy in Greensboro, North Carolina.

passage to begin, "If an enemy attacks you ...," or something similar to that.

Instead, the Torah seems to assume that there will be war. The primary objective of the passage is to limit the destructive potential of war. It never tries to define a just cause for war, though it does identify specific enemies of the Israelites. It is not particularly merciful toward these enemies. But that is not the same as saying, "Under the following circumstances, you are justified in going to war." Rather, the Torah just assumes that war is something that nations do. Because war is regarded as inevitable, it is best to limit laws to prohibiting the worst excesses of war.

In fact, if we look at the limitations that Deuteronomy imposes, we will see that those limitations actually make war a remarkably bad choice.

Ordinarily, if you want to win wars, you send your best soldiers, that is, young adult males in the prime of their life. Instead, the passage exempts the following from military service:

> Is there anyone who has built a new house but has not dedicated it? Let him go back to his home, lest he die in battle and another dedicate it. Is there anyone who has planted a vineyard but has never harvested it? Let him go back to his home, lest he die in battle and another harvest it. Is there anyone who has paid the bride-price for a wife, but who has not yet married her? Let him go back to his home, lest he die in battle and another marry her.
>
> (Deuteronomy 20:5–7)

Notice the order of these three categories of exemption—in increasing amounts of time. Who knows how long one waited before dedicating a house? A vineyard? One is not permitted to harvest its crop for personal use for five years (Leviticus 19:25). What about marriage? In ancient times, a family might pay the bride-price many years before the marriage takes place.

Then, as if this weren't enough, the text seems to exempt anyone else who doesn't want to fight: "The officials shall go on addressing the troops and say, 'Is there anyone afraid and disheartened? Let him go back to his home, lest the courage of his comrades flag like his'" (Deuteronomy 20:8).

The Rabbis add that when the officials called forth those who were exempt, they would ask them all to present themselves at the same time, so that no one would know who was actually afraid (Midrash, *Sifrei Devarim* 20:8).

And the few soldiers who are left? They are supposed to tiptoe around the fruit trees and make sure they don't get stepped on (Deuteronomy 20:19–20). In one of the best rhetorical questions in the Torah, we read, "Are trees of the field human to withdraw before you into the besieged city?" (Deuteronomy 20:19).

Kings don't usually write laws like these that deprive themselves of able soldiers and limit their ability to conduct war. But priests do. Deuteronomy reflects the interests of priests, who wanted to make sure that there were houses, farms, and families and didn't care so much whether the king could wage war. The priests didn't like idolatry, and they didn't speak kindly of other nations that lured Israel into the worship of foreign gods. But they sure didn't have a good handle on how to win wars. If Israel had followed their laws, it is unlikely that they would have ever won any wars.

These laws, then, are more utopian than realistic. What does the author really care about? A strong society, with housing and jobs and families, and protecting the land itself. Ironically, the part of the Torah most concerned with the conduct of war undermines the very ability of the king to wage war.

"Just war" is something that philosophers debate. The authors of the Torah were not concerned with that intellectual exercise. It is almost as if they knew that all nations try to defend their own wars as "just."

Instead, they set priorities: You want to wage war?

Fine.

Just don't ruin the country in the process.

# כי תצא
# *Ki Tetzei*

## You Must, Because You Can
### Rabbi Edward Feinstein

**You shall not abuse a needy and destitute laborer, whether a fellow countryman or a stranger in one of the communities of your land.** (Deuteronomy 24:14)

Among those who left Egypt, there were two—Berel and Shmerel.

As slaves, these two had grown so accustomed to looking down at the ground that they could no longer lift their eyes. And so when Moses brought Israel across the Red Sea, Berel asked Shmerel, "What do you see?"

"I see mud," he responded.

"I see mud, too," said Berel. "What's all this about freedom? We had mud in Egypt; we have mud here!"

When Israel stood at Mount Sinai, Shmerel asked Berel, "What do you hear?"

"I hear someone shouting commands," he answered.

"I hear commands, too," said Shmerel. "What's all this about Torah? They shouted commands in Egypt; they shout commands here!"

Finally, after forty years, when Israel arrived at the Promised Land, Berel asked Shmerel, "How do you feel?"

"My feet hurt," he replied.

---

**Rabbi Edward Feinstein** is senior rabbi of Valley Beth Shalom in Encino, California.

"My feet hurt, too," said Berel. "What's all this about a Promised Land? My feet hurt in Egypt; my feet hurt here!"

Removing the external chains of slavery doesn't make a person free. Sure, the body might be free, but the mind remains in bondage. "One of the great liabilities of life," declared Rev. Dr. Martin Luther King in one of his last sermons, "is that all too many people find themselves living amid a great period of social change, and yet they fail to develop the new attitudes, the new mental responses, that the new situation demands. They end up sleeping through a revolution."

In the Torah, freedom comes in two parts: the Exodus from Egyptian slavery, and the revelation of law on Mount Sinai.

Why law? Law seems like an odd place to find spirituality. Law is technical and dry. Law is about conflict and confrontation. Law is a necessary restraint on our "lowest" parts. In Western culture, law is an instrument for achieving social order—a way to keep us from killing one another.

Now, consider a law from the *Mishneh Torah*, the code of Jewish law written by the great medieval sage Maimonides. To paraphrase: You must give charity to the poor. You must give at least one-tenth of your income, but you may not give more than one-fifth. When you give charity to the poor, the dignity of the poor must be respected. You may not humiliate the recipient of charity. Anonymous giving, where neither donor nor recipient is aware of one another's identity, is best. Even better is to provide employment or a business opportunity, thus alleviating the need for further assistance.

Notice how this is phrased.

It doesn't say the poor have a *right* to receive charity. This isn't an entitlement program. It says you have an *obligation*. It is a mitzvah—a commandment. This is the core concept of Jewish law: you are obligated because you are covenanted.

This law speaks not to the lowest in us, but to the highest. "You shall be holy, for I, the Eternal your God, am holy" (Leviticus 19:2). The purpose of law in the Torah is to cultivate the holy, the compassionate, the just, and the sensitive within us—to cultivate the divine within us. Law has an educational purpose.

Law is a meeting place between what is and what should be. Law rests upon a paradox: because we're human, we need law. Because we have drives, because we often forget who we are, because we have the ability to rationalize any behavior or attitude—because we're human, we need law.

But we can live up to the law only because we have the divine within us. Every "ought" implies a "can." The command to be holy— to live a life of justice and compassion—is the strongest possible confirmation that we have the capacity to be holy. We have godliness in us.

The Protestant preacher Phillips Brooks wrote:

> The great danger facing all of us is not that we shall make an absolute failure of our life. Nor that we shall fall into outright viciousness. Nor that we shall be terribly unhappy. Nor that we shall feel that life has no meaning. The danger is that we shall fail to perceive life's greatest meaning, fall short of its highest good, miss its deepest and most abiding happiness, be unable to tender the most needed service, be unconscious of life ablaze with the light of the Presence of God, and be content to have it so.

The danger is that we will wake up to find we've missed life itself. The danger is that we will be satisfied too soon with too little—with a life that falls short of the best.

# The Ties That Bind

Rabbi Joseph B. Meszler

**You shall make fringes on the four corners of the clothes you wear.** (Deuteronomy 22:12 [my translation—JBM])

Many people get a *tallit*, or prayer shawl, as a present for their bat or bar mitzvah. Mine is a "Joseph's coat" *tallit*. It has many colors going down the sides. My mother picked it out because my name is Joseph. I like to wear my *tallit* not only because it is colorful and meaningful but also because it gives me something to fiddle with during services—the *tzitzit*, the fringes hanging from the corners, the most important part of the *tallit*.

The *tzitzit* are tied in a specific way. On each fringe are five knots, recalling the Five Books of Moses. Look closely, and you will see the five knots are actually double knots, which symbolize the Ten Commandments. From the knots dangle eight threads, symbolizing the eighth day of the covenant of circumcision for a baby boy. When we see these knots and threads, we are supposed to remember God and the mitzvot (commandments).

Some define *mitzvah* as a "good deed" or as something nice that you do—if you have the time. *Mitzvah*, however, literally means "divine commandment." It is something God *wants* you to do.

Let me tell you the day that I learned the meaning of *mitzvah*.

---

**Rabbi Joseph B. Meszler** serves Temple Sinai of Sharon, Massachusetts, and teaches at Kehillah Schechter Academy in Norwood, Massachusetts.

It happened when I was growing up in Maryland. It was a snowy day. As my mother and I were driving up to the house, we noticed our neighbor, Mr. Mercier, chopping ice off of his driveway.

"Go out and help him," my mother said. I began to complain that I didn't feel like it.

Wrong move.

About 0.2 second later, my mother's boot landed in my butt, and as I was flying out through the car door, she said, "Do it because it's a mitzvah!"

Sometimes, a mitzvah comes with a boot in your butt.

The *tzitzit* are supposed to be like a string tied around your finger, reminding you to do God's commandments—even if you don't feel like it. They symbolize our responsibilities to our neighbors—whether they live next door, in the next bedroom, or in the next country.

With our new, contemporary knowledge, the fringes of the *tallit* have taken on even deeper meaning. In the twenty-first century, scientists overwhelmingly accept the big bang theory (how the universe originated at one point in space and time) and evolution (how all living things on our planet go back to one original organism with the same DNA). We are all connected because we were all originally one, coming from the same single starting point.

Similarly, if we look at the *tzitzit*, we can see how they are all knotted and tied together. The strings and knots can remind us of the interconnectedness of all things, our connections with each other, and our relationships and responsibilities—the "ties that bind." Each of us is the end of a dangling thread going back to the same Source.

You are connected to people and nature. The different people who grow your food, who deliver and package it, and who put it on your table; the electricity that comes to your home, and the impulses that run through your nerves; the water that comes through the pipes, and the blood in your arteries; the tree breathing through its leaves, and you breathing through your lungs; the person writing you a note from the chair next to you, and the person driving away your trash: everything and everyone is interdependent. We are tied to and affect each other.

We are also tied to the people who came before us and those who will come after us. We all go back to a common ancestor (whom we can call Adam, if we want), and even before that—to a single point of extraordinary light that exploded ("Let there be light"; Genesis 1:3).

"Only connect!" wrote the novelist E. M. Forster in his novel *Howard's End*. The *tzitzit* remind us of what we should do for each other because we are irrevocably tied together. If we are the threads, then God is the Knot.

# כי תבוא
# *Ki Tavo*

## An Unholy Mash-Up
### Rabbi Joseph Black

**After you have crossed the Jordan, the following shall
stand on Mount Gerizim when the blessing for the
people is spoken: Simeon, Levi, Judah, Issachar, Joseph,
and Benjamin. And for the curse, the following shall
stand on Mount Ebal: Reuben, Gad, Asher, Zebulun,
Dan, and Naphtali.** (Deuteronomy 27:12–14)

When my family and I were moving to New Mexico in 1997, my wife
and I went on a house-hunting trip, and we stayed for a few nights
in a downtown Albuquerque hotel room that was located one floor
above two adjacent ballrooms. We discovered the disadvantages of
our location when, upon returning in the evening from a long day
of activities, we were greeted by a noise that sounded like an unholy
mash-up of rhythm and blues and mariachi, coming through the
uninsulated floor from the two ballrooms below us.

As you can imagine, we didn't get a lot of sleep that night.

*Ki Tavo* shows us a different type of "noise." In Deuteronomy
27:12–14, we learn that the leaders of the tribes are commanded
to shout blessings and curses at the people from atop two different
mountains: the blessings from Mount Gerizim, and the curses from

---

**Rabbi Joseph Black** is senior rabbi of Temple Emanuel in Denver,
Colorado.

Mount Ebal. The basic idea is that if we follow God's commandments, we will be blessed. If we don't, we will be cursed.

The text then goes on to list the curses and the blessings. The blessings are pretty standard: long life, health, and prosperity. The curses, on the other hand, are pretty brutal: everything from plagues and famine, to actually (and this is hard to take) being forced to eat your own children. As curses go, it doesn't get any worse than that one.

Every time I read this text, I picture a valley with a mountain on each side. The leaders of the tribes are divided up on the mountains, and the people are located in the valley. Sometimes, I imagine that all the blessings are shouted first, and then the curses follow.

Other times, I "hear" the people on each mountain answering one another: blessing/curse, blessing/curse.

But sometimes, I hear both sides screaming at the same time— with the people in the valley hearing curses in one ear and blessings in the other. After a while, it becomes impossible to tell the difference between the two sides. Blessings and curses become intertwined and interchangeable.

The last image is the one that sticks with me the most. Sometimes blessings and curses *do* get mixed up. Think about it: have you ever found yourself in a situation that you thought was going to be horrible, but after it was over, you realized that it actually was pretty cool? Or, on the other hand, have you ever looked forward to something, but afterward you realized that it wasn't what you thought it was going to be at all? Sometimes blessings turn into curses. Sometimes curses turn into blessings. Life can be funny that way.

There are times where it can take a while to tell whether something is going to be a blessing or a curse. When we are in the middle of a situation, it can sometimes be hard to distinguish what's really happening. All too often, we tend to jump to conclusions and label things before we have a chance to sort them out. Usually this is harmless. Other times, however, jumping to conclusions and acting on them can have a tragic effect. Allowing yourself the time to step back and sort things out can be a powerful and vital tool in discovering both the blessings and the curses in your life.

# Remember Who You Are
# (and Then, Party)

Rabbi David Steinhardt

**You shall then recite as follows before the Eternal your
God: "My father was a fugitive Aramean. He went down
to Egypt with meager numbers and sojourned there...."**
(Deuteronomy 26:5)

*Ki Tavo* might be all you need to know in order to learn how to live
successfully.

The Jewish people are about to leave their wanderings and enter
the Land of Israel. And it *is* a Promised Land—truly an *eretz zavat
chalav ud'vash*, a "land flowing with milk and honey" (Exodus 3:8).

But what are their concerns? Probably the same concerns any
one of us would have if we were moving to a new place and starting
a new life. There are many challenges. You can imagine them; you
might even have experienced them already. When you go to college
or do something else after you graduate from high school, you will
experience those challenges then. Trust me—that is the truth, and
there is no way of getting around it.

But God's concerns are different. God understands that the
people will be successful. But God seems to be concerned that the
people will forget where they come from, that they will lose their

**Rabbi David Steinhardt** is senior rabbi at B'nai Torah Congregation in
Boca Raton, Florida.

identities, that they will lose their sense of self and no longer be faithful.

And so, God presents a four-point program.

First, the people must bring an offering of their finest first fruits.

Then, they must recite a statement that would remind them of their history.

Third, they have to share with others, especially those who are less fortunate.

Then—and only then—they can enjoy the fruit of their work—which means that they can celebrate and party!

These requirements speak to each one of us, and they address the challenge of preserving what's important in a "new land" (whatever that "new land" of opportunity might be) and how to spiritually survive when we are faced with the challenge of living comfortable lives.

> **Step one reminds us:** There is something beyond ourselves that determines our well-being. We should never lose our humility. We should bring God into the larger picture of our lives.
>
> **Step two:** Remember where you come from. What were the struggles of our grandparents and ancestors? What brought us to this place?
>
> **Step three:** We have obligations to those who aren't as fortunate as we are. We measure the value of a society by how it treats people on the fringes.
>
> **Step four:** We should enjoy life, and our religious life and observances should bring us joy and fulfillment!

*Ki Tavo* presents a wonderful blueprint for us whenever we enter a new place. Our fears are often misdirected. Typically, our true challenge is to work on ourselves.

# נִצָּבִים

# *Nitzavim*

## The Ultimate Network

### Rabbi Dr. Analia Bortz, MD

**I make this covenant ... not with you alone but both with those who are standing here ... and with those who are not with us here this day.** (Deuteronomy 29:13–14)

Everyone knows what social networking is, and everyone knows how it has contributed to the way that we establish and maintain our relationships.

A definition: according to www.whatissocialnetworking.com, social networking is the grouping of individuals into specific groups, like small rural communities or a neighborhood subdivision. Although social networking is possible in person, especially in the workplace, universities, and high schools, it is most popular online.

Whether it is Facebook, Twitter, LinkedIn, or Ning networks, it has never been as simple to establish relationships, to connect, and to reconnect with people as it is today.

Great—as long as we use it wisely and with common sense.

Let me tell you about a similar idea that occurred around thirty-two hundred years ago.

God says to the people of Israel, "You stand this day, *all of you*, before the Eternal your God ... to enter into the covenant.... I make this covenant ... not with you alone, but both with those who are

---

**Rabbi Dr. Analia Bortz, MD,** is a bioethicist and serves as rabbi at Congregation Or Hadash in Sandy Springs, Georgia.

standing here … and with those who are not with us here this day" (Deuteronomy 29:9–14 [my emphasis—AB]).

For those who were present, that was simple. It was face time!

Who are those who are not present? Have any of your ancestors "tagged" you in this picture? What does it mean to be "tagged"? Even if you were not aware, now you are part of this social network, and that makes you an active partner in a collective responsibility.

Now that you have a message to convey, you are part of this "fan club"—"fans" that follow the covenant. This covenant demands commitments, actions, and a deep level of understanding, criticism, and argument. If you are a seeker, you belong in here! This is an ancient "Facebook"—a book of faces that allows different interpretations, and your interpretation is very important. The Torah gives us hints; it is written in an interesting style of few words, and those words invite us to discover new horizons. Each one is a link to another source.

LOL? No, don't laugh out loud.

Give yourself the opportunity to see something new.

It is written in this Torah portion: *Lo va-shamayim hi*, "The Torah is not in the heaven" (Deuteronomy 30:12). Rather, it is *b'fichah u'vilivavecha la'asotah*, "the Torah is in your mouth and in your heart to take it to action" (Deuteronomy 30:14). That's right— it's not just about talking the talk; it's also about walking the walk.

And, as for BRB—if you are planning to "be right back," remember that you are always welcome.

In this ancient Facebook, this book of our Jewish faces, you might think about "unfriending" the entire Jewish people.

Are you sure?

Just try to stay in the network. It's worth it, and you will not regret it.

# Standing for Civility

## Rabbi Peter J. Rubinstein

**You stand this day, all of you, before the Eternal your God—your tribal heads, your elders and your officials, all the men of Israel, your children, your wives, even the stranger within your camp, from woodchopper to water drawer—to enter into the covenant of the Eternal your God, which the Eternal your God is concluding with you this day....** (Deuteronomy 29:9–11)

We Jews especially love this Torah portion. It is one of the few portions that we read twice a year—once as part of the weekly Torah cycle, and again on Yom Kippur morning.

The portion begins with Moses's powerful words to the Israelites:

> *Atem nitzavim ha-yom*—You stand this day, all of you, before the Eternal your God—your tribal heads, your elders and your officials, all the men of Israel, your children, your wives, even the stranger within your camp, from woodchopper to water drawer—to enter into the covenant of the Eternal your God, which the Eternal your God is concluding with you this day....
>
> (Deuteronomy 29:9–11)

---

**Rabbi Peter J. Rubinstein** is senior rabbi of Central Synagogue in New York City.

When Moses describes the people as *nitzavim*, "standing," he doesn't mean that the people are simply "standing." If he meant that, he would have used the Hebrew word *omdim*.

But, it's not as if the Israelites are just "hanging out" and standing around. The word *nitzavim* implies that the people are standing with a certain *attitude*. They seem to be standing proudly and defiantly, with intention and at attention.

Now that doesn't seem extraordinary. But, it wasn't all that long ago that this same people were complaining about food and water and even challenging Moses's leadership. They kvetched (complained) continuously.

So, why now are they *nitzavim*-ing? Why do they suddenly stand quietly at attention and listen?

Perhaps they have figured out that no one expects that they have to like all those others with whom they are standing. Perhaps they have finally figured out that they are in this venture together. All of the Israelites stand there with the people they like and the people they don't like at all, and they need to be civil to each of them.

That's an enormous accomplishment, isn't it? People standing civilly, packed together, shoulder to shoulder: whether they agree about Moses's ability as a leader or not; whether they share common devotion to God or not—it makes no difference.

Even if they have issues with members of their own family or hate the other tribes on the far side of the encampment, even if they consider their neighbors unworthy, all of those Israelites stand together. They have finally embraced a basic Jewish value: you have to treat other people well, even if you don't want to. That is what it means to care about others as you would want them to care about you.

Each of us has an obligation to embody generosity of spirit and to do what is right, even for people we may not like.

This is a great lesson to hear twice a year—and especially on Yom Kippur! And it is something that we can practice all year long.

# וילך

## *Vayelech*

# Tunes

Joel Lurie Grishaver

**Moses wrote down this Teaching and gave it to the priests, the sons of Levi, who carried the Ark of the Eternal's Covenant, and to all the elders of Israel.**
(Deuteronomy 31:9)

Jane and I drove to work today. The radio was on softly—almost too quiet to hear. A bass line started to play in the background. It was not one that I could have hummed. I really didn't recognize it, but I knew it. Useless information, but it was an ancient guitar play—Peter Frampton—from the classic album *Frampton Comes Alive.*

The whole tune, from an album I never bought—and from a time way before downloads—had been stored without effort, without intent, in my brain.

This Torah portion is the end of Moses. It will take him a few more weeks to die, but here he retires, sees himself as old, and turns the Jewish people over to Joshua. Here is where he says, "The Eternal has said to me, 'You shall not go across yonder Jordan'" (Deuteronomy 31:2).

He appoints Joshua, gives him a pep talk, and then we read, "Moses wrote down this Teaching ..." (Deuteronomy 31:9). Ten verses later, Moses says, "Therefore, write down this poem and teach

---

**Joel Lurie Grishaver** is a partner in Torah Aura Productions and is a teacher, writer, storyteller, and cartoonist.

it to the people of Israel" (Deuteronomy 31:19). Moses writes down his version of the Torah, and then he talks to the young'uns who are taking over and writing down their own Torah remix. The Hasidic commentary *Sefat Emet* says, "Everyone has their own version of the Torah, and it might take a whole lifetime to discover it all."

Moses gets this when God tells him, "Have the Jews create their own list of tunes—and invite them to make Torah out of it."

Think of it—iPod lists, a soundtrack of your life—as Torah. Each of us has our own list of tunes. These are tunes that speak the truth to us. They are our expression of the Torah. Collecting our music is one way of sorting out the truth.

We always get one Torah handed to us—the one that comes from Moses.

And then we turn the Torah that we have received into our own song.

Judaism needs tunes to get the words off the paper and into our hearts. Music has its own way of telling the truth.

# Facing the End

Rabbi James Ponet

**Moses went and spoke these things to all Israel. He said to them, "I am now one hundred and twenty years old, I can no longer be active. Moreover, the Eternal has said to me, 'You shall not go across yonder Jordan.'"**
(Deuteronomy 31:1–2)

Here's the skinny: Moses is really old, apparently 120 years old, yet he feels pretty good—still strong and clear-eyed. Somehow, a brand-new thought captures him. Although he once killed a man, it has never ever occurred to him that he, too, would someday die.

He thinks, "These children of slaves will not always have me around as their guide and defender. How will they manage when I am gone? How is it that I have never thought of this before?" His eyes glisten with tears, as a deep sorrow sobs silently in his chest and stomach.

These people are not going to have an easy time of it, he realizes. They will encounter hardships, face enemies, and suffer losses. He knows. And he will not be there to comfort them, fight for them, and make sense of things for them. He wishes that he would not need to leave them, but he knows that soon he will.

He tries to talk to them about this. "I am old," he tells them. "I cannot get about as easily as I used to. Things are gonna happen."

**Rabbi James Ponet** is the Jewish chaplain at Yale University.

But, guess what? They will not believe him, because they cannot imagine a world without Moses.

No Moses? Impossible.

He tries to scare them, to prod them—until he realizes that he cannot prepare them for the shock that is coming.

But what he might do is leave them a written story that might be sung like a ballad or a lullaby—maybe even a poem, or a song.

Yes, it would be a song that they could sing when he is gone, a song that will let the people remember his voice, see his face, and know that they are not alone.

Remember: this was before video cameras, digital recorders, smartphones, and things like that. How could he assure them that although he will disappear alone into the mystery of death, he will still be there, available, present?

He climbs alone to the top of a high mountain that gives him a view westward into the Promised Land. Sitting on the summit, he begins to hum and dream and listen. Soon, words flow from him, and he writes these words down, meticulously and with great pleasure.

If you watched him writing, you would see a man utterly absorbed, his tongue gently caressing his lower lip as his hand moves over the calfskin parchment like a conductor leading a great symphony orchestra. He sits like this for hours, and by day's end, as the sun turns scattered clouds scarlet and purple at the horizon, two poems face him atop his rock desk.

The first poem came to him as he remembered the day, forty years ago, when he had thought the entire people would leap to their deaths in the roiling Sea of Reeds. Reckless Nachshon had already jumped in and looked about to disappear beneath the waters, when Moses, inspired, lifted his shepherd's staff as if it were a mighty pen and wrote a different ending. As we know, the waters parted, the people crossed the sea on dry land, and then they watched as the Egyptian army, hot in pursuit, drowned beneath the resurgent waters.

That was Moses's first song—"The Song at the Sea" (Exodus 15:1–18): "The Eternal is my strength and song.... Who is like You, O Eternal, among the celestials...."

But then a second song came to him. It came to him as he realized that he would never descend this mountain on whose summit he now sat. The elders would look for him, but they would discover only these two poems.

That second song is Psalm 90, "a prayer of Moses." He wrote, "Teach us to count our days rightly, that we may obtain a wise heart.... Let the works of our hands prosper ..." (Psalm 90:12, 90:17).

Like Moses, you and I are singers and writers, ever wondering, "Who are You?" as we search for our own ways into a wise life.

# האזינו

## *Haazinu*

### Driven To Non-distraction

Rabbi Denise L. Eger

**Give ear, O heavens, let me speak....** (Deuteronomy 32:1)

*Haazinu* is the second to last Torah portion in the book of Deuteronomy—which is to say, it is the second to last Torah portion in the entire Torah. We always read it on the Shabbat between Rosh Hashanah and Yom Kippur. In the Torah scroll, it is a poem that appears in a special layout of two columns.

I think that I know why it is laid out this way, and not in the "usual" way. The portion wants to get our attention.

Because this is the point of the entire portion. *Haazinu* means "to listen." We must listen to this farewell address of Moses before he ascends Mount Nebo and is gathered to heaven. We must listen to and hear the words that admonish us to follow the Torah that has been entrusted to our keeping. We must listen to the voice of the One God and make *teshuvah*, repentance, whenever we can (a timely message between Rosh Hashanah and Yom Kippur!). We must listen to the story of our history.

But listening is often hard. You might *hear*, but do you really *listen*?

The television might be on, but you can be distracted, texting or talking on the phone. You hear the sound, but you don't really hear the conversation. It has certainly happened to all of us. You hear,

**Rabbi Denise L. Eger** is founding rabbi of Congregation Kol Ami, West Hollywood, California.

but you don't really listen. You can have your attention diverted even when you are in a conversation with another person. So the words are there, but you don't really hear them.

Parents frequently complain about this to their kids: "You're not listening." Teens frequently complain about this to their parents: "You don't hear me"—which can also be code for "You don't understand me." It can be difficult for teens and parents to communicate with each other.

So how can you take the message of the Torah portion— listening—to heart? How can you hear the voice of the Torah? How can you hear the voices of your parents? How can you really listen with your whole self to the words and to the meaning beyond the words?

Here's one way: for just one minute, *stop multitasking*. When you're in a face-to-face conversation with another person, put down the phone. Or, if you're on a phone call, stop doing something else at the same time. Or, when you are text messaging or Skyping, pay attention to the person in front of you. Listening—really hearing what is said—matters. And when we are doing so many different things at once, we often don't really hear what is being said.

The Torah and Jewish tradition try to get your attention—not only by the words on the page but also by *how* they are laid out on the page. If it has a different layout style, then it must be really important. The words must matter.

After all, what is Moses telling you? Follow God and don't be distracted by the many different gods and goddesses that are in the cultures that surround you. *Idolatry is, at its very root, a distraction.* It is as good advice today as it was back in ancient times. You can't really hear or listen when you are distracted.

So stop for a moment. Focus, and then you might really hear the voice of another.

You might even hear the voice of the One God.

# Listening—with Our Eyes

## Rabbi David B. Rosen

**Moses came, together with Hosea son of Nun, and recited all the words of this poem in the hearing of the people.** (Deuteronomy 32:44)

When my daughter was young, she once came over to me while I was doing stuff on my computer. She had a lot to say, and I acknowledged everything by saying, "Wow, great, that's amazing." I thought we were having a great father-daughter conversation, but apparently she didn't. She grabbed my head and turned it toward her, saying, "Daddy, you're not listening to me with both eyes!"

Both eyes? Surely, she meant both ears—but no, she knew what she was saying.

I was listening, but I wasn't really paying attention, because the whole time she was talking to me, my eyes never left the computer screen. She was right: it's one thing to "listen"; it's quite another thing to really pay attention.

I think that's what Moses has in mind when he stands before all the Israelites for the last time. He has a lot of important things he wants to share with them. After all, they are about to enter the Land of Israel for the first time after a forty-year journey in the desert. They are about to run into some pretty rough people who won't be so glad to see the Israelites converging on their land.

---

**Rabbi David B. Rosen** is senior rabbi of Congregation Beth Yeshurun in Houston, Texas.

But when Moses stands up and starts to talk, he discovers what a lot of speakers see: lots of people standing around "listening," but not with both eyes, or even with both ears. Because while they are listening, they are also thinking about what they will need to do the next morning, maybe what clothes they will want to wear, or how much food they will need for the last leg of their journey. Maybe some of the Israelites are listening to Moses while they play with their children.

And maybe that's why Moses begins his last speech with the word *Haazinu*, "Listen up!" He doesn't use the word *Shema*, as in *Shema Yisrael*, "Hear, O Israel," but a stronger word. What he has to say is really important, and he needs everyone to look at him and really give him his or her full attention.

I was once teaching a class when I saw a student with his head down on his desk. I went over to him and gave him a gentle nudge.

"I'm listening," he said.

"Right," I replied, "so tell me what I just said."

He gave me an answer that was half right—and half wrong. He may have heard my words with his ears, but he hadn't even given me one eye's worth of attention, let alone two.

When our parents or our teachers talk to us, do we just "listen" or do we really "listen up"? There's a big difference. That's what my daughter taught me a long time ago when I was sitting at my computer—and what Moses taught the Israelites as he spoke to them for the very last time.

# וזאת הברכה
## Ve-zot Ha-brachah

### Building a Better World:
### A Vision, a Plan, and the Workers

Rabbi Andrew Davids

**Moses went up from the steppes of Moab to Mount Nebo, to the summit of Pisgah, opposite Jericho, and the Eternal showed him the whole land: Gilead as far as Dan; all Naphtali; the land of Ephraim and Manasseh; the whole land of Judah as far as the Western Sea; the Negev; and the Plain—the Valley of Jericho, the city of palm trees—as far as Zoar.** (Deuteronomy 34:1–3)

I love the Empire State Building. Not because it is an attractive building—the nearby Chrysler Building is certainly more beautiful. Nor is it because my father worked there, high above Manhattan, where the cars and people below look like tiny grasshoppers. The Empire State Building is dear to me because it represents the culmination of a powerful vision, a sophisticated plan, and more than seven thousand workers coming together to erect a landmark known throughout the world.

The Empire State Building is constructed out of 57,000 tons of steel, transported so efficiently that it took just three days for the steel to move from furnaces in Pittsburgh to being riveted into the

**Rabbi Andrew Davids** is head of school at the Beit Rabban Day School in Manhattan.

building's skeleton; 200,000 cubic feet of Indiana limestone and granite join 10 million bricks and 730 tons of aluminum and stainless steel to complete the structure. New technologies, such as self-lifting cranes and bathrooms that would move up with the workers as the building rose a floor a day, contributed to the amazing fact that this building was constructed in only one year and forty-five days.

Standing as the tallest building in the world for forty-two years, until the late, lamented World Trade Center surpassed it, it is, unfortunately, once again the tallest building in New York. It is an incredible structure—the culmination of vision, planning, and combined effort.

Far away in Jordan, a country I have visited twice, lie the mountains of Moab. I have climbed these peaks, and like Moses, I have looked from the heights of Mount Nebo and gazed eastward into Israel.

Although the Torah claims that Moses had clear eyesight even at the age of 120, there is no way he could have seen all of that land. When I tried, at best I could see parts of the Jordan River Valley, the Aravah, and the Judean hills.

Moses must have seen not what *was*, but what *would be*. Moses, always a man of vision, must have seen how the Jewish people, once in our own land, would build ourselves into a mighty nation, capable of creating a rich spiritual culture that would produce the Bible, monotheism, and an unbroken tradition connecting each of us to him. For *Ve-zot Ha-brachah*, "This is the blessing," is not just the final speech of Moses. The blessing is the entire Torah, a plan for how to build a society of righteousness and compassion, a way for people to work together to create a better way of life. Our tradition inspires us to join this workforce and make our own contribution toward building a better world.

The next time you find yourself in New York, I invite you to visit the Empire State Building. Look out from this high point and imagine the future you see for yourself, our country, Israel, and the Jewish people. Then come back downstairs and figure out how you will quickly lay the next brick in this ancient project.

# ... And Ready to Start Again

### Rabbi Elie Kaplan Spitz

**This is the blessing with which Moses, the man of God, bade the Israelites farewell before he died.** (Deuteronomy 33:1)

God wrote $E = MC^2$.

"Einstein," you say.

Yes—him, too.

I once asked Dr. David Lieber, my teacher and the editor of the *Etz Hayim Torah and Commentary*, "Who wrote the Bible?"

"People," he replied.

"And what was God's role?" I persisted.

"God enables genius, whether in Shakespeare, Mozart, or a great scientist," he replied. "The Torah is a work of spiritual genius."

My teachers in rabbinical school shared the modern perspective that ideas have a history. They taught that the Torah unfolded over time and that it emerged from specific historical settings. During the exile in Babylonia, Dr. Lieber taught, Jewish sages wove many different oral traditions together into a magnificent, written tapestry.

This description of the Torah's origins conflicted with that of my childhood teachers, who instructed me that God had dictated the words to Moses, letter by letter.

---

**Rabbi Elie Kaplan Spitz** is rabbi of Congregation B'nai Israel in Tustin, California.

In *Ve-zot Ha-brachah*, the Torah closes by reminding us of the uniqueness of Moses, "whom the Eternal singled out, face to face" (Deuteronomy 34:10). On the holy day of Simchat Torah, we chant these last words of Torah, and with the next *aliyah*, we immediately begin reading the Torah all over again. And when we conclude our readings, we hold the Torah aloft, and we sing, "And this is the Torah that Moses placed before the children of Israel; the Torah given by God to Moses."

The Torah contains many distinctive laws and rituals, such as demanding that one day a week we not work or go shopping. Shabbat teaches us that God is in charge and that we need to create time to enjoy our relationships with those around us and with God. Our Torah demands that landowners provide for the poor—an idea that was radical for the ancient world and still exists as a challenge today. When the Torah states, "And God spoke to Moses, saying" (the Torah's most often repeated phrase), it means that what follows is our people's best understanding of God's will and values.

For the Jewish people, the Torah is like a sacred love letter from God. Yes, people wrote it, but the wisdom of Torah emerged from having reached deeply within and beyond ourselves to hear a hushed sliver of voice calling us toward justice, discipline, and love.

So here is what I invite you to do.

Read the Torah as a modern person.

Embrace the Torah because it is sacred. It is sacred even if people wrote it. They wrote it because they sensed that God was "calling" out to them to make the world better.

Embrace the Torah as sacred because it invites us to enter into a relationship with God.

Embrace the Torah because it is a blessing that gives and gives, and when you are finished reading it, you can go back to "the beginning" and read it again.

# Notes

## Introduction

1. Ben Tracy, "Many Teens Sending 3,000 Texts a Month," *CBS Evening News*, April 21, 2010, www.cbsnews.com/stories/2010/04/20/evening-news/main6415699.shtml.

## *Bereshit*/Genesis

1. Martin Buber, *Tales of the Hasidim*, vol. 2, *Later Masters* (New York: Schocken Books, 1987).
2. Aaron Wildavsky, *Assimilation versus Separation: Joseph the Administrator and the Politics of Religion in Biblical Israel* (New York: Transaction Publishers, 2001).

## *Shemot*/Exodus

1. Rabbi William Hamilton thanks his wife, Debra Block, for her guidance and help in writing this essay.
2. This piece is based on Adina Gerver's *dvar tzedek* on *Bo*, which can be found at http://ajws.org/what_we_do/education/publications/dvar_tzedek/5769/bo.html.
3. Nelson Mandela, *Long Walk to Freedom: The Autobiography of Nelson Mandela* (New York: Little, Brown and Company, 1994), 622.
4. Reuven Bulka, *Torah Therapy: Reflections on the Weekly Sidra and Special Occasions* (New York: Ktav, 1983), 48.

## *Vayikra*/Leviticus

1. Daniel Matt, *The Zohar: Pritzker Edition*, vol. 1 (Stanford: Stanford University Press, 2003), 1:3b and commentary, 17; *The Zohar: Pritzker Edition*, vol. 5 (Stanford: Stanford University Press, 2009), 2:132a.
2. Ben Zion Bokser, *Abraham Isaac Kook: The Lights of Penitence, the Moral Principles, Lights of Holiness, Essays, Letters, and Poems* (New York: Paulist Press, 1978), 135–139.
3. Midrash, *Vayikra Rabbah*; also quoted in Rashi's commentary.
4. Rashi on Deuteronomy 9:20.

5. Michael Perlstein, "For Tales of Life and Death, the Writing's on the Walls," *New Orleans Times-Picayune*, September 17, 2005.
6. Elie Wiesel, *One Generation After* (New York: Schocken, 2011), 77.

## *Bemidbar*/Numbers

1. Michael Carasick, ed., *The Commentator's Bible: Numbers* (Philadelphia: Jewish Publication Society, 2011), 38.
2. Joseph B. Soloveitchik, *Reflections of the Rav: Lessons in Jewish Thought*, vol. 1 (New York: Ktav, 2003).
3. Elizabeth Goldstein, "*Matot*," in *The Torah: A Women's Commentary*, ed. Tamara Cohn Eskenazi and Andrea L. Weiss (New York: URJ Press, 2008), 992.

# NOTES

# NOTES

# NOTES

# Inspiration

**God of Me:** Imagining God throughout Your Lifetime
*By Rabbi David Lyon* Helps you cut through preconceived ideas of God and dogmas that stifle your creativity when thinking about your personal relationship with God. 6 x 9, 176 pp, Quality PB, 978-1-58023-452-8 **$16.99**

**The God Upgrade:** Finding Your 21st-Century Spirituality in Judaism's 5,000-Year-Old Tradition *By Rabbi Jamie Korngold; Foreword by Rabbi Harold M. Schulweis* A provocative look at how our changing God concepts have shaped every aspect of Judaism. 6 x 9, 176 pp, Quality PB, 978-1-58023-443-6 **$15.99**

**The Seven Questions You're Asked in Heaven:** Reviewing and Renewing Your Life on Earth *By Dr. Ron Wolfson* An intriguing and entertaining resource for living a life that matters. 6 x 9, 176 pp, Quality PB, 978-1-58023-407-8 **$16.99**

**Happiness and the Human Spirit:** The Spirituality of Becoming the Best You Can Be *By Rabbi Abraham J. Twerski, MD* Shows you that true happiness is attainable once you stop looking outside yourself for the source. 6 x 9, 176 pp, Quality PB, 978-1-58023-404-7 **$16.99**; HC, 978-1-58023-343-9 **$19.99**

**A Formula for Proper Living:** Practical Lessons from Life and Torah
*By Rabbi Abraham J. Twerski, MD* 6 x 9, 144 pp, HC, 978-1-58023-402-3 **$19.99**

**The Bridge to Forgiveness:** Stories and Prayers for Finding God and Restoring Wholeness *By Rabbi Karyn D. Kedar* 6 x 9, 176 pp, Quality PB, 978-1-58023-451-1 **$16.99**

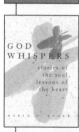

**The Empty Chair:** Finding Hope and Joy—Timeless Wisdom from a Hasidic Master, Rebbe Nachman of Breslov *Adapted by Moshe Mykoff and the Breslov Research Institute* 4 x 6, 128 pp, Deluxe PB w/ flaps, 978-1-879045-67-5 **$9.99**

**The Gentle Weapon:** Prayers for Everyday and Not-So-Everyday Moments—Timeless Wisdom from the Teachings of the Hasidic Master, Rebbe Nachman of Breslov *Adapted by Moshe Mykoff and S. C. Mizrahi, together with the Breslov Research Institute* 4 x 6, 144 pp, Deluxe PB w/ flaps, 978-1-58023-022-3 **$9.99**

**God Whispers:** Stories of the Soul, Lessons of the Heart *By Rabbi Karyn D. Kedar* 6 x 9, 176 pp, Quality PB, 978-1-58023-088-9 **$15.95**

**God's To-Do List:** 103 Ways to Be an Angel and Do God's Work on Earth
*By Dr. Ron Wolfson* 6 x 9, 144 pp, Quality PB, 978-1-58023-301-9 **$16.99**

**Jewish Stories from Heaven and Earth:** Inspiring Tales to Nourish the Heart and Soul *Edited by Rabbi Dov Peretz Elkins* 6 x 9, 304 pp, Quality PB, 978-1-58023-363-7 **$16.99**

**Life's Daily Blessings:** Inspiring Reflections on Gratitude and Joy for Every Day, Based on Jewish Wisdom *By Rabbi Kerry M. Olitzky* 4½ x 6½, 368 pp, Quality PB, 978-1-58023-396-5 **$16.99**

**Restful Reflections:** Nighttime Inspiration to Calm the Soul, Based on Jewish Wisdom *By Rabbi Kerry M. Olitzky and Rabbi Lori Forman-Jacobi* 4½ x 6½, 448 pp, Quality PB, 978-1-58023-091-9 **$16.99**

**Sacred Intentions:** Morning Inspiration to Strengthen the Spirit, Based on Jewish Wisdom *By Rabbi Kerry M. Olitzky and Rabbi Lori Forman-Jacobi* 4½ x 6½, 448 pp, Quality PB, 978-1-58023-061-2 **$16.99**

# Kabbalah/Mysticism

**Jewish Mysticism and the Spiritual Life:** Classical Texts, Contemporary Reflections *Edited by Dr. Lawrence Fine, Dr. Eitan Fishbane and Rabbi Or N. Rose* Inspirational and thought-provoking materials for contemplation, discussion and action. 6 x 9, 256 pp, HC, 978-1-58023-434-4 **$24.99**

**Ehyeh:** A Kabbalah for Tomorrow
*By Rabbi Arthur Green, PhD* 6 x 9, 224 pp, Quality PB, 978-1-58023-213-5 **$18.99**

**The Gift of Kabbalah:** Discovering the Secrets of Heaven, Renewing Your Life on Earth
*By Tamar Frankiel, PhD* 6 x 9, 256 pp, Quality PB, 978-1-58023-141-1 **$16.95**

**Seek My Face:** A Jewish Mystical Theology *By Rabbi Arthur Green, PhD*
6 x 9, 304 pp, Quality PB, 978-1-58023-130-5 **$19.95**

**Zohar:** Annotated & Explained *Translation & Annotation by Dr. Daniel C. Matt; Foreword by Andrew Harvey* 5½ x 8½, 176 pp, Quality PB, 978-1-893361-51-5 **$15.99**
*(A book from SkyLight Paths, Jewish Lights' sister imprint)*

See also *The Way Into Jewish Mystical Tradition* in The Way Into... Series.

# Holidays/Holy Days

## Prayers of Awe Series

An exciting new series that examines the High Holy Day liturgy to enrich the praying experience of everyone—whether experienced worshipers or guests who encounter Jewish prayer for the very first time.

### We Have Sinned—Confession in Judaism: Ashamnu and Al Chet
*Edited by Rabbi Lawrence A. Hoffman, PhD*
A varied and fascinating look at sin, confession and pardon in Judaism, as suggested by the centrality of *Ashamnu* and *Al Chet*, two prayers that people know so well, though understand so little.   6 x 9, 250 pp (est), HC, 978-1-58023-612-6 **$24.99**

### Who by Fire, Who by Water—Un'taneh Tokef
*Edited by Rabbi Lawrence A. Hoffman, PhD*   6 x 9, 272 pp, HC, 978-1-58023-424-5 **$24.99**

### All These Vows—Kol Nidre
*Edited by Rabbi Lawrence A. Hoffman, PhD*   6 x 9, 288 pp, HC, 978-1-58023-430-6 **$24.99**

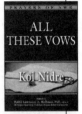

### Rosh Hashanah Readings: Inspiration, Information and Contemplation
### Yom Kippur Readings: Inspiration, Information and Contemplation
*Edited by Rabbi Dov Peretz Elkins; Section Introductions from Arthur Green's These Are the Words*
Rosh Hashanah: 6 x 9, 400 pp, Quality PB, 978-1-58023-437-5 **$19.99**
Yom Kippur: 6 x 9, 368 pp, Quality PB, 978-1-58023-438-2 **$19.99**; HC, 978-1-58023-271-5 **$24.99**

### Reclaiming Judaism as a Spiritual Practice: Holy Days and Shabbat
*By Rabbi Goldie Milgram*   7 x 9, 272 pp, Quality PB, 978-1-58023-205-0 **$19.99**

### The Sabbath Soul: Mystical Reflections on the Transformative Power of Holy Time
*Selection, Translation and Commentary by Eitan Fishbane, PhD*
6 x 9, 208 pp, Quality PB, 978-1-58023-459-7 **$18.99**

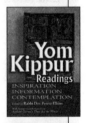

### Shabbat, 2nd Edition: The Family Guide to Preparing for and Celebrating the Sabbath
*By Dr. Ron Wolfson*   7 x 9, 320 pp, Illus., Quality PB, 978-1-58023-164-0 **$19.99**

### Hanukkah, 2nd Edition: The Family Guide to Spiritual Celebration
*By Dr. Ron Wolfson*   7 x 9, 240 pp, Illus., Quality PB, 978-1-58023-122-0 **$18.95**

## Passover

### My People's Passover Haggadah
Traditional Texts, Modern Commentaries
*Edited by Rabbi Lawrence A. Hoffman, PhD, and David Arnow, PhD*
A diverse and exciting collection of commentaries on the traditional Passover Haggadah—in two volumes!
Vol. 1: 7 x 10, 304 pp, HC, 978-1-58023-354-5 **$24.99**
Vol. 2: 7 x 10, 320 pp, HC, 978-1-58023-346-0 **$24.99**

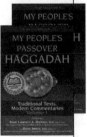

### Freedom Journeys: The Tale of Exodus and Wilderness across Millennia
*By Rabbi Arthur O. Waskow and Rabbi Phyllis O. Berman*
Explores how the story of Exodus echoes in our own time, calling us to relearn and rethink the Passover story through social-justice, ecological, feminist and interfaith perspectives.   6 x 9, 288 pp, HC, 978-1-58023-445-0 **$24.99**

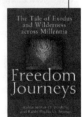

### Leading the Passover Journey: The Seder's Meaning Revealed,
the Haggadah's Story Retold   *By Rabbi Nathan Laufer*
Uncovers the hidden meaning of the Seder's rituals and customs.
6 x 9, 224 pp, Quality PB, 978-1-58023-399-6 **$18.99**

### Creating Lively Passover Seders, 2nd Edition: A Sourcebook of Engaging Tales,
Texts & Activities   *By David Arnow, PhD*   7 x 9, 464 pp, Quality PB, 978-1-58023-444-3 **$24.99**

### Passover, 2nd Edition: The Family Guide to Spiritual Celebration
*By Dr. Ron Wolfson with Joel Lurie Grishaver*   7 x 9, 416 pp, Quality PB, 978-1-58023-174-9 **$19.95**

### The Women's Passover Companion: Women's Reflections on the Festival of Freedom
*Edited by Rabbi Sharon Cohen Anisfeld, Tara Mohr and Catherine Spector; Foreword by Paula E. Hyman*
6 x 9, 352 pp, Quality PB, 978-1-58023-231-9 **$19.99**; HC, 978-1-58023-128-2 **$24.95**

### The Women's Seder Sourcebook: Rituals & Readings for Use at the Passover Seder
*Edited by Rabbi Sharon Cohen Anisfeld, Tara Mohr and Catherine Spector*
6 x 9, 384 pp, Quality PB, 978-1-58023-232-6 **$19.99**

# Bar/Bat Mitzvah

**The Mitzvah Project Book**
Making Mitzvah Part of Your Bar/Bat Mitzvah ... and Your Life
*By Liz Suneby and Diane Heiman; Foreword by Rabbi Jeffrey K. Salkin; Preface by Rabbi Sharon Brous*
The go-to source for Jewish young adults and their families looking to make the world a better place through good deeds—big or small.
6 x 9, 224 pp, Quality PB Original, 978-1-58023-458-0 **$16.99** For ages 11–13

**The Bar/Bat Mitzvah Memory Book, 2nd Edition:** An Album for Treasuring the Spiritual Celebration
*By Rabbi Jeffrey K. Salkin and Nina Salkin*
8 x 10, 48 pp, 2-color text, Deluxe HC, ribbon marker, 978-1-58023-263-0 **$19.99**

**For Kids—Putting God on Your Guest List, 2nd Edition:** How to Claim the Spiritual Meaning of Your Bar or Bat Mitzvah  *By Rabbi Jeffrey K. Salkin*
6 x 9, 144 pp, Quality PB, 978-1-58023-308-8 **$15.99** For ages 11–13

**The Jewish Prophet:** Visionary Words from Moses and Miriam to Henrietta Szold and A. J. Heschel  *By Rabbi Dr. Michael J. Shire*
6½ x 8½, 128 pp, 123 full-color illus., HC, 978-1-58023-168-8 **$14.95**

**Putting God on the Guest List, 3rd Edition:** How to Reclaim the Spiritual Meaning of Your Child's Bar or Bat Mitzvah  *By Rabbi Jeffrey K. Salkin*
6 x 9, 224 pp, Quality PB, 978-1-58023-222-7 **$16.99**; HC, 978-1-58023-260-9 **$24.99**

**Putting God on the Guest List Teacher's Guide**
8½ x 11, 48 pp, PB, 978-1-58023-226-5 **$8.99**

# Teens / Young Adults

**Text Messages:** A Torah Commentary for Teens
*Edited by Rabbi Jeffrey K. Salkin*
Shows today's teens how each Torah portion contains worlds of meaning for them, for what they are going through in their lives, and how they can shape their Jewish identity as they enter adulthood.
6 x 9, 304 pp (est), HC, 978-1-58023-507-5 **$24.99**

**Hannah Senesh:** Her Life and Diary, the First Complete Edition
*By Hannah Senesh; Foreword by Marge Piercy; Preface by Eitan Senesh; Afterword by Roberta Grossman*
6 x 9, 368 pp, b/w photos, Quality PB, 978-1-58023-342-2 **$19.99**

**I Am Jewish:** Personal Reflections Inspired by the Last Words of Daniel Pearl
*Edited by Judea and Ruth Pearl*  6 x 9, 304 pp, Deluxe PB w/ flaps, 978-1-58023-259-3 $18.99
Download a free copy of the *I Am Jewish Teacher's Guide* at www.jewishlights.com.

**The JGirl's Guide:** The Young Jewish Woman's Handbook for Coming of Age
*By Penina Adelman, Ali Feldman and Shulamit Reinharz*
6 x 9, 240 pp, Quality PB, 978-1-58023-215-9 **$14.99** For ages 11 & up

**The JGirl's Teacher's and Parent's Guide**
8½ x 11, 56 pp, PB, 978-1-58023-225-8 **$8.99**

**Tough Questions Jews Ask, 2nd Edition:** A Young Adult's Guide to Building a Jewish Life  *By Rabbi Edward Feinstein*
6 x 9, 160 pp, Quality PB, 978-1-58023-454-2 **$16.99** For ages 11 & up

**Tough Questions Jews Ask Teacher's Guide**
8½ x 11, 72 pp, PB, 978-1-58023-187-9 **$8.95**

# Pre-Teens

**Be Like God:** God's To-Do List for Kids
*By Dr. Ron Wolfson*
Encourages kids ages eight through twelve to use their God-given superpowers to find the many ways they can make a difference in the lives of others and find meaning and purpose for their own.
6 x 9, 150 pp (est), Quality PB, 978-1-58023-510-5 **$15.99** For ages 8–12

**The Book of Miracles:** A Young Person's Guide to Jewish Spiritual Awareness
*By Lawrence Kushner, with all-new illustrations by the author.*
6 x 9, 96 pp, 2-color illus., HC, 978-1-879045-78-1 **$16.95** For ages 9–13

## Bible Study/Midrash

**The Book of Job:** Annotated & Explained
*Translation and Annotation by Donald Kraus; Foreword by Dr. Marc Brettler*
Clarifies for today's readers what Job is, how to overcome difficulties in the text, and what it may mean for us. Features fresh translation and probing commentary.
5½ x 8½, 220 pp (est), Quality PB, 978-1-59473-389-5 **$16.99**

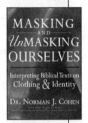

**Masking and Unmasking Ourselves:** Interpreting Biblical Texts on Clothing & Identity   *By Dr. Norman J. Cohen*
Presents ten Bible stories that involve clothing in an essential way, as a means of learning about the text, its characters and their interactions.
6 x 9, 240 pp, HC, 978-1-58023-461-0 **$24.99**

**The Other Talmud—*The Yerushalmi*:** Unlocking the Secrets of The Talmud of Israel for Judaism Today   *By Rabbi Judith Z. Abrams, PhD*
A fascinating—and stimulating—look at "the other Talmud" and the possibilities for Jewish life reflected there.   6 x 9, 256 pp, HC, 978-1-58023-463-4 **$24.99**

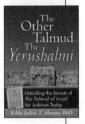

**The Torah Revolution:** Fourteen Truths That Changed the World
*By Rabbi Reuven Hammer, PhD*   A unique look at the Torah and the revolutionary teachings of Moses embedded within it that gave birth to Judaism and influenced the world.   6 x 9, 240 pp, HC, 978-1-58023-457-3 **$24.99**

**Ecclesiastes:** Annotated & Explained
*Translation and Annotation by Rabbi Rami Shapiro; Foreword by Rev. Barbara Cawthorne Crafton*
5½ x 8½, 160 pp, Quality PB, 978-1-59473-287-4 **$16.99**

**Ethics of the Sages:** Pirke Avot—Annotated & Explained   *Translation and Annotation by Rabbi Rami Shapiro*   5½ x 8½, 192 pp, Quality PB, 978-1-59473-207-2 **$16.99**

**The Genesis of Leadership:** What the Bible Teaches Us about Vision, Values and Leading Change   *By Rabbi Nathan Laufer; Foreword by Senator Joseph I. Lieberman*
6 x 9, 288 pp, Quality PB, 978-1-58023-352-1 **$18.99**

**Hineini in Our Lives:** Learning How to Respond to Others through 14 Biblical Texts and Personal Stories   *By Rabbi Norman J. Cohen, PhD*   6 x 9, 240 pp, Quality PB, 978-1-58023-274-6 **$16.99**

**A Man's Responsibility:** A Jewish Guide to Being a Son, a Partner in Marriage, a Father and a Community Leader   *By Rabbi Joseph B. Meszler*   6 x 9, 192 pp, Quality PB, 978-1-58023-435-1 **$16.99**

**The Modern Men's Torah Commentary:** New Insights from Jewish Men on the 54 Weekly Torah Portions   *Edited by Rabbi Jeffrey K. Salkin*
6 x 9, 368 pp, HC, 978-1-58023-395-8 **$24.99**

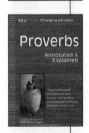

**Moses and the Journey to Leadership:** Timeless Lessons of Effective Management from the Bible and Today's Leaders   *By Rabbi Norman J. Cohen, PhD*
6 x 9, 240 pp, Quality PB, 978-1-58023-351-4 **$18.99**; HC, 978-1-58023-227-2 **$21.99**

**Proverbs:** Annotated & Explained
*Translation and Annotation by Rabbi Rami Shapiro*
5½ x 8½, 288 pp, Quality PB, 978-1-59473-310-9 **$16.99**

**Righteous Gentiles in the Hebrew Bible:** Ancient Role Models for Sacred Relationships
*By Rabbi Jeffrey K. Salkin; Foreword by Rabbi Harold M. Schulweis;*
*Preface by Phyllis Tickle*   6 x 9, 192 pp, Quality PB, 978-1-58023-364-4 **$18.99**

**Sage Tales:** Wisdom and Wonder from the Rabbis of the Talmud
*By Rabbi Burton L. Visotzky*   6 x 9, 256 pp, HC, 978-1-58023-456-6 **$24.99**

**The Wisdom of Judaism:** An Introduction to the Values of the Talmud
*By Rabbi Dov Peretz Elkins*   6 x 9, 192 pp, Quality PB, 978-1-58023-327-9 **$16.99**

*Or phone, fax, mail or e-mail to:* **JEWISH LIGHTS** Publishing
Sunset Farm Offices, Route 4 • P.O. Box 237 • Woodstock, Vermont 05091
Tel: (802) 457-4000 • Fax: (802) 457-4004 • www.jewishlights.com
*Credit card orders:* **(800) 962-4544** (8:30AM–5:30PM EST Monday–Friday)
*Generous discounts on quantity orders. SATISFACTION GUARANTEED. Prices subject to change.*

## About Jewish Lights

People of all faiths and backgrounds yearn for books that attract, engage, educate, and spiritually inspire.

Our principal goal is to stimulate thought and help all people learn about who the Jewish People are, where they come from, and what the future can be made to hold. While people of our diverse Jewish heritage are the primary audience, our books speak to people in the Christian world as well and will broaden their understanding of Judaism and the roots of their own faith.

We bring to you authors who are at the forefront of spiritual thought and experience. While each has something different to say, they all say it in a voice that you can hear.

Our books are designed to welcome you and then to engage, stimulate, and inspire. We judge our success not only by whether or not our books are beautiful and commercially successful, but by whether or not they make a difference in your life.

For your information and convenience, at the back of this book we have provided a list of other Jewish Lights books you might find interesting and useful. They cover all the categories of your life:

| | |
|---|---|
| Bar/Bat Mitzvah | Life Cycle |
| Bible Study / Midrash | Meditation |
| Children's Books | Men's Interest |
| Congregation Resources | Parenting |
| Current Events / History | Prayer / Ritual / Sacred Practice |
| Ecology / Environment | Social Justice |
| Fiction: Mystery, Science Fiction | Spirituality |
| Grief / Healing | Theology / Philosophy |
| Holidays / Holy Days | Travel |
| Inspiration | Twelve Steps |
| Kabbalah / Mysticism / Enneagram | Women's Interest |

Stuart M. Matlins, Publisher

Or phone, fax, mail or e-mail to: **JEWISH LIGHTS Publishing**
Sunset Farm Offices, Route 4 • P.O. Box 237 • Woodstock, Vermont 05091
Tel: (802) 457-4000 • Fax: (802) 457-4004 • www.jewishlights.com
**Credit card orders:** (800) 962-4544 (8:30AM–5:30PM EST Monday–Friday)
Generous discounts on quantity orders. SATISFACTION GUARANTEED. Prices subject to change.

## For more information about each book, visit our website at www.jewishlights.com